The French Riviera: A Literary Gui ╎
journey along this fabled coast, fr
the west to the Italian border in tl
and work of writers who passed ⁺
Nobel laureates to new authors v
Ted Jones's encyclopedic work cov╌╌ ╌╌╌ ╌╌
Graham Greene and W. Somerset Maugham, who spent much of
their lives there; F. Scott Fitzgerald and Guy de Maupassant,
whose work it dominates; and the countless writers who simply
lingered there, including Louisa M. Alcott, Hans Christian
Anderson, J. G. Ballard, Samuel Beckett, Arnold Bennett,
William Boyd, Bertholt Brecht, Anthony Burgess, Albert Camus,
Bruce Chatwin, Joseph Conrad, Charles Dickens, T. S. Eliot,
Ian Fleming, Ernest Hemingway, Aldous Huxley, James Joyce,
Rudyard Kipling, D. H. Lawrence, A. A. Milne, Vladimir Nabokov,
Dorothy Parker, Sylvia Plath, Jean-Paul Sartre, George Bernard
Shaw, Robert Louis Stevenson, Anton Tchekhov, Leo Tolstoy,
Evelyn Waugh, H. G. Wells, Oscar Wilde, P. G. Wodehouse, Virginia
Woolf and W. B. Yeats – and many others.

Ted Jones is a writer and journalist who specialises in travel and
the arts. He divides his time between Villefranche-sur-Mer on the
French Riviera and Windsor, England.

'The ultimate travel book for anyone who likes sun and literature. I found it irresistible.'   Peter Mayle

'There are two views of the French Riviera. One says it is an over-developed blot on the landscape; the other that it is the epitome of style. If you veer towards the latter, and enjoy literary history, this book is for you. Drawing on the stories of more than 150 writers, Jones does a great job of buffing up the legend.'
Anthony Sattin, *Sunday Times*, Books of the Week

'Thoughtful, entertaining and vivid, Jones's *The French Riviera* sweeps us along the coast ... Jones's book is sad only because it reminds us of how much of the Riviera's tranquil beauty has been sacrificed. The list of literary lovers of the Riviera almost beggars belief. It is delightful to have their eloquent, acerbic, lyrical responses collected here, in a book that deserves to become a favourite with all travellers.'   Miranda Seymour, *Sunday Times*

'There is much to relish. The author is assiduous in recording who wrote what where and when, in seeking out memorial plaques and mourning lost landmarks.'
E. S. Turner, *Times Literary Supplement*

'A vivid guide to the Cote d'Azur in the eyes of some of the greatest writers of their time.'   Jane Mays, *Daily Mail*

'Certainly among the best of recent books on the area. Jones has done a lot of research and presents his results in a clear and lively style. The book will appeal obviously to those with literary interests but it's also designed to please those who enjoy Sunday paper-style gossip (broadsheet, of course).'
Patrick Middleton, *The Riviera Reporter*

'Unsurpassed in literary name-dropping'
David Armstrong, *San Francisco Chronicle*

Tauris Parke Paperbacks is an imprint of I.B.Tauris. It is dedicated to publishing books in accessible paperback editions for the serious general reader within a wide range of categories, including biography, history, travel and the ancient world. The list includes select, critically acclaimed works of top quality writing by distinguished authors that continue to challenge, to inform and to inspire. These are books that possess those subtle but intrinsic elements that mark them out as something exceptional.

The Colophon of Tauris Parke Paperbacks is a representation of the ancient Egyptian ibis, sacred to the god Thoth, who was himself often depicted in the form of this most elegant of birds. Thoth was credited in antiquity as the scribe of the ancient Egyptian gods and as the inventor of writing and was associated with many aspects of wisdom and learning.

THE FRENCH RIVIERA

A Literary Guide
for Travellers

TED JONES

TPP

TAURIS PARKE
PAPERBACKS

Published in 2007 by Tauris Parke Paperbacks, reprinted 2009, 2014
an imprint of I.B.Tauris and Co Ltd
6 Salem Road, London W2 4BU
175 Fifth Avenue, New York NY 10010
www.ibtauris.com

In the United States of America and Canada distributed by
Palgrave Macmillan, a division of St. Martin's Press
175 Fifth Avenue, New York NY 10010

First published in 2004 by I.B.Tauris and Co Ltd

Cover image: *La Cote d'Azur* poster by M. Tangry, ca. 1910 © Swim Ink 2,
LLC/CORBIS

ISBN: 978 1 84511 455 8

A full CIP record for this book is available from the British Library
A full CIP record is available from the Library of Congress

Library of Congress Catalog Card Number: available

Printed and bound by CPI Group (UK) Ltd, Croydon, CRO 4YY

To Joan, for her help, encouragement and belief.

Contents

Acknowledgements

I should like to thank Bernard Payet for his atmospheric drawings, Eric Paul, a fellow writer of the Riviera, for leading my steps where they may not otherwise have gone, and Alison Worthington for correcting them when they took the wrong direction. My thanks go also to Wally Storer for the jump-start when the project seemed stalled, and to the staff of the British Library, the Windsor and Maidenhead libraries, the Pompidou Library in Paris, the Bibliothèque Municipale in Nice and the Princess Grace Irish Library in Monaco.

With a cast of more than 150 authors, from many countries, it would have been impossible to research original documentation in every case. Where I have not, I am indebted to those many writers who have gone before me, and hope they will accept my thanks.

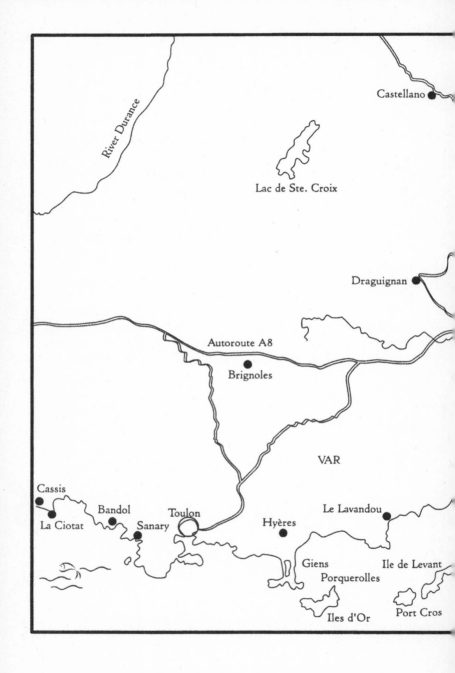

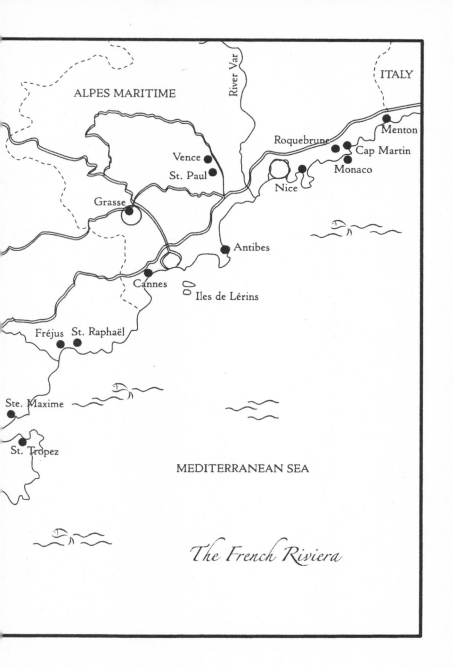

The French Riviera

Preface

I was drawn to the French Riviera by my earliest reading of adult fiction. Whether by coincidence or choice I don't remember, but my literary preference at the time would often light upon the likes of Scott Fitzgerald, Georges Simenon, Somerset Maugham and Guy de Maupassant. It was these authors and their contemporaries and their stories of azure skies and sun-drenched beaches that first aroused my ambition to visit this wonderful land where, it seemed, winter never ventured and the sun always shone.

It was many years before I finally came to live in south-eastern France, still remembering the writers who had first lured me here. I was fascinated to find that there were many more reminders of its literary past than I had imagined. In almost every town and village, plaques, street names, statues, tombs and monuments proclaimed with pride the authors who had been there before me. At least a dozen laureates of the Nobel Prize for Literature have lived here: the Italian poet, Dante, came here in the thirteenth century and described the region in his *Divine Comedy*. Yet, despite the fact that the region had attracted writers for more than seven centuries, I was surprised to find that no one – not even its resident writers – had attempted a literary history of the region.

The prospect of travelling the length and depth of this most beautiful and fortunate corner of Europe recording its literary heritage suddenly seemed to me to be the most exciting adventure imaginable.

When the biographer Richard Holmes was in south-western France following the trail taken by Robert Louis Stevenson a hundred years earlier in his *Travels with a Donkey in the Cevennes*, he befriended an itinerant painter whom he called 'La Paille' because of his straw hat. When Holmes explained the purpose of his journey,

La Paille said, 'You must be madder than I am. You should have a life of your own.' But La Paille missed the point: Holmes's life was no different from his own. Both were artists travelling in search of subjects – the only difference was in their materials.

As a travel writer I had always begun my journeys with a specific destination in mind, but this book began life by retracing the footsteps of those writers who had made the Riviera their home and whose work and lives most interested me. The writers themselves would dictate the destinations: Graham Greene in Antibes where, despite his wealth, he roughed it for the last 26 years of his life in a humble one-bedroom apartment; Somerset Maugham who, by contrast, lived in a palatial mansion on Cap Ferrat in which he spent his last 40 years; Robert Louis Stevenson in Hyères; Rudyard Kipling in Cannes; H. G. Wells in Grasse; Katherine Mansfield in Bandol and Menton and D. H. Lawrence just about everywhere along the coast until he died in Vence in 1930. I would walk where they walked, visit their former homes and surroundings, read their journals and letters and find out what drew them to this enchanted coast, what were their impressions of it and how it influenced their lives and work. It would be a book about writers – the places would be incidental.

I had not anticipated how many other writers would emerge along the way – serendipitous discoveries that would sidetrack me from my intended journey. Wherever I went in search of one I would discover a dozen more. So many novelists, poets, playwrights, historians and biographers came to light that my cast of authors grew exponentially like a chain letter until the pressure of numbers meant that I had to start eliminating some who were less well known to Anglo-Saxon readers. Gradually, the book took on a life of its own and before long it had evolved from a sentimental essay into a literary guide.

What had started as a personal adventure had become a quest. It was a quest that was to take me from one end of the Riviera to the other: from Toulon in the west to the borders of Italy in the east and from the sandy beaches and rugged Mediterranean coastline of the south to the snow-capped mountains of the southern Alps. No plaque went uninvestigated, no cemetery unvisited, no tombstone unread. The result, after several immensely satisfying years, was this book.

Far from being the end of my journey, it turned out to be only the beginning. The book was a moveable feast: after it was published, readers began to add their own first-hand recollections of authors in the book. A man in Monaco wrote to tell me of his escape from the Riviera with W. Somerset Maugham in the summer of 1940 on the *Saltersgate*, the last coal ship to leave the area as the German troops marched in. A lady in Germany sent me underwater photographs of the wreckage of the Lockheed P38 fighter plane – thought to have been lost forever – in which Antoine St Exupéry, author of *The Little Prince*, went missing over the Mediterranean in 1944. My correspondents included the former neighbours and friends of writers; landlords and incumbents of their former homes (Jules Verne's home on the Cap d'Antibes is now the Irish Consulate); the literary-minded postman who helped me to find H. G. Wells's love-nest and swore me to secrecy lest it should become a shrine (my photograph of it shows an angry concierge threatening to set the dogs on me) and a lady who shared a dustbin with Graham Greene. Other writers have discovered the Côte d'Azur: Nobel Prize winners like the Irish poet Seamus Heaney and the American novelist Toni Morrison and, inevitably, I have met resident authors whom I missed in the first edition but who are now close friends.

The search continues. I thank these readers for their interest and hope to hear from many more. Their recollections have helped to make the quest an endless one. No doubt I will continue to find new links with past and present writers of the Riviera and will unearth more memories of its literary past. Perhaps one day they will find their way into yet another edition.

Ted Jones
Villefranche-sur-Mer
tedjon@aol.com

Introduction

In the south-eastern corner of France, squeezed between the southern Alps and the Mediterranean Sea, is a place of palm-fringed beaches, picturesque mountain villages, bustling towns and deserted islands, where the sun shines on more than 320 days in the year. And even in these days of traffic-induced smog, there are still those unforgettable, sparkling days – usually after the mistral, the chill wind that rushes down the Rhône valley and sweeps through Provence like an automatic car wash – when the mountains seem almost within touching distance, and sea and sky form mosaics of blues and greens. The place is the French Riviera.

The Riviera has been a magnet for writers for 700 years. Early in the fourteenth century, the exiled Florentine poet Dante passed through, and wrote of its vertiginous mountain roads in his *Inferno*. Since then, generations of literary migrants, of every nationality and genre, have followed.

You do not have to travel far to be reminded of them: every town and village proclaims its literary associations. Street names – from the boulevard Somerset Maugham to the avenue Katherine Mansfield – recall memories of former residents. A plethora of plaques record their passing – outside a turn-of-the-century hotel in Nice: 'Anton Tchekhov lived here'; on a pretty villa in Roquebrune: 'William Butler Yeats lived and died in this house'.

More recently known as the Côte d'Azur, the French Riviera is a 120-mile stretch of coastline that meanders north-eastwards from the purple rocks of the Esterel in the west to the border town of Menton in the east.

Even its name is a writer's creation. In 1887, Stephen Liégeard, French novelist, playwright and poet, wrote a book about a journey along the coast of Provence. Although the book is long forgotten, his title, *La Côte d'Azur* - the Azure Coast - has lived on to spawn a million glossy brochures.

The literary connection with the region continued in the seventeenth and eighteenth centuries. The earliest British diarists were sons of the landed gentry, at the time the only people who could afford to travel - male inheritors rounding off their education with 'The Grand Tour' of Europe before returning to their estates. The nobility of the time felt that their sons' classical studies would be incomplete without their exposure to the glories of Athens and Rome - even if, like the young James Boswell, their main exposure was to sexually transmitted diseases.

But the Côte d'Azur remained a sighting from a passing ship, or at best an excursion, incidental to the travellers' main cultural goal. John Milton, author of *Paradise Lost*, called at Nice in 1638 en route to Genoa, and in October 1644, the English diarist and art historian John Evelyn stopped off in Fréjus to admire the ruins of the Roman port before sailing on to Italy.

All this was to change with the arrival, in 1763, of the 42-year-old Scottish surgeon and writer Tobias Smollett. Not only was Smollett a pioneering author in his own right, later much admired by Charles Dickens, who had discovered his novels as a child, but he had a reputation as a prolific translator from the French, especially of Voltaire.

But Smollett had a handicap that was incompatible with the role of an eighteenth-century travel writer: he hated sea voyages. Not only did he suffer from chronic seasickness, but he dreaded a more daunting hazard - pirates. He would certainly have known of the French playwright Jean-François Regnard, who, in the autumn of 1678, was returning from Rome along the coast, having been offered a passage in a British Royal Navy frigate from the nearby port of Civitavecchia. Off the coast of Corsica, two ships hove into view flying French flags, but when they got within firing range, switched them to the dreaded crescent of the Saracen pirates. The captain and most of the English crew were killed and the writer and his companion, a French noblewoman named Madame de Prade, were taken to Algeria and sold as slaves to the sultan, Achmet-Talem.

Regnard, having some skill as a chef, was put to work in the kitchens, but Mme de Prade was installed in the sheikh's harem - a warning that even aristocratic young ladies should learn how to cook. It took Regnard's family ten months to scrape together the £12,000 ransom – which was good business for the sheikh, who had bought him for only £1,500. Mme de Prade was never heard of again.

It is not surprising, therefore, that Smollett chose to make his way by land along the almost trackless, often bridgeless and mosquito-infested coast.

Smollett's phobias became the Riviera's bonanza. He based himself in Nice, and collected his letters from there into a book: *Travels through France and Italy.* The book was published in 1766, and although less than complimentary to the town, Smollett's grudging praise put Nice on the map, and, in appreciation, the people of Nice put him on theirs, naming one of its streets the rue Smollett. After Smollett, the French Riviera, instead of being a mere diversion, became a destination – and writers have flocked there ever since.

This book is the story of those writers – why they came here, where they lived, and how their stay influenced their lives and work.

Their reasons for coming were as many and varied as their origins. Many came in search of freedom of various kinds. The British censor drove a number of writers abroad, including D. H. Lawrence, James Joyce and Frank Harris. Some authors fled despotic regimes: after Hitler became German chancellor in 1932 the future looked bleak for writers with communist leanings, such as Bertolt Brecht, or who were Jewish – or had Jewish partners – like Vladimir Nabokov. Book-burning cultures are not conducive to creative thought.

And after the trial and imprisonment of Oscar Wilde in 1895, many British homosexual artists left the country, threatened by the surge in public hostility. The hostility was even extended to those condemned by association, whatever their sexual orientation: Wilde was never a contributor to *The Yellow Book*, a contemporary literary review, but because the newspapers reported that he had been carrying a copy when he was arrested the mob attacked its premises. A number of its contributors emigrated, many of them finishing up on the Riviera.

For some writers, the Côte d'Azur offered an escape from domestic complications: Somerset Maugham left a token marriage and H.G. Wells one that he found restrictive, and P.G. Wodehouse,

Graham Greene and Anthony Burgess decamped a few steps ahead of the Inland Revenue Department.

To some French writers, the Riviera was a national shrine. When Napoleon escaped from Elba in 1815 while his jailer was on the mainland seeing his girlfriend, he paddled ashore on to the beach at Golfe Juan, near Antibes. Victor Hugo trod the same beach 'in a state of religious fervour' at having 'walked in the emperor's footsteps'.

Jules Verne and Guy de Maupassant came to sail their yachts, away from the distractions of Paris and, during the Second World War, Jean-Paul Sartre and André Gide were among the many who sought freedom from the constraints of German occupation.

The 1920s invasion by American writers was a result partly of a revolt against Prohibition and partly of an extremely favourable exchange rate. Another attraction was the largesse of wealthy expatriate patrons, beneficiaries of which included Ernest Hemingway, F. Scott Fitzgerald, and humorists Dorothy Parker and James Thurber – who, as the creator of *The Secret Life of Walter Mitty*, became one of the few writers to be attributed by the *Oxford English Dictionary* with the coinage of a new word.

Some writers, like Hans Christian Andersen, Arnold Bennett and Baroness Orczy, came as fugitives from northern winters, while some simply succumbed to the general post-First World War artistic restlessness, like the Waugh brothers, Alec and Evelyn, and Aldous Huxley.

But the most distressing immigrants were those who came on medical advice – which often proved to be a well-intentioned ticket to eternity. Again, the culprit was a writer: in 1866, an English doctor living in Menton, James Henry Bennet, wrote a book called *Winter and Spring on the Shores of the Mediterranean*. It was part medical treatise and part tourist brochure, and, coinciding with the completion of the railway in 1868, attracted British consumptives in their coughing hordes, making Bennet famous and greatly enlarging his client base – which was later to include Robert Louis Stevenson and Queen Victoria.

The Côte d'Azur owed much of its nineteenth-century prosperity to Dr Bennet and to the misplaced faith of northern European doctors in the curative powers of its climate. In pre-antibiotic times,

British and Russian doctors who might otherwise have sent their tubercular patients to Blackpool or the Black Sea shipped them to Monaco and Menton.

Bennet, like Tobias Smollet a hundred years earlier, was not only a physician, but was similarly afflicted by both tuberculosis and the compulsion to write about it. He had come to the Riviera 'to die in some quiet corner', but made a dramatic recovery, the result, he believed, of wintering by the Mediterranean. The next year he tried northern Italy, but was less successful, because of 'the unhygienic state of the large towns of that classical land'.

So he settled in Menton, encircled, he said, by 'a phalanx of cured and arrested consumption cases', and was followed, like some pulmonary Pied Piper, by tubercular travellers from all over the world, many of them writers: from nineteenth-century authors such as Tchekhov, Nietzsche and Carlyle to the likes of Katherine Mansfield, W.B. Yeats and Alan Sillitoe in the twentieth.

To follow in the footsteps of these hundreds of expatriate writers (the locals have made relatively little international impact), whatever the reasons for their migration, is a rapturous journey. It takes in every corner of these lettered shores, where every road sign evokes leisure and literature.

Its gateway is the old Roman port of Hyères, the Riviera's southernmost town, for until the railway began to inch its way along the coast, Hyères was the only convenient option for northern travellers. Its literary ghosts include the Russians Tolstoi and Turgenev, Americans Henry James and Edith Wharton, and Britons Rudyard Kipling and Robert Louis Stevenson.

Hyères is the hub of a ring of coastal towns with strong reader associations: resorts like Bandol and Sanary-sur-Mer, with their memories of Brecht, the Lawrences and Huxley, and St-Tropez, which became the haunt of French writers like Sartre, Françoise Sagan and Colette.

Next is trendy Cannes, at whose film festival stars and writers have romped for over 60 years, the city that Kipling called 'a music-hall revue' and Wodehouse 'a loathly hole', where novelist Arnold Bennett wrote his sequel to *The Card* - and entertained a young Rupert Brooke (before he became a Great War poet) to tea - and where de Maupassant cut his own throat.

At the eastern end of the Bay of Cannes, the Cap d'Antibes stretches out into the Mediterranean like a basking dolphin, at its nose the famous Eden Roc Hotel – host to the fabulously rich.

Antibes is also rich in literary links. Here Jules Verne moored his yacht and wrote his scenario for *Around the World in 80 Days*, Scott Fitzgerald wrote *Tender is the Night* on its 'bright tan prayer-rug of a beach', and Graham Greene spent his last 24 years in a modest one-bedroom apartment, where he wrote his last seven novels.

Nice, the capital of the Côte d'Azur, is a treasure house of literary memories. Here Hans Christian Andersen and the German philosopher Nietzsche used to winter, Oscar Wilde recuperated after his release from Reading Gaol, and travel writer Bruce Chatwin died from AIDS.

Scores of writers have strolled the sweeping palm-fringed crescent of Nice's Promenade des Anglais, from Nabokov to James Joyce. Louisa M. Alcott set parts of *Little Women* on it, H.G. Wells, Hemingway and Scott Fitzgerald cavorted in its posh Negresco Hotel, and on its sky-blue chairs, a young American poet, Sylvia Plath, wrote a euphoric postcard to her mother. Here the Russian playwright Tchekhov watched Queen Victoria drive by, and the dancer Isadora Duncan was strangled with her own scarf.

Around the bay of Villefranche, the Cap Ferrat dangles like an earring into the Mediterranean. Around its coast, the manicured lawns of sumptuous villas – many of which belonged to King Leopold II of Belgium – roll down to the water's edge.

One of these villas, the Villa Mauresque, originally built in the Moorish style to house King Leopold's personal priest, was bought in 1926 by the English novelist and playwright W. Somerset Maugham, who lived there until his death almost 40 years later. The villa was a writers' Mecca, its pampered pilgrims including the leading artists, musicians and writers of the day.

A 'mini-Manhattan' is what Anthony Burgess, the author of *A Clockwork Orange*, called Monaco. Ever since the granting of the gambling franchise in 1863, writers – and their characters – from A.A. Milne, creator of Winnie the Pooh, to Ian Fleming's 007 have contributed to the Casino's coffers. Dorothy Parker and Harpo Marx left their offerings on its green baize tables (but his tetchy namesake Karl called the Casino's clients 'lunatics').

Sandwiched between Monaco and the Italian border are Cap Martin and the city of Menton. At the peak of the Cap, in the Hôtel Idéal-Séjour, the Irish poet and playwright William Butler Yeats spent the last flagging months of his life in 1939. He wanted his remains to be buried in his beloved Sligo, but a war intervened, and it was nine years before the Irish navy came to collect them.

The last town on this journey is that most Italian of French cities, Menton. Here, in the Villa Isola Bella, the consumptive New Zealand short-story writer Katherine Mansfield finally found peace – 'this little place is and always will be for me – the only place' – and published a succession of stories until her death in 1923. Sadly, her much-loved villa is now overgrown and crumbling – 'bella' no longer.

Also in Menton, in 1947, the Irish playwright Samuel Beckett, author of *Waiting for Godot,* lived in the avenue Aristide Briand. It is the last street in France – appropriately, for the author of *Endgame* – and, like this journey, ends at the Italian border.

Writers created the legend of the Côte d'Azur, and, down the ages, writers have perpetuated it. 'Here,' wrote Aldous Huxley, 'all is exquisitely lovely.' Rebecca West called it 'the nearest thing to paradise'; Lawrence Durrell was 'convinced it is the only place to live'; to Vita Sackville-West it was 'a perfection of happiness'; and Kipling hailed its 'great leap forward into summer'.

Such is the wealth of literature written from and about the Côte d'Azur that its inspirational force is undeniable. Not only were established writers, their day-to-day career pressures left behind, free to explore new styles, genres – and even new languages – but many new writers, inspired by the combination of sunshine and serenity, and stimulated by the proximity of other artists, found their voices here.

When Simone de Beauvoir wrote of 'looking forward to sun, silence, and time to work', she may well have been speaking for all the writers of the Côte d'Azur, from Alcott to Zola, from Hyères to eternity.

CHAPTER ONE

I wish to God I had died in Hyères.
(Robert Louis Stevenson)

Hyères: Gateway to the Riviera

Hyères is the southernmost point of the Côte d'Azur, and its gateway. It lies 12 miles east of Toulon; from here the coastline meanders north-east through the French and Italian Rivieras until Genoa. In the years before 1859, when the railway reached only as far as Marseilles, Hyères was the easiest option for northern European travellers because it was the nearest seaside haven to Marseilles. But as the railway inched its way along the coast, Hyères, lacking the convenience of Nice - with its TGV (high-speed trains) and busy airport - and the sophistication of Cannes, began to attract the seeker of calm.

It is in fact two towns: the old town, three miles from the sea, which has been a winter retreat since Roman times, centuries before sea bathing was invented, and the modern town, with its shops, beaches and yachting marina.

The ancient chateaux of the old town are of mixed heritage: built by Romans, enlarged and fortified by medieval French, and restored by more recent residents, they retain a hybrid harmony. Winding streets slope down into sunlit squares, and ruined ramparts look out on to lovingly manicured vineyards.

Like so much of the coast that it heralds, Hyères has suffered its share of modern urbanization, but it has managed to contain the development, and with its spacious gardens and its wide, palm-tree-lined avenues, retains the sense of quietude that has attracted artists and tourists as diverse as Tolstoi and Queen Victoria.

Its writers are commemorated in its street names - unless, it seems, they happened to be British. Thus Victor Hugo and Voltaire have their respective *rues*, and Georges Simenon an eponymous two. Eisenhower and Édith (sic) Wharton even merit *avenues*, but staunch

Hyères-ophiles like Scotland's Robert Louis Stevenson and the singularly English Rudyard Kipling don't rate even an *allée*.

The earliest writers to discover Hyères were Russian: Leo Tolstoi in 1840, and Ivan Turgenev eight years later. Neither visit was auspicious. Tolstoi was there to care for his tubercular brother, Nicolas, on what it was hoped would be a curative visit. Nicolas, who was accompanied by his wife and three children, survived only a few months, and died in a local nursing home. He was buried in the little cemetery of Hyères.

Turgenev stayed at the Hôtel d'Europe, but not for long. He wrote of his visit, 'Everything would be fine if it were not for the rain, which has not stopped falling for four days.' He left a week later.

Robert Louis Stevenson, author of *Treasure Island* and *Kidnapped*, had discovered the Côte d'Azur in January 1863, at the age of 12, when he visited Nice and Menton with his parents as part of a family European tour. Consumptive from an early age, he had returned at ten-year intervals, again staying mostly at the eastern end of the Riviera.

In September 1882, on his doctor's advice, he went south again, initially to the St Marcel quarter of Marseilles, where Fanny, his Californian wife who was ten years his senior, joined him a month later. Marseilles proved disastrous for his health: the house was 'as damp as a sponge and poisonous with marshes' and as soon as they could break the lease they moved along the coast to Hyères.

In March 1883, he wrote to his mother, 'We have found a house up a hill, close to the town, an excellent place though very, very little'. It was Le Chalet de la Solitude, a pseudo-Swiss folly that had been exhibited at the Paris Exhibition of 1878. Stevenson's eccentric landlord liked the chalet so much that he bought it and had it shipped to Hyères.

Having been built for show rather then habitation, it was minuscule, but Stevenson thought it 'the loveliest house you ever saw, with a garden like a fairy story and a view like a classical landscape'. He wrote at the time, 'I live in a most sweet corner of the universe, sea and fine hills before me, and a rich variegated plain; and at my back a craggy hill, loaded with vast feudal ruins.' Fanny described it 20 years later:

It was made more conspicuous by its position, clinging to a low cliff almost at the entrance of the old town. From this cliff the ground rose with a gentle gradient and just outside our garden gate, where it became more rugged and steep, breaking out near the summit into rocky crags that were crowned with the ruins of an ancient Saracen castle ... it was like a doll's house, with rooms so small that we could hardly turn around in them; but the view from the verandas was extensive, the garden was large and wild, with winding paths and old gray olive trees where nightingales nested and sang. Looking in one direction we could see the Îles d'Or and in another, the hills beyond Toulon.

Stevenson still suffered bouts of severe illness: in addition to the tuberculosis, at one point he went temporarily blind from an infection resulting from the local authority's policy of using town effluent as road fill.

The 16 months spent at La Solitude were both idyllic and productive, and Stevenson enjoyed what for him was a long stay, in relatively good health. He was able to finish *The Silverado Squatters*, which he had started in America, to work on a number of stories and articles, and to send off his book of poems, *A Child's Garden of Verses*, which he dedicated to his childhood nurse, Alison Cunningham ('Cummy') - to 'lighten my burthen of ingratitude'.

He also started *The Black Arrow*, a nautical adventure story, in an abortive attempt to repeat the success of *Treasure Island*, and the much more successful *Kidnapped*, and would probably have stayed longer if Fanny, a regular reader of *The Lancet*, had not read an item about a cholera outbreak in Hyères. So in June 1884, not realizing that the annual cholera outbreak was as much a part of the summer schedule as the Battle of the Flowers, she whisked him off to Royat, in the hills near Clermont-Ferrand in central France, and thence home.

It was his last stay on the Riviera, and for once he did not leave gladly. His contentment at La Solitude shouts from his correspondence of the time: 'that garden, the arbour, the flight of stairs that mount the artificial hillock, the plumed blue gum trees that hang trembling, become the very skirts of Paradise'.

He even lauded it in a mock epitaph:

Here lies
The carcase
Of
Robert Louis Stevenson
An active, austere, and not inelegant
writer,
who,

...

owned it to have been his crowning favour
TO INHABIT

LA SOLITUDE

He was to travel extensively among the islands of the south Pacific, eventually settling in Samoa, where he died ten years later. But, as he wrote from there: 'I was only happy once: that was at Hyères.'

La Solitude still stands, 'clinging to a low cliff almost at the entrance of the old town', as Fanny said. Now much enlarged and with a garage and a satellite dish, its gardens are still much as Stevenson described them:

> This spot, our garden and our view, are sub-celestial. I sing daily with my Bunyan, that great bard, 'I dwell already the next door to Heaven!' If you could see my roses, and my aloes, and my olives, and my view over a plain, and my view of certain mountains ... you would not think the phrase exaggerated.

Today that view, with its foreground of terracotta rooftops and its 180-degree Mediterranean backdrop, is still, despite the fact that the 'rich variegated plan' now includes an airport, 'sub-celestial'.

Eighteen years after Stevenson's departure, another English writer arrived in Hyères. It was the novelist and poet Richard Le Gallienne. He had told his father and his wife that the reasons for his choice of Hyères were his asthma and the need to finish a novel. He did not reveal until later the 'paramount association': that he had been attracted by Stevenson's association with the town. Less than a year before he died, Stevenson had written to Le Gallienne from Samoa bemoaning the 'artificial popularity of style' that he thought was infiltrating English writing, and metaphorically passing on a literary baton to the younger writer: 'You are still young, and you may live to do much.'

Le Gallienne checked into the Grand Hôtel des Hespérides in Hyères on 16 March 1900. Like Stevenson, he was enchanted. On the same day, he wrote to his wife, Julie, 'If I cannot write a book here, it must certainly be because I have no more books in me.' From his balcony, he could see the mountains and the Mediterranean, the olive groves, cypresses and palm trees. 'Think of palm trees,' he wrote. 'I have never seen one before, and indeed never thought I should care too much about them. They didn't seem like real trees in the pictures – but they are fascinating in reality – particularly the little ones planted thick along the boulevards and looking like large pineapples.'

To a young accountant from Liverpool, it must have seemed a magical world – especially the sunshine:

> I never seem to have seen sunshine before. It seems richer and more scented than other sunshine, a sort of musky tropical sunshine – which I shouldn't care for always, but which is wonderful all the same, and especially good just now, after all those leaden skies that make the heart sink.

But the rapture he saved for the traces of Stevenson:

> For me the paramount association of Hyères is the fact that some eighteen years ago, Robert Louis Stevenson was living in a little chalet just behind my hotel, and that as he lifted his eyes from his painfully growing manuscript, they rested on just the same landscape, those mountains, those very cypresses – as mine do now ... It was reading in Stevenson's letters that I first thought that, whenever I went south, I would go to Hyères. As I write, there is a jar of flowers on my desk. I gathered them this morning in Stevenson's garden – and I have just been reading again the letters that relate to his stay here.

Le Gallienne went on:

> Having forgotten to bring my own copy [of Stevenson's letters], they were handed to me by a kindly librarian, who eighteen years ago was handing volumes to Stevenson himself. He remembers him vividly, and with that affectionate lighting-up of the face with which everyone who has only met him for five minutes recalls the pleasant incident ... How strange it is to walk by that little bungalow, with its

wooden verandah and carved eaves – to read the rather faded name on the gate, 'La Solitude' – to think of its openings and shuttings, the witty high-spirited welcomes, and all the good talk and the fine silences on that verandah under the moon. God bless you, R. L. S.

But soon, Le Gallienne was complaining about the loneliness of life at Hyères. He wrote to his wife Julie, 'I shall never again voluntarily face a loneliness like these last weeks. I am not well enough to stand it. It is not good for me.' This must have gone down well with the long-suffering Julie, leading an impecunious existence with their daughter in suburban Chiddingford, and unable to pay the rent. He arrived home, tanned, mosquito-bitten and penniless, on 9 May – two months after he left – and without the book he left to write. 'For,' he wrote to his mother, 'in spite of all the lovely scenery, roses and nightingales, etc. etc. the Mediterranean, and all the romantic surroundings, I have never felt so lonely in my life.'

But Julie had had enough. Within a week of his return, they were quarrelling again, and soon they had separated for good, Julie and their daughter going to Paris and Richard to New York. He did not see his daughter again until he saw her name on a theatre billboard in New York 15 years later, and bought a ticket. And he did not return to Europe until after the First World War, when he went to live in Paris with his third wife, Irma, with whom he later moved to Menton.

South of the old town is the beach resort of Hyères-Plages, blessed with sandy beaches and sheltered from the worst of the mistral – the westerly storm that rises in the Rhone valley, bringing what Stevenson called 'vomitable' weather. Stretching even further south is La Presqu'Île de Giens – the Giens peninsula. This is a *presqu'île* which really lives up to its literal translation: it is almost an island, and is only prevented from being a fully fledged *île* by the twin parallel bars of land: the result of an accumulation of coastal silt.

The eastern stretch is the higher of the two, bordered on its western side by salt marshes and on its eastern side by a sandy beach.

It was here on the Giens peninsula, in December 1874, that young Józef Teodor Konrad Korzeniowski, said farewell to his lover, Thérèse Chodzka.

Korzeniowski was to sail the world for the next 20 years, storing up experiences which were to colour his plays, stories, and novels for the succeeding 30 years. By then he had become Joseph Conrad. Many of his works became films, some in as many as five versions: his *Heart of Darkness* became most famous as the Vietnam War film, *Apocalypse Now*.

Korzeniowski had boarded a train in Cracow, Poland, two months earlier, at the age of 17, headed for Marseilles. His heart was set on becoming a sailor, and his head full of dreams of the Mediterranean:

> Happy he who, like Ulysses, has made an adventurous voyage, and there is no such sea for adventurous voyages as the Mediterranean – the inland sea which the ancients looked upon as so vast and so full of wonders. And, indeed, it was terrible and wonderful.
>
> (*The Mirror of the Sea*)

He was also looking for freedom, believing that the only way to find it was to distance himself from an overbearing uncle. While waiting for a ship from Marseilles, he met a fellow Pole and former merchant seaman, Wiktor Chodzka, who kept an hotel on the nearby Giens peninsula. Wiktor had a daughter, Thérèse.

The young Conrad had a teenage romance with Thérèse. But he was also in love with the Mediterranean: his first long trip was a five-month voyage on the *Mont Blanc*, which left Marseilles on 11 December 1874. 'The charm of the Mediterranean dwells in the unforgettable flavour of my early days, and to this hour this sea, upon which the Romans alone ruled without dispute, has kept for me the fascination of youthful romance,' he wrote in *The Mirror of the Sea*.

But it was not just a 'youthful romance' to Thérèse: on 11 December 1875, a year to the day after Conrad sailed, she committed suicide.

For the next three years he sailed with the French Mercantile Marine based in Marseilles, and came to know the Côte d'Azur well, particularly the creeks and gullies of the area around Hyères – a knowledge which served him well when he made his living as a gun-runner for the Spanish army. Then, in the late winter of 1878–79, Conrad pointed a gun at himself and fired. The actual date is not known: could it have been 11 December?

Fortunately, the bullet entered his chest and went straight through him without damaging any vital organs, but in a way it was the end of one life and the beginning of another. He decided to become a career seaman in the British merchant navy: 'if a seaman, then an English seaman', he wrote at the time – in Polish.

> I yet longed for the beginning of my own obscure Odyssey, which, as was proper for a modern, should unroll its wonders and terrors beyond the Pillars of Hercules.

He signed on to a ship to Newcastle, and during the next 15 years worked his way up to ship's captain, perfected his English, became a British citizen, changed his name, married an English woman (whom he described to a friend as 'no bother at all') and settled in England to become a writer.

But the Mediterranean was to feature in his work for the rest of his life – which is fortunate, because he was uniquely qualified to write about it from a mariner's viewpoint:

> The blue level of the Mediterranean, the charmer and the deceiver of audacious men, kept the secret of its fascination, ... hugged to its calm breast the victims of all the wars, calamities and tempests of its history, under the marvellous purity of the sunset sky. A few rosy clouds floated high up over the Esterel range. The breath of the evening breeze came to cool the heated rocks of Escampobar; and the mulberry tree, the only big tree on the head of the peninsula, standing like a sentinel at the gate of the yard, sighed faintly in a shudder of all its leaves.
>
> (The Rover)

He was to return to the Côte d'Azur on a number of occasions, but never to Hyères – until, that is, April 1921, when, after a research visit to Corsica with Jessie, the wife he had married when he gave up the sea in 1896, he took the ferry from Ajaccio to Nice, and a train to Hyères. A photograph shows him leaning against a grounded boat at La Madrague on the Giens peninsula, looking old and, although a woman is standing close to him – alone. We will never know why he went back to the exact spot at which he had left Thérèse 45 years earlier, or what thoughts were in his mind, but it seemed as if he had always intended to return, and decided that this would be his last opportunity. Though he was never one to waste research, he did not write any 'Corsica' book: was that trip too a pretext to return to Giens?

The theme of the lover abandoned by a sailor has been recurrent in a number of Conrad's works, none more so than *Nostromo*, of whose heroine, Antonia, Conrad once said, 'I used my first love as a model'.

The answer seems to be found in *The Rover* (1923), the novel he wrote on his return to England:

> In the dusk the clump of pines across the road looked very black against the quiet clear sky; and Citizen Peyrol gazed at the scene of his young misery with the greatest possible placidity. Here he was after nearly fifty years, and to look at things it seemed like yesterday. He felt for all this neither love nor resentment. He felt a little funny as it were, and the funniest thing was the thought which crossed his mind that he could indulge his fancy (if he had a mind to it) to buy up all this land to the furthermost field, away over there where the track lost itself sinking into the flats bordering the sea where the small rise at the end of the Giens peninsula had assumed the appearance of a black cloud.

It was his last completed work. He died on 3 August 1924 at his home near Bishopsbourne in Kent and is buried in Canterbury. His epitaph, from a speech in Spenser's *The Faerie Queene*, exhorting suicide, is a fitting farewell:

> Sleep after toyle, port after stormie seas,
> Ease after war, death after life, does greatly please.

Fifty years later, the same epitaph was requested by another Riviera writer, Agatha Christie.

Conrad's guide on that last visit to Giens in 1921, and the woman who stands beside him leaning against the beached boat, was the wealthy New York divorcee and novelist, Edith Wharton. She came to Paris in 1911, and lived in France until her death. She had won the prestigious Pulitzer Prize in 1920 – the first woman to do so – with her *The Age of Innocence*, and had been living in Hyères for two years. In 1919, staying at the Hôtel du Parc in Hyères while her Paris mansion was being redecorated, she had been enchanted by a ruined convent, Ste Claire du Vieux Château, a few hundred yards uphill from the chalet in which Robert Louis Stevenson had lived, and bought it. 'I am thrilled to the spine,' she wrote at the time - and it became her annual winter home for the rest of her life.

Visitors to the chateau were usually warned by previous guests of Mrs Wharton's passion for tidiness. According to Kenneth - later Lord - Clark, art historian and writer and presenter of the BBC *Civilization* series, her books snapped back into their shelves on elastic cords, and every time one left a chair a footman would leap forward and plump up the cushions.

Wharton would be pleased to see her Château Ste Claire today. It is now a lovingly tended public park, its turreted tower and Romanesque arches leading to a panoramic south-facing terrace on which it is easy to imagine the heiress from Manhattan entertaining her guests - many of them writers.

They included the French poet and novelist Paul Bourget, who lived in the nearby villa, Le Plantier, from 1894 until his death; Aldous Huxley, author of *Brave New World*, a frequent visitor in his Bugatti from his home in Sanary-sur-Mer, on the western side of Toulon; Scott and Zelda Fitzgerald, who were staying at the Hôtel du Parc in 1924 (to whom she wrote afterwards 'to your generation ... I must represent the literary equivalent of tufted furniture and gas chandeliers'); and on many occasions the American novelist and prolific short-story writer Henry James.

James first came to Europe as a baby with his Anglophile father, and lived in what are now the grounds of Windsor Castle. He graduated from Harvard in 1862 and moved to Europe permanently in 1875. He first arrived in Hyères in April 1899, in response to an invitation from Bourget. But he did not stay for long. It was during France's shameful 'Dreyfus' period, after Alfred Dreyfus, a Jewish officer in the French army, had been convicted on a false charge of spying and sent to Devil's Island for life in 1894. He was not totally cleared until 1906, but in the interim, most French writers campaigned for his release, most notably Émile Zola (1840-1902), whose letter to the president entitled *J'Accuse* was, according to James, 'one of the most courageous things ever done'. Zola was put on trial for libel, found guilty, stripped of his Legion of Honour, and fled to England.

The case became an icon of anti-Semitism, and James, horrified to find that his right-wing, Catholic-establishment host was against Dreyfus's release, delayed his arrival and brought forward his departure in order to avoid spending too much time with him. Bourget finally survived James by almost 20 years but his *anti-dreyfusard* views appear not to have concerned Mrs Wharton – he is the third person in the 1921 photograph at La Madrague with her and Conrad.

James later moved to England and, in 1915, became a British citizen – as did many Americans during wartime. A year later he died and, after a funeral service held at London's Chelsea Old Church, his body was cremated and the ashes smuggled into the USA to be buried beside his mother's grave.

One of the many literary figures who paid his tribute to James at Chelsea Old Church on that day in 1916 was Rudyard Kipling. In the 1920s, at about the time when Conrad was visiting Hyères for the last time, Kipling was discovering it. He and his family would sometimes winter in Hyères as a change from their usual hibernation in Cannes. He enjoyed relaxing walks in the pinewoods and collecting shells on the beach, and they would take train trips along the coast to Nice and Monaco. They used to stay at a Victorian hotel in the old town: although a lover of Provence, he clung to English-run hotels and cuisine: 'same as one gets in England y'know – and committees to run everything. But the air, the flowers, the scent of hot pinewoods, the butterflies, the blue sea, and the island cannot be spoiled by the English.'

One wonders if Kipling recognized Stevenson's little home on the hill near his hotel. As a 12-year-old, Kipling was taken by his father to that same Paris Exhibition of 1878 at which La Solitude was exhibited. Another exhibit was the head of the Statue of Liberty that was about to be presented to the United States. The young Kipling climbed inside the head and looked out, claiming later that 'it was through the eyes of France that I commenced to see'.

The islands that Fanny Stevenson could see from her veranda, Les Îles d'Or (the Golden Islands), are a few miles to the south and east of Hyères. They take their name from the effect of the setting sun on the quartz and mica layers of the formations of schistose rock.

Over the centuries, the islands have provided sheltered moorings for Greek and Turkish traders, and the two largest islands still show the remains of Saracen fortresses. The restored fortress on the island of Port Cros was rented in the winter of 1928–29 by the English novelist and biographer Richard Aldington.

The three main islands, Porquerolles, Port-Cros and Île du Levant, are less than an hour by ferry from Hyères-Plages, and are noted for their quiet beaches, shaded by umbrella pines, and for the excellent walking and cycling trails. Tolstoi found great solace in walking these trails following the death of his brother, and he would bring Nicolas's children to the islands for picnics. The loss of Nicolas had a visible impact on the subject matter and tone of Tolstoi's later work.

Roger Martin du Gard, Nobel Literature prize winner in 1937, stayed on the largest of the islands, Porquerolles, and was joined there by André Gide in 1922, during which visit, 'at the water's edge, in the morning stillness of a beautiful day,' Gide fathered a child by a woman he did not name until many years later. The daughter was later adopted by his friend Pierre Herbart. On the same island, 20 years later, he conceived the plot of *Les Mouches* (*The Flies*).

To protect the islands – whose sheltered bays were a favourite anchorage for Guy de Maupassant in his yacht *Bel-Ami* – and their wildlife from the pollution afflicting much of the coast, they are today mostly designated national park areas, and are both chemical-free and, except for residents, out-of-bounds to cars.

To the west of Toulon the coastline turns north-west towards Marseilles. At the turning point, another peninsula protrudes from the coast, its craggy creeks and fjords forming a mini-Riviera, which, although not geographically part of the Côte d'Azur, merits its place here because it is spiritually no less Azuréen than Nice, and, politically, is more closely linked to the French Riviera than the independent principality of Monaco.

The coastal villages of this rugged shoreline, convulsed by rocks and riven by deep *calanques* (creeks), are not so much vacation resorts as weekend rallying points for trippers from the neighbouring cities of Toulon and Marseilles – respectively ten and 30 miles away. By

Riviera standards, they are relatively tranquil in mid-week – so much so that one of the creeks is a nudist colony.

The best way to see the *calanques* – and the nudists – is the one-hour boat trip from Cassis. Alphonse Daudet brought his bride here on their honeymoon in 1867. She wrote ecstatically to her mother about her new life of leisure 'in the beautiful south', where the almond trees blossom in February.

Inland, it is Peter Mayle country, where tired executives from northern cities live out their *A Year in Provence* fantasies in restored Provençal villas cordoned by vast vineyards and olive groves. Little surprise then, that the crepuscular coastline between Cassis and Sanary-sur-Mer has also harboured writers.

In the years 1925, 1927, 1928 and 1929, Virginia Woolf came to Cassis: on the last three occasions to visit her sister, Vanessa, the painter who had married fellow artist Clive Bell and set up her workshop in Cassis, a virtual *ménage à trois* with her lover, Duncan Grant. Most of Vanessa's paintings for her first London show were painted in Cassis and St-Tropez.

Virginia recorded her impressions in her journal:

I am waiting to see what form of itself Cassis will finally cast up in my mind. There are the rocks. We used to go out after breakfast & sit on the rocks, with the sun on us. L.[eonard] used to sit without a hat, writing on his knee. One morning he found a sea urchin – they are red, with spikes which quiver slightly. Then we would go for a walk in the afternoon, right up over the hill, into the woods, where one day we heard the motor cars & discovered the road to La Ci-ota[t] just beneath. It was stony, steep & very hot.

Moths fluttering around a lamp on Vanessa's veranda gave Virginia the idea for a novel, which, originally called *The Moths*, became *The Waves*.

Leonard and Virginia Woolf were so enraptured with the area that they almost bought a house there. Virginia wrote in her journal:

This island means heat, silence, complete aloofness from London; the sea; eating cakes in the new hotel in La Ciotat; driving off to Aix; sitting on the harbour dining; seeing the sardine boats come in; talk with people who have never heard of me and think me older, uglier than [Va] Nessa ... Leonard in his shirt-sleeves; an Eastern private life

for us both; an Indian summer running in & out of the light of
common day; a great deal of cheap wine and cigars.

Although the Woolfs continued to be enthusiastic visitors to France
until the eve of the Second World War, they never came back to
Cassis. When travelling, they played a continuous game of comparing meals, hotels, etc with English counterparts. They never agreed:
'In this great argument I am always for France; L[eonard] for England.'

La Ciotat is an ancient port five miles west of Cassis. It was built by
the Phoceans hundreds of years before the Romans got here. The
French novelist and journalist Stendhal, who visited La Ciotat in
1830, was one of the earliest writers to describe this coast, and
Bertolt Brecht, the German dramatist, visited the town in 1928, as a
break while writing *The Threepenny Opera* in Le Lavandou. He was
inspired by a statue he saw there to write *The Soldier of La Ciotat*.

A further 14 miles along the coast is the little town of Bandol, to
which the New Zealand author Katherine Mansfield came in November 1915.

She was there primarily on her doctor's orders – she was suffering
from rheumatic fever – but also in grief at the loss of her beloved
brother Leslie, killed on the Western Front. He had spent his em-
barkation leave with Mansfield in London immediately before sailing
for France, where he was killed soon after his arrival.

Yes, though he is lying in the middle of a wood in France and I am
still walking upright and feeling the sun and the wind from the sea, I
am just as much dead as he is.

Her friend D.H. Lawrence wrote to her:

Do not be sad. It is one life which is passing away from us, one 'I' is
dying, but there is another coming into being, which is the happy,
creative you ... Don't be afraid, don't doubt it, it is so.

When Mansfield had left New Zealand in 1908, she had been intent
on achieving fame either as a musician or a writer, but her musical
aspirations were short-lived: eight months after her arrival, pregnant
from an unrequited affair and fearful of the reaction of her parents,
who were planning a trip to England, she hastily married her music

teacher, George Bowden, in Paddington registry office, left him immediately – and sold her cello. Friends thought that, had she known that she would have a miscarriage soon after her parents returned to New Zealand, it is unlikely that she would have married Bowden. (It was also suspected that her mother knew all along about the shameful pregnancy: as soon as she got back to Wellington, she cut Katherine out of her will without explanation.)

Success as a writer came slowly, but after several rejections, she was eventually accepted by John Middleton Murry, editor of a short-story magazine, *Rhythm*, first as a contributor, then as mistress.

On arrival in Bandol, she stayed first at the Hôtel Beau Rivage on the sea front, and, when feeling well enough, would take evening walks on the promenade. In anticipation of a visit from Murry, she rented a villa on a cliff-top, with views across the bays towards Sanary, which she found reminiscent of the New Zealand coast. Excited with her find, she wrote to him:

> I have found a tiny villa for us, which seems to me almost perfect in every way ... It has a stone verandah and a little round table where we can sit and eat and work ... It is very private and stands high on the top of a hill. It is called the Villa Pauline.

As Lawrence had predicted, Leslie's death had an immediate, and dual, impact on Mansfield's writing. First, it motivated her to record the New Zealand of their childhood that they had discussed so nostalgically during his last visit. ('Why don't I commit suicide?' she wrote in her journal on his death. 'Because I feel I have a duty to perform to the lovely time when we were both alive. I want to write about it and he wanted me to.') Secondly, it was an incentive to try to achieve things that he never would. The evocation of life in New Zealand helped her to introduce the family element into her fiction that she had been unable to create in England, and she began one of her most industrious periods, publishing *Prelude* in 1918. She divorced Bowden and married Murry in the same year.

There is still a house at No. 75 rue des Écoles, overlooking the Renecros beach, with a wrought-iron sign which reads 'Villa Pauline'. But it is not a 'tiny villa': it is a large, box-like, two-storeyed cream and salmon-pink edifice – certainly not a love-nest, where the two writers would sit working at the single round table, on seats 'scooped out of stone' occasionally passing romantic notes to each other.

It is a relief to find, hidden in the garden behind the big house, a cosy little cottage with a faded, barely readable plaque outside, saying, in French: 'Katherine Mansfield wrote *Prelude* here, January–April 1916'. All is explained by another sign in the same wrought-iron, but smaller. It reads 'La Petite Pauline'.

It is easy to imagine the sick and grieving Mansfield, sitting alone on the cliff-top, watching the sun go down over the Île Rousse – the russet island – writing her wartime journal on that Sunday evening in December 1915:

> I am ill today – and in pain. This afternoon I did not go for a walk. There is a long stone embankment that goes out into the sea. Huge stones on either side and a goat path in the centre. When I came to the end the sun was going down. So, feeling extremely solitary and romantic, I sat me down upon a stone and watched the red sun, which looked horribly like a morsel of tinned apricot, sink into a sea like a huge junket.

Goat paths would be hard to find in today's Bandol. Unusually for the generally south-easterly orientation of the rest of the Côte d'Azur, its port faces south-west. Even more unique is that it is the only town on the coast whose wines merit their own *appellation contrôlée*. It is now a bustling, commercial tourist resort, especially in summer, when the gentle curve of its sandy beach becomes a living human barbecue and the promenade is lined with dozens of tiny stalls. Everyone has something to sell, from T-shirts to villas – and especially wine.

In addition to her many reminiscences of New Zealand life, the Provençal landscape has found its way into a number of Mansfield's stories. Cassis is the setting for 'The Escape', and 'The Man Without a Temperament' draws an acutely observed picture of the run-down Edwardian-age hotel:

> ... the dim hall with its scarlet plush and gilt furniture – its Notice of Services at the English Church, its green baize board with the unclaimed letter climbing the black lattice, huge 'Presentation' clock that struck the hours at the half hours, bundles of sticks and umbrellas and sunshades in the clasp of a brown wooden bear, past the crippled palms.

From Mansfield's description, the town of Bandol itself is unmistakable:

> The gates of the Pension Villa Excelsior were open wide, jammed open against some bold geraniums. Stooping a little, staring straight ahead, walking swiftly, he passed through them and began climbing the hill that wound behind the town like a great rope looping the villas together ... On, on – past the finest villas in the town, magnificent palaces, palaces worth coming any distance to see, past the public gardens with the carved grottoes and statues and stone animals drinking at the fountain.

Just as she uses real locations, Mansfield does not attempt to disguise her domestic situation. 'The Man Without a Temperament' is a realistic portrayal of a consumptive, demanding wife, who, like Mansfield, also complains of a weak heart, and of her uncaring writer husband who reluctantly joins her in her dingy Riviera pension. In case the reader is in any doubt, Mansfield dedicates the book to her own writer husband, John Middleton Murry.

Mansfield returned to Bandol, again on her doctor's advice, in November 1917, towards the end of the war, but, like much of Provence, the little town had suffered during the war and was now 'dirty and neglected'. By this time she had been diagnosed with tuberculosis; travel was still difficult, and, to make it worse, on the overnight train from Paris to Marseilles, she had shared a compartment with two women in funereal black who spent the night discussing medical case histories which proved 'what a fatal place this is for anyone threatened with lung trouble'.

As if to prove them right, her own health deteriorated, and she could not find the inspiration of her previous visit. But now bureaucratic travel restrictions prevented her from returning to England: she was held up for three weeks in a wintry Paris awaiting paperwork, and she did not get to London until 11 April 1918. She never returned to Bandol, and did not regain her inspiration until she returned to the Riviera in 1920 – to the Villa Isola Bella in Menton, where, despite gradually worsening health, she wrote continuously until her death in Fontainebleau in January 1923.

Of the Îles d'Or that the Stevensons and Edith Wharton had viewed from their sunny terraces in Hyères, Port Cros is one of the smaller islands. In the sixteenth century it had been a prison colony – until the prisoners turned to piracy as a sideline.

It was here that the author of *Lady Chatterley's Lover*, David Herbert (D.H.) Lawrence, came in October 1928 as a guest of his friend and subsequent biographer – Richard Aldington, who had rented an old fortress there. Lawrence was to have come with his wife, Frieda, but she was involved in one of her extra-marital dalliances – this time with the Italian army officer, Angelo Ravagli (of whom more later) – and arrived ten days late.

Port Cros was yet one more stage in Lawrence's trek around Europe – visa problems prevented him from returning to his ranch in Taos, New Mexico – in his attempt to find relief from the tuberculosis that was killing him. The island was virtually uninhabited at the time – as it almost is today – and although the visit was not a social success, the climate suited Lawrence, so much so that he returned to the area the following winter and stayed in Bandol.

By this time all the signs pointed to tuberculosis, but Lawrence could never bring himself to utter the word, despite the fact that he had been thrown out of a hotel in the French Savoy Alps because his coughing upset the other guests. In the stopover before that, in Bavaria, he had written the premonitory 'Ship of Death':

> It is now autumn and the falling fruit
> And the long journey towards oblivion ...

> Oh build your ship of death, your little ark
> and furnish it with food, with little cakes, and wine
> for the dark flight down oblivion.

Lawrence and Frieda stayed at first in the Hôtel Beau Rivage – the same hotel in which Katherine Mansfield had stayed only 13 years earlier, in 1915. Although he did not acknowledge Mansfield's influence in his choice, they had been close friends at the time – she and Murry had been witnesses at his marriage to Frieda in 1914 – so it would have been unlikely for him not to have known of her visit.

Like Mansfield and Murry, the Lawrences soon left the hotel and rented a villa. Theirs was called Beau Soleil, and his condition seemed to improve there. Sick or well, he worked with the compulsion of a man who knows that time is running out. Despite his growing reputation, he had not been able to find a publisher bold enough to accept *Lady Chatterley* because of its deemed obscenity, so he decided to have it printed in Italy. He took on the heavy publishing and marketing load himself, with considerable success – until it started to run into censorship difficulties.

(Lawrence was never to know the full impact of *Lady Chatterley's Lover* on the publishing world. The book was not finally cleared for publication until the famous *Regina v. Penguin Books* trial in 1960, 30 years after Lawrence's death, with its judgement which marked the virtual end of literary censorship in England. Lawrence may not have expected it to take 30 years, but he always claimed that his work would result in greater freedom for future writers.)

Towards the end of the winter his health deteriorated and he reluctantly agreed to Frieda's request that he see an English specialist who was staying in the region – while still insisting that there was nothing wrong with his lungs. Dr Morland diagnosed that he had had tuberculosis for at least ten years, and, although still in denial of the disease, Lawrence grudgingly accepted the recommended treatment: that he move inland and to a higher altitude.

Early in 1930, he moved to what he called a 'sort of sanatorium' in Vence, in the hills above Nice, but, as we shall see in Chapter 4, it was too late.

Among the small group who accompanied Lawrence's body to the cemetery in Vence were the English poet Robert Nichols, who lived in Villefranche but was later to become professor of English at Tokyo University, and the Lawrences' close friends, Aldous Huxley and his wife, who, hearing that Lawrence was seriously ill, had driven from Paris to be at his side.

In their younger days, both Lawrence and Huxley had been members of the Bloomsbury set, a loose – in every sense of the word – association of artists and intellectuals whose vortex, in the period during and following the First World War, was that quarter of London, plus occasional country houses within convenient access of the city. It was at the home of one of the Bloomsbury benefactors, Lady Ottoline Morrell, whom he described as 'naturally, congenitally, aristocratic and eccentric to an outrageous degree', that Huxley met his Belgian wife, Maria.

The Bloomsburies (Mansfield called them 'the Bloomsbury *tangi*' – the Maori word for a noisy, wailing funeral) and their fringe included many writers who appear elsewhere in this book, such as Virginia Woolf, James Joyce and Rupert Brooke.

After helping the impractical Frieda through the funeral formalities, Aldous and Maria Huxley made for Bandol, where they had enjoyed a ten-day stay at the Hôtel Beau Rivage with Lawrence and Frieda the previous year. They intended to look for a permanent residence there, and within a few days bought a house in Sanary-sur-Mer, a small fishing port five miles east of Bandol.

The name painted on the villa's gate posts by a well-meaning, but apparently dyslexic, stone mason was Villa Huley. The family so liked this charming contraction of their name that it remained the Villa Huley and was their main residence for the next eight years.

'Here, all is exquisitely lovely,' wrote Huxley. 'Sun, roses, fruit, warmth. We bathe and bask.'

He also worked. At Sanary, Huxley wrote his first play, *A World of Light*, some of his most famous novels, including *Brave New World* and *Eyeless in Gaza*, and many essays, stories and poems; he also edited a collection of Lawrence's letters.

When it was published in 1932, *Brave New World* was an instant success in Britain, but not in the United States, where much of its irony was lost. Christopher Hitchens, author of *Orwell's Victory* (entitled *Why Orwell Matters* in the USA), tells that Orwell's *Animal Farm* was rejected by an American publisher because 'there's no market here for animal stories'.

Years later, Huxley said that *Brave New World* started as 'a little fun pulling the leg of H.G. Wells'; and when, during a trip to Grasse, he dined with Wells at Lou Pidou, Wells's Provençal villa nearby, he reported that Wells 'wasn't best pleased with it'. In the 70 years since *Brave New World* was published, much of its then science fiction – human cloning, genetic manipulation and mind-changing and relaxational drugs – has become science fact.

Huxley still found time at Sanary to relax with family and friends. He visited Cannes, Nice and Monaco – and other writers, in particular Edith Wharton at her chateau in Hyères. He also swam, boated, walked, painted and enjoyed the quietude of early summer nights:

Moonless, this June night is all the more alive with stars. Its darkness is perfumed with faint gusts from the blossoming lime trees, with the smell of wetted earth and the invisible greenness of the vines. There is silence; but a silence that breathes with the soft breathing of the sea and in the thin shrill noise of the cricket ...

There is, at least there sometimes seems to be, a certain blessedness lying at the heart of things.

Maria put it another way: 'You have never been here when the cumulative madness of five months of sun and country and stars make the world unreal in its pleasures and beauties – and when the northern sobriety is very northern and unreal indeed. I shall be so sensible this winter, *but I am so happy now.*'

The idyll could not last for ever. In 1937 they moved to California and left the Villa Huley for the last time. Huxley gave a number of reasons for the move, including offers of well-paid work from Hollywood studios, and finding the year-round Californian summers beneficial for his health. Coming from the writer who, in *Point Counter Point*, wrote, 'Several excuses are less convincing than one', one is inclined to believe that the over-riding reason was the increasing rumble of war clouds.

But they did return to Sanary, staying for a nostalgic break at the Villa la Rustique in 1950. The gateposts of the Villa Huley still bore its idiosyncratic name.

Huxley died in Los Angeles on 22 November 1963. Nursing staff in the hospital were looking at television sets. He had once again shown his disregard for the machinery of publicity; for it was the day on which the bullet was fired from a book repository in Dallas, Texas, that killed John F. Kennedy.

One Sanary writer who was less than pleased with Huxley's industriousness during the early 1930s was the literary critic Cyril Connolly. A keen admirer of Huxley in London, Connolly had somehow formed the impression that Aldous and Maria were impatiently awaiting his and his wife Jean's relocation to Sanary. The Connollys had gone there on the Huxleys' recommendation and taken a long lease on Les Lauriers Roses – The Oleanders – on the coast road. It must have been a bitter disappointment, then, to find their access to

Huxley repeatedly barred by Maria, 'the watchdog', with the mantra 'Aldous is working'.

Part of the reason for the snub was that Huxley had over-committed to his publisher in return for a generous monthly ad-vance, and – even if he did occasionally 'bathe and bask' – he probably *was* working. Another was that Maria did not like Jean as much as she did their other neighbours. And finally, it seems that the Connollys' over-casual lifestyle, with their odd range of domestic animals, did not appeal to the punctilious Maria and the hypochon-driac Aldous. 'The ferrets stank,' wrote Maria later, and she did not think it cute when her brandy glass was taken from her by a lemur.

But, whatever the reason, to Connolly the cut was deep and long-lasting. 'The Huxleys,' he said, 'have added ten years to my life'. He was to write later of the only occasion on which he was invited, together with the Huxleys, to Edith Wharton's chateau. All four squeezed into Huxley's three-seater Bugatti:

> Jean and Maria were highly suspicious of each other, and Aldous was quite unaware that my deep admiration for him – which was respon-sible for us settling in Sanary – had curdled.

> We entered the dining-room like two opposing tennis teams before an already biased umpire.

But Connolly recovered, and was later to set his only novel, *The Rock Pool*, in Cagnes-sur-Mer and St-Paul-de-Vence. He forgave Huxley and they became friends again – and when given the accolade of an entry in *Who's Who?* he gave 'the Mediterranean' as his hobby. Also his reminiscences 15 years later, in his *The Unquiet Grave* (1944), showed that the charm of little Sanary was undiminished:

> October on the Mediterranean, blue skies scoured by the mistral, red and golden vine branches, wind-fretted waves chopping round the empty yachts; plane trees peeling; palms rearing up their dingy underlinen; mud on the streets, and from doorways at night the smell of burning oil.

> On dark evenings I used to bicycle in to fetch our dinner, past the harbour with its bobbing launches and the bright cafes with their signs banging. At the local restaurant there would be one or two *plats à emporter* ... then I would bowl back heavy-laden with the mis-tral behind me, a lemur buttoned up inside my coat with his head

sticking out. Up the steep drive it was easy to be blown off into the rosemary, then the dinner would be spoilt. We ate with our fingers beside the fire, - true beauty lovers.

Mansfield also wrote of Sanary, which she knew from her walks along the cliffs from Bandol:

The shimmering, blinding web of sea
Hung from the sky, and the spider sun
With busy frightening cruelty
Crawled over the sky and spun and spun
She could see it still when she closed her eyes
And the little boats in a web like flies.

Leaving Hyères and its peninsular, the road squeezes between the Massif des Maures and its contorted shoreline to Le Lavandou. Opinions as to the derivation of its name are equally divided between 'lavender' and 'laundry'.

Le Lavandou has seen more artistic days. Its literary connections are tenuous, and writer sightings have been scant since 1928. But in May of that year, a German trio arrived. Bertolt Brecht had committed to staging *The Threepenny Opera*, the adaptation by Elisabeth Hauptmann of John Gay's *Beggar's Opera*, in Berlin at the end of August, and was urgently looking for a place to work. At the time, neither the music nor the libretto were complete, so Brecht brought with him to Le Lavandou his collaborator, Kurt Weill, to write the music, and Weill's wife, Lotte Lenya. It is an interesting thought that the opening line of the show's most famous song *Mack the Knife* - 'Oh, the shark has pretty teeth, dear' - may well have been born in this now sprawling Mediterranean resort.

Brecht was to visit the area more frequently later: after his pro-Stalinist sympathies caused the Nazis to revoke his German citizenship, he adopted an even more peripatetic life style.

He stayed in Sanary-sur-Mer in the autumn of 1937 as a guest of the prolific German novelist and playwright Lion Feuchtwanger. (After Hitler came to power in 1932, Sanary-sur-Mer was colonized by expatriate German intellectuals - Thomas Mann, Bruno Frank and others - and came to be known as Sanary-les-Allemands.) Brecht was filling in time between a Russian-organized conference in Paris to discuss means of helping the government cause in the Spanish

Civil War (attended also by Ernest Hemingway), and the rehearsals for the Paris performance of *The Threepenny Opera*.

Huxley's biographer, Sybille Bedford, describes a disastrous attempt to bring the two Sanary communities together at a garden party, with the Anglo-Saxons in shorts and cotton shirts at one end of the garden and the stiff-collared Germans at the other.

Feuchtwanger, being both Stalinist and Jewish, had thought it prudent to leave Germany immediately after Hitler became chancellor. He was right: in May 1933, when Goebbels published his infamous list of writers whose books were to be burned, Feuchtwanger's name was on it. After the war started, many of the Germans expatriates were arrested by the French and either interned or deported to Germany. Feuchtwanger managed to escape to the USA and worked in the film industry.

For those who think that the Côte d'Azur is entirely a foreign invention, the short drive north-eastwards across the hills from Hyères – the coastline is impassable by road – will reveal a resort that, in concept and atmosphere, is indisputably French.

Unlike the towns to the east of the Var River, St-Tropez bears few signs of Genoese domination. In fact in the seventeenth and eighteenth centuries it belonged to the French family Suffren – one of whom, the admiral Bailli de Suffren, plundered English ships in the Atlantic during the American War of Independence, and was honoured for defeating an English fleet in the West Indies in 1781. He is proudly commemorated by a statue on the sea front.

The very feature that made St-Tropez easy to defend against the Saracens and, later, the Spanish navies, its inaccessibility by land, is now its biggest problem. Access to the town from the north is restricted by the narrow bridge at Grimaud: and the fact that its maze of narrow cobbled streets is, surprisingly, open to cars, ensures that its summer traffic jams are the longest and most ill-tempered in France.

Formerly a Greek settlement, the town takes its name from a Roman soldier, Torpes, who in 68 AD was beheaded on the orders of Nero for the peculiarly Christian offence of refusing to renounce his faith in public. The body was never found, but the head was rescued by local Christians, and is now revered in a chapel in Torpes's native Pisa.

Today, decapitations are relatively rare: the only scalpers are the waterfront artists who sell mass-produced 'original' paintings to gullible tourists.

St-Tropez first came into artistic prominence in the late nineteenth century with the arrival of the painters – Paul Signac led the way, and Matisse, Braque, Seurat, Dufy and others followed, attracted by its rugged coast, colourful countryside, and its long twilight, deriving from the fact that it is one of the few Riviera harbours that faces north-west.

As so often happens, writers followed the artists. Guy de Maupassant's *Bel-Ami II* was becalmed here in 1887, at a time when, except for an occasional stage coach, the sea was the main means of access to the little fishing port.

The town's modern era dates from the 1920s. In 1925, the French writer Colette was brought there for the first time by Maurice Goudeket, her third husband. She fell in love with St-Tropez, and immediately sold her second home in Brittany and bought the villa La Treille Muscate, which she kept until 1938. Colette, former artists' model and music hall performer, was the most important French woman writer of her age, and the novels that she began writing in her 20s – the most famous of which, *Gigi*, was adapted for stage and screen – are still enchanting her readers today.

Her years in St-Tropez and her life there with Goudeket are movingly recorded in *La Naissance du jour*, an autobiographical novel that she began there in 1927:

> After our five-o'clock swim, a swim lashed with wind and freezing cold despite a formidable sun – everything is antithesis on the Mediterranean coast – we didn't seek shelter in the rose room, but on the warm and living bank of earth, under the shadow of the widely spaced trees. Five o'clock in the afternoon is an unstable, golden moment, a transitory change from the eternal blue of sky and water in which we bathe down here. The wind was no longer blowing, though slight eddies were still visible in the more responsive leaves such as the feathery mimosas.

It was, not surprisingly, Goudeket's favourite of Colette's books, because, he wrote, 'I see in it the flower of her full maturity. Bathed in poetry and of unequalled density, richness and eloquence.'

Its last paragraph begins:

> The cold blue has crept into my bedroom, trailing with it a very faint tinge of flesh colour that clouds it. It is the dawn, wrested from the night, drenched and drawn. The same hour tomorrow will find me cutting the first grapes of the vintage.

But, sadly, the writers of the 1920s and 1930s – Colette, working on *La Naissance du jour,* Jean-Paul Sartre sitting in the Café Sénéquier writing *Les Chemins de la liberté* (*The Roads to Freedom*), the French novelist Anaïs Nin, and Goudeket himself – probably saw St-Tropez at its best.

Colette was one of the first to note the decline, when she herself started to become a tourist attraction. Goudeket records their decision to leave:

> The first result of this encroaching renown was to make Saint-Tropez uninhabitable for Colette. The peaceful village of our first years, devoted to fishing and pottering, had turned into a hive of tourists. On the wharves a double row of cars hid the view of the port. The yachts had chased away the old boats, the bars had become dance-halls where every imaginable kind of couple stayed on until the first light. The few hundred yards which separated *La Treille Muscate* from the village hardly protected us. A visit to Colette formed part of every holiday programme. Even the morning bathe had henceforth its spectators, many of whom came by sea.

Today its once picturesque harbour is a place of joyless fun, frequented by those who want to see who else is there to see them – a Disneyland for adults, where all is artificial and nothing real. One does not go there to write. But around the cluster of rocks at the eastern end of the harbour, out of sight of the artists and their serried rows of easels, it is still possible to visualize the St-Tropez of Colette:

> When night has shut down, the sea is reduced to a language of splashings, of throaty noises and obscure chewing sounds made by the hulls of the moored boats; the marine immensity is diminished to one dark little wall, low and vertical, across the sky, the sweeping vividness of blue and gold shrinks to tiny harbour lights, and the few

bulbs of the business section with its two cafés and its sleepy little bazaar.

In the years following the Second World War, the fame of St-Tropez grew in parallel with that of the Cannes Film Festival. The little town became popular with itinerant film stars, and some – most famously Brigitte Bardot – made their homes here. But the writer most recently associated with St-Tropez was Françoise Sagan, whose *Bonjour Tristesse*, written at the age of 18, sold almost one million copies and established her as a bestselling author. It is an apt metaphor for the St-Tropez of today.

Sagan's precocious success with this and her next work, *Un Certain Sourire* (*A Certain Smile*), did little to lay the foundations of a glittering literary career: work that the reading public was willing to accept from a teenager was less acceptable from a mature author. In the almost 50 years since *Tristesse*, none of her many published works has had the same success, and she has never won a Prix Goncourt – the French 'Booker Prize'.

Although St-Tropez is still a mainly French resort, the threat of globalization seems to have been spotted by de Maupassant as early as 1889:

> It was already daylight, and I could distinctly see the coast of Saint Raphaël ... and the sombre mountains of the Maures, themselves running out seawards till they came to an end, far away in the open sea, beyond the gulf of Saint Tropez.

> Of all the southern coast, this is the spot I am fondest of. I love it as though I had grown up in it, because it is wild and glowing, and because the Parisian, the Englishman, the American, the man of fashion, and the adventurer have not yet poisoned it.

The port of Toulon has remained a *lieu de passage* for writers: Rudyard Kipling, Gustave Flaubert, Alexandre Dumas and Hans Christian Andersen all passed through, and Evelyn Waugh sampled its brothels, but none made a permanent home there.

But the perimetric shore encircling its coastline from Hyères all the way round to Bandol seems a fitting prologue to a story of the writers of the Côte d'Azur. Cyril Connolly best summed up the literary essence of this hallowed crescent through the cynical Naylor in *The Rock Pool*:

All along the coast from Huxley Point and Castle Wharton to Cape Maugham little colonies of angry giants had settled themselves: there were [Patrick] Campbell in Martigues, [Richard] Aldington at Le Lavandou, anyone who could hold a pen in Saint Tropez, [Michael] Arlen in Cannes, and beyond, Monte Carlo and the [E. Phillips] Oppenheim country.

CHAPTER TWO

I like Cannes excessively, especially for its climate and scenery.
(Edward, Prince of Wales, to his mother, Queen Victoria)

Cannes: City of Festivals

Cannes is the queen of the French Riviera. Like much of the coast, it enjoys a benign climate, cobalt seas and picture-postcard skies, beaches and snow-white villas. But in Cannes the sea is smoother, the beaches sandier and the passers-by more elegant. It has casinos, a sun-facing old port surrounded by restaurants, and a wide, palm-fringed promenade lined with luxury hotels: La Croisette.

Its history as a resort began with the arrival of Lord Brougham. Although a Scot, he was Lord Chancellor of England, co-founder of London University and designer of the one-horse coach that bore his name. In 1834, Lord Brougham was prevented by an outbreak of cholera from crossing the Var river – the then border with Italy – to enjoy his usual winter in Nice, and decided to stay 20 miles west, in this small fishing port with a population of about 3,000.

Its name came from the abundant *roseaux*, or canes, that flourished in its swamps, and its most recent distinguished guest had been Napoleon, who had camped there 19 years earlier, on 1 March 1815, after escaping from Elba.

A memorial plaque outside the main Cannes post office in the rue Bivouac Napoleon commemorates his short stay. The next morning he set off through the mountains, reaching Paris on 20 March, establishing himself as emperor, and the Route Napoleon as a national tourist attraction.

When Napoleon landed, a local butcher pointed a gun from his window, saying he would 'kill the Corsican ogre', but was dissuaded by his neighbours, who feared that reprisals might follow. It seems a pity that the 40,000 men who were to die at Waterloo 100 days later were not given a vote on the matter.

Napoleon had little support in Cannes. A Scottish lady who followed Lord Brougham to Cannes in 1856 was Lady Margaret

Maria Brewster, the wife of an eminent Edinburgh physicist, Sir David Brewster. (He also followed Lord Brougham – as Chancellor of Edinburgh University.) She was travelling with a maid and companion and, finding that there were no guidebooks, decided to publish her *Letters from Cannes and Nice* (1857). She wrote from Cannes:

> The inhabitants of Cannes were lukewarm in the Imperial cause. The father-in-law of Mr. Borniel Père (who is a resident in Cannes, and a most pleasing specimen of the old, courteous French gentleman) was then *préfet*. When applied to by Napoleon for assistance and fealty, he replied that he would pay him respect, and assist him with provisions, but that he could not serve him, as he was the King's servant. 'Sir, I esteem you for it,' was Napoleon's answer.

So enchanted was Lord Brougham with his discovery of Cannes that he built a luxury villa, named the Château Eléanore in memory of a daughter, Eleanore-Louise, who had died, and he returned every winter for the next 34 years, until his death in 1868. Prudently acquiring land in the surrounding hills while it was cheap, he sold it on to the cream of British aristocracy who every winter joined him there, bringing their gardeners – and some even their lawns – with them.

The grateful Cannois – who today number 70,000 – erected a statue in his honour. He stands in the minuscule Lord Brougham Square overlooking the open-air market, his finger pointing at the ground as if he were refereeing one of the *boules* matches being played in front of him.

The poem inscribed on the plinth of the statue was written by Stephen Liégeard – poet, playwright, politician and the very inventor of the term Côte d'Azur. Its closing lines translate as: 'He points to where palm trees entwine with English roses, as if to say, this is the place!'

Lady Margaret Brewster was equally enchanted. 'Cannes is the loveliest of all lovely places!' she said:

> the sea so exquisitely blue – the sky so bright and cloudless – the rich sun upon the gleaming white houses so lovely in all its phases from the early roseate flush to the last glowing smile of evening – the Hill of Cannes, or the Mont Chevalier, crested with a square tower, and château in ruins, and an old church; – '*La Croisette*,' a long

point of land jutting out into the sea; – the Isles of the Lérins just in front; – and the subdued tints of the olive-trees, and the rounded heads of the orange-groves, laden at once with blossoms and with ripening fruit. It is a lovely scene; perhaps still more beautiful last night in the moonlight, which was so clear that one could easily read by it; and the hills, and sea, and olives, and oranges, were all exqui-site in the purity of light and depth of shadow, while in the foreground the painted balustrades of this château, pink and white, and characteristically French by day, looked quite graceful and picto-rial.

Cannes is also a city of festivals. The conference industry began as an attempt to encourage tourism after the end of the Second World War, and has already outgrown two conference centres. In 1982 the beautiful old *Belle Époque* casino was flattened and replaced by the vast concrete bunker that is the new Palais des Festivals.

The pride of its annual programme is the Cannes Film Festival, held every May, and a rendezvous for writers since its inception in 1946. The film festival began as a protest after the jury at the 1938 Venice Festival bowed to Fascist pressure and awarded its top prize to a German documentary – despite the fact that the festival did not accept documentaries.

The French gesture was ill timed: the brand new film festival of Cannes was scheduled to open on 1 September 1939, the day that Hitler goose-stepped into Poland. Two days later, the Second World War started, so that when star guests Mae West, Tyrone Power and George Raft arrived by sea, they had to turn around and go home.

Jean-Paul Sartre trod the famous red carpet at the first film festival in 1946, and hundreds of writers have followed. Its presi-dents have included Jean Cocteau (three times), Marcel Pagnol, Georges Simenon, Tennessee Williams, Françoise Sagan and Dirk Bogarde. Henry Miller, Lawrence Durrell and Anthony Burgess have been among its jurors. There have been 'writers' years', like 1952, when Graham Greene and Orson Welles occupied adjacent cabins on Sir Alexander Korda's yacht, writing screenplays for the legendary film producer – whom Greene later caricatured in his novel, *Loser Takes All*. Or 1957, when Cocteau and André Maurois were joint presidents and Pagnol was juror. That was also the year that France's greatest crime writer, Georges Simenon, met America's, James Hadley Chase.

It is now the world's largest film marketplace - and keeps on growing. Today more than 30,000 professionals and 5,000 journalists jostle to see as many as possible of the 1,200 or so films on view. Hotels, yachts and stars are commandeered for nightly publicity parties - as Cocteau once put it, 'my name is the plural of cocktail'. But the general public, corralled by crush barriers and herded by armed security guards, are lucky if they catch a distant glimpse of red carpet.

Directly across the Croisette from the Palais des Festivals is the square Prosper Mérimée. A plaque outside No. 3 records that the author of *Carmen* - the story that was used by Bizet for his opera - lived there. Mérimée was also an historian and archaeologist, and author of, among many stories and novels, *Colomba*, a novel set on the island of Corsica.

Originally from Normandy, Mérimée had discovered Cannes on an archaeological tour in 1834. He was enchanted from his first visit: 'Although it is December, there's not a cloud in the sky, there's no wind, the sun is magnificent - and there are wild strawberries growing in the woods.' He finally moved there in 1861, thus overlapping the last six years of Lord Brougham's life.

Lord Brougham had tried to get into the French National Assembly in 1848, and only gave up the attempt when told he would have to give up his British citizenship and peerage to do so.

The Anglophile Mérimée enjoyed socializing with the British aristocracy, and chronicled the declining health of the ageing peer in letters to Sir Anthony Parizzi, chief librarian of the British Museum. In 1862: 'Lord Brougham looks extremely well for a man of 80'; 1865: 'Lord Brougham has just lost his wife, but he does not know too much about it, and when it is mentioned, says, "We can only hope she will get better" '; and in 1866: 'His Lordship is very deaf, and shrieks when he speaks. The fact that he has stopped wearing his dentures makes him even less intelligible.'

Mérimée's *Colomba*, published in 1841, has the unusual distinction, for a novel, of having precipitated a murder. It tells the story of a bloody feud between two Corsican families. Although the story was based on fact, Mérimée went to some trouble to disguise the names and places, and then, in an attempt to add a touch of realism, wrote a footnote to the effect that, if anyone should doubt the existence of such long-standing vendettas, they should talk to a Monsieur Jérôme Roccaserra of Sartène, one of that town's 'most distinguished and agreeable citizens', who would authenticate the story.

Unfortunately, Monsieur Roccaserra was head of one of two formerly feuding clans. The other, the Pietri family, had lost three of their sons in ambushes. Despite the fact that the two families had attended Mass together and signed a witnessed agreement to terminate the vendetta, so incensed were his protagonists at his being publicly honoured in this way that in 1843 he was ambushed and killed.

No one was ever accused of the crime, but the next day, the local priest, the Abbé Sebastien Pietri, uncle of the murdered men and a signatory to the truce, who had sworn never to shave until the death of his nephews was avenged, appeared without his beard.

Mérimée lived a bachelor, but not celibate, existence with his valet and two English maids – 'they are devoted and they aren't bothered by cigars' – and corresponded copiously with many women, including the Empress Eugénie herself, to whom he had been a tutor, and the French writer George Sand. Her unflattering description of him – 'ce n'est pas grand-chose' (it's no big thing) – is capable of a number of interpretations. Of marriage, he said, 'The only benefit it would bring me would be some gentle care when I am ill, and when I have to depart for the other world.'

Despite his many illnesses – bronchitis, chronic asthma and heart problems – he managed to postpone that departure until his 67th year, and died peacefully in his sleep in his beloved Cannes, where he is buried in the local cemetery.

Edward Lear was another of Mérimée's English *confrères*. The English landscape artist and travel writer was also the pioneer of nonsense verse and popularized the limerick form. As the youngest of 21 children, it is not surprising that he should develop a flair for the absurd.

On Mérimée's recommendation, Lear spent the winters of 1865–66 and 1866–67 in Cannes, and wrote possibly his best-known work, *The Owl and the Pussycat*, there. Appropriately, his literary tribute to the city is a limerick:

> There was an Old Person of Cannes,
> Who purchased three fowls and a fan.
> Those she placed on a stool, and to make them feel cool
> She constantly fanned them at Cannes.

Children's literature has come a long way since 1867.

Urban street names in France abound with literary eponyms, but the rue Guy de Maupassant in Cannes is appropriately named, because in the early 1890s the writer of over 300 short stories lived at No. 42 – the Chalet de l'Isère – at the point where it meets the avenue de Grasse.

He was impressed by the concentration of foreign royalty to be seen in Cannes, as distinct from the streets of post-revolutionary Paris:

> Princes, Princes, everywhere, Princes! ... No sooner had I set foot yesterday morning on the promenade of the Croisette than I met three, one behind the other. In our democratic country, Cannes has become a city of titles ... Some men gather together in gambling houses because they are fond of cards, others meet on racecourses because they are fond of horses. People gather together at Cannes because they love Imperial and Royal Highnesses.

After women, his other great passion was sailing, and he kept his yacht, *Bel-Ami* – named after his first successful novella, about the rise to wealth of an unscrupulous journalist – in the nearby harbour, today known as the Old Port. He called the yacht his 'great white bird', and if in contemporary pictures it does not look white, with its three flying jibs it was certainly bird-like. It was formerly the coastal yawl *Zingari*, built in Lymington, Hampshire, in 1879. *Bel-Ami* was a well-known sight along the Côte d'Azur, from Hyères as far as Portofino in Italy. The coast is the setting of de Maupassant's book *Sur l'Eau (Afloat)* and his yacht *Bel-Ami* is its key character.

One evening he was unable to berth at Cannes because the surf was too strong, so he dined aboard ship.

> After dinner I went up and sat in the open air. Around me Cannes stretched forth her many lights. Nothing can be prettier than a town lighted up and seen from the sea. On the left, the old quarter with its houses that seem to climb one upon the other, mingled its lights

with that of the stars; on the right, the gas lamps of the Croisette extended like an enormous serpent a mile and a half long.

On New Year's Day 1892, de Maupassant took the train to Nice to lunch with his mother in the elegant suburb of Cimiez. With syphilis beginning increasingly to affect his mind, his behaviour was so irrational that his mother begged him to stay, but he insisted on returning to Cannes: he had asked his captain to make *Bel-Ami* ready to sail in the afternoon. He did not go sailing: according to the journal of his valet, François Tassart, he dined, went for a long walk, and went to bed. At midnight, a telegram arrived from a mysterious woman who had been visiting de Maupassant for a year and a half, whom Tassart knew only as 'the woman in grey'.

At a quarter to two in the morning, valet and captain were awakened by violent noises from de Maupassant's room on the first floor, and on opening the doors they found him standing with his razor in his hand, his throat cut and bleeding, and shouting at Tassart for having removed the bullets from his revolver.

A doctor came, reported the injuries 'not serious', and stitched up the gaping gullet. But the throat was now the least of the damage. As soon as he was well enough to travel, he was sent to an asylum in Passy, near Paris, which – since it was identified by a doctor's name, Dr Blanche – was luxurious and expensive.

On the way to Cannes railway station, the little group – the straight-jacketed de Maupassant, his valet, nurses and doctors – stopped by the port for him to say a tearful goodbye to his 'great white bird'. It was more than a farewell to sailing: it was an end to writing, to pleasure and to freedom. He did not leave the asylum until 18 months later, in July 1893 – on his way to the cemetery. He was just one month short of his 43rd birthday.

Despite its springtime and summer bustle, for most of the year Cannes is relatively peaceful. So at least thought the mother of the poet Rupert Brooke when she met him off the train at Nice station in the first week of 1912. Brooke was 25, and had yet to achieve fame through his wartime sonnets. His London neurologist, alarmed at his mental and physical condition – he had lost 14 pounds in a month – had ordered immediate rest in a sunny climate.

Brooke's rather domineering mother – he called her 'the Ranee' – decided, when she met him at the station, that Nice was no place for an invalid, and she drove him directly to the Hôtel du Pavillon in Cannes.

At the time, Brooke was in love with Katherine ('Ka') Cox, a fellow student at Cambridge and later intimate of Virginia Woolf. He wrote to Ka from Cannes: 'Outside there are large numbers of tropical palms, a fountain, laden orange trees, and roses. There's an opal sea and jagged hills, with amazing sunsets behind.'

Ka was not in the least interested in Brooke and had told him so – an action guaranteed to send him into frenzies of desire – and he sent her letters and telegrams by the hundred, begging her to meet him in Munich when he was better.

He sent her several pleading missives a day, but said she need not answer them all: 'I desire very short, but not too infrequent, statements'; and 'I've no faith or strength. If only you were with me an hour, I'd have both'. That they were followed immediately – sometimes in the same letters – with accusation and contrition is indicative of his unbalanced state of mind: 'One changes so if one's ill on a rainy Riviera'; and 'You are quite the nicest person in the world ... And I am a beast and a toad.'

The problem was that, since Ka loved someone else, he had to keep telling her how ill he was. The pleading only stopped when he told her he was dying. She telegraphed immediately saying she was coming to see him, and, knowing that he had gone too far and that his deception was about to be discovered, he sent off more sheaves of telegrams claiming that he had made a miraculous discovery and begging her not to come on his account. It would have been even more embarrassing because he was keeping the affair secret from his mother, who was staying in the same hotel.

To his relief, Ka never came to Cannes, but they did eventually meet in Munich, and the relationship remained, with the exception of one single, benevolent gesture, one of friendship. The objective of sacrificing his heterosexual virginity finally achieved, Brooke could write only a few months later, 'I'd not care if I saw Ka dying of some torture I could inflict on her slowly.'

When war broke out he was given a commission in the Royal Navy, and was on his way to the invasion of Gallipoli when he fell ill and was transferred to a French hospital ship. In his notebook at the end of the boozy Christmas Day of 1914, he started a sonnet with the words, 'If I should die, think only this of me', and put it aside to finish later. Thus one of Britain's most famous First World War poets never reached the war: he died off the Greek island of Skyros in April 1915, at the age of 27, from septicaemia following mosquito bites.

His poetry has remained popular. His 'The Old Vicarage, Grantchester' ('Stands the church clock at ten to three'), and his wartime sonnets, caught the mood of the early wartime, expressing an idealism that was not to be found in the work of those later poets who actually experienced the horrors of war in the trenches. Yet if asked to quote from a Great War poem, most people would recite the famous lines from 'The Soldier':

> If I should die, think only this of me:
> That there's some corner of a foreign field
> That is for ever England.

In April 1912, while young Rupert Brooke was in Cannes, his mother took him to the posh Grand Hôtel Californie, where they had tea with another expatriate writer, Arnold Bennett. At the time, the prolific novelist from the Potteries – he wrote 30 novels in all, many of them portrayals of the five Staffordshire towns which are now incorporated in the Borough of Stoke-on-Trent – was working on *The Regent*, a sequel to his immensely successful *The Card* (in America *Denry the Audacious*). He was in Cannes awaiting completion of his new house in Essex.

Bennett had moved to Paris in 1903, at the age of 35. He had had a productive stay in Menton in 1904, working in collaboration with the Indian-born, Devon-based British writer Eden Phillpotts, during which, in three weeks, they completed a play, two short stories, three articles and a chapter of a novel.

He had always said that he would marry at 40, and, precisely as planned, married the French actress Marguerite Soulié in 1907. But he gradually reverted to his bachelor lifestyle, and she eventually left him in 1921.

Another visitor to Bennett at La Californie was his friend from Paris, the French writer André Gide, who was impressed with Bennett's work rate and lavish lifestyle. Gide noted in his journal after the visit, 'Arnold Bennett, installed at the Hôtel Californie. Earns around a thousand francs a day; he is paid at the rate of a shilling a word.' Since Bennett's word rate over most of his writing career was seldom less than a prodigious 400,000 per year, he could easily afford to stay at La Californie. (He wrote 78,200 words of *The Regent* there in two months and three days.)

He also wrote the novel *Accident*, the story of a train journey from London to the Riviera, which was based on a report of a train accident that happened in France the previous year.

But perhaps the most surprising work that Bennett was inspired to write during his stay beside the Mediterranean was his only published poem, 'Night on the Riviera', of which the following is an extract:

Out of the blind disorder and the plague
Of ravelled dreams that coil the pillow round,
Reluctantly I rise.

And lo!
Spectacular and cold,
Between the moonstruck sea-sward and the sky
Whose violet arches span the silver waste,
Flashes and burns the Mediterranean night,
Consuming in its frigid fire the sense
Of human, intimate things. And far below,
Gently the palms wave on the murmurous shore
In acquiescence. But not I will yield
To that pale dominance. Within my heart
The latent pantheism of endless time
Leaps proudly to self-consciousness and cries:
This peace is my peace and this kingdom mine!

Photographs from the time show Bennett and his wife in the exotic gardens of the Croisette, she with a muff and matching ostrich-feather hat, he in an elegant three-piece woollen suit, wing collar and black bow tie. Marguerite may have been the actress, but body language leaves no doubt as to whom Bennett thinks is being photographed.

Somerset Maugham deplored such pretension, and thought that Bennett had got too big for his Potteries roots. In his autobiographical *The Summing Up* in 1938, seven years after Bennett's death, he said of Bennett:

> He never knew anything intimately but the life of the Five Towns ... and it was only when he dealt with them that this work had character.

> When success brought him into the society of literary people, rich men and smart women, and he sought to deal with them, what he wrote was worthless.

It was during this stay in Cannes that Bennett's journal note read 'Very ill': he had been struck down by a severe illness which, although it never left him, was to remain undiagnosed until it killed him 19 years later. It was typhoid.

The illness made him late in returning to London, and some American friends who were waiting there cancelled their sailing reservations so that they could hear *The Regent*, thus missing the maiden voyage of the *Titanic*.

Exactly ten years later, Rudyard Kipling made the same train journey in reverse on his way to Cannes. Kipling was born in Bombay, India, where his father was a museum curator. His unusual first name is that of the lake in Staffordshire – that same West Midlands pottery county in which Bennett set *The Card* – where his parents met on a picnic.

Because of the high child mortality rate in India at the time, it was the custom for the children of expatriate parents to be fostered with English families. So, without warning – his parents did not want him to worry in advance – the six-year-old Rudyard was committed to six forlorn years in what he called 'The House of Desolation', bullied and abused by his foster mother and her teenage son. Under this regime of what he called 'calculated torture', he found that lying could sometimes reduce the severity of his punishment. It was, he said, 'the foundation of [my] literary effort'.

A Francophile from his first trip with his father to the Paris exhibition of 1878 at the age of 12 – which 'set my lifelong love for France' – he was a frequent visitor to the Côte d'Azur, and from the early 1920s until his death in 1936 he and his wife Carrie spent most of their winters there.

He was an avid student of French, even when it was unfashionable: 'French as an accomplishment was not well seen at English schools in my time, and knowledge of it connoted leanings towards immorality.'

After the First World War, in which his only son John was killed at the Battle of Loos, Kipling worked as an adviser to the War Graves Commission on the construction of the vast military cemeteries ubiquitous in northern France. It was Kipling who chose the familiar epitaph from the Book of Ecclesiasticus: 'Their name liveth for evermore'. He also wrote the epitaph for the graves of the hundreds of thousands of unidentified dead and missing in action: 'Known unto God'.

The loss of John in his first action of the war had an indelible impact on Kipling's life. He barely mentioned him in his work – with the exception of the poignant reference in his *Epitaphs of the War*:

My son was killed while laughing at some jest, I would I knew
What it was, and it might serve me in a time when jests are few.

But he stopped spending winters in Switzerland, where he and his son had made their first attempts at skiing – he wrote to the hotelier in Engelberg, 'We have not the heart to come out there again' – and began to winter in the south of France.

Although the Kiplings sometimes stayed in Hyères and Monte Carlo, Cannes was their destination of choice. He once wrote from there in the middle of a mistral – those sudden thunderous storms that grow in the Rhone valley and burst upon the normally tranquil south-eastern coast – 'When the sun comes out again all nature will take another leap forward into summer, and there will be a vast hatch-out of butterflies.'

Staying with his family at the elegant twin-towered Carlton Hotel on the Cannes Croisette in the spring of 1921, he described the town as 'like the third act of a music-hall revue', with its 'pink and white houses, blinding sun, blinding green vegetation, roses, wisteria, irises, judas trees, even hydrangeas and rhododendrons all out together; and wonderfully dressed females of surpassing beauty promenading up and down through it all'.

Another of the consequences of the loss of John was an ongoing mistrust of German imperialism, and he warned stridently of the dangers of a second world war. He became more ill as his warnings were ignored, and did not live to see them confirmed: on 18 January 1936, he died from a perforated ulcer. The last entry in the diary of his ever-present wife Carrie was 'Rud died at 12.10 a.m. Our Wedding Day.'

Two days later, his friend King George V, for whom he had written many speeches, died, inspiring a newspaper of the day to the famous headline: 'The King has gone – and taken his trumpeter with him.'

Not everyone was as enthusiastic about Cannes as Kipling. The English humorist Pelham Grenville (P.G.) Wodehouse, one of the few writers apart from Tom Stoppard who might have had an alternative career as a cricketer – as a fast bowler he once took six wickets for Dulwich College – was there in 1925. 'Plague-spot' was one of his more polite terms for the town.

Wodehouse's output of work in his long life is staggering. His acknowledged work alone – he sometimes wrote under noms de plumes to avoid tax – included 96 books, 16 plays, 28 musicals (he wrote the words of songs like *Bill* in *Showboat*) and at least 300 short stories. This was in addition to light verse, film scenarios and thousands of letters.

'Plum', as he was familiarly known, was staying with his wife at the Hôtel Gallia. His early views on Cannes are inconsistent, but, on the whole, scathing. On 30 March, he wrote to his stepdaughter:

Two days ago ... Mummie [was] saying that Cannes was really a delightful spot ... Today, suddenly, we both exclaimed that we thought Cannes the most loathly hole in the known world and that, once we got out of this damned Riviera, nothing short of armed troops would induce us to return. Of all the poisonous, foul, ghastly places, Cannes takes the biscuit with absurd ease.

His later comments suggest an explanation for his truculence: that the Wodehouses were, at the time, inexperienced travellers, and probably homesick: 'Mummie and I have come to the conclusion that we loathe foreign countries. We hate their ways, their architecture, their language and their food.'

That his xenophobia was later reversed is evidenced by the fact that he was later to live in Paris and Le Touquet, on the northern coast of France. Cannes even mellowed over the next 24 hours: the next day he wrote, 'Cannes doesn't seem so bad after all. I think the secret is not to go into it'; and the day after that, 'Not such a bad place, Cannes! We went to the Casino last night and I won 500 francs ... Italian musicians have been singing under our window this morning. All very jolly.'

Wodehouse's remark about 'armed troops' proved prophetic: prevented by the breakdown of his car from leaving Le Touquet ahead of the German advance in 1940, they were interned and taken to a lunatic asylum in Upper Silesia. Again under armed guard, he was taken to Berlin, where the Nazi High Command asked him to broadcast to America, which he did. And, on their return to Paris after their release, they and their Pekingese dog Wonder were arrested by French police on a charge of espionage.

Whether or not Wodehouse knowingly committed treason by broadcasting for the enemy during wartime was never tried in court. His supporters claimed naivety. He said that he thought he was thanking his American friends for their kindness. Some, on the other hand, might question why it should have taken five broadcasts to do that.

In 1945 he wrote, 'I made an ass of myself, and must pay the penalty', and, after the war, moved permanently to the United States, becoming a US citizen in 1955. Although the popularity of his books never waned in Britain, it was as a symbolic gesture of reconciliation that the Queen made him a knight in 1975, the year in which he died, aged 94.

In February 1939, while staying at the Carlton, the most luxurious of the hotels that line the Croisette, the Wodehouses visited another writer friend, E[dward] Phillips Oppenheim, author of *The Moving Finger*, at his large villa in Roquefort-les-Pins, about five miles inland from Cagnes-sur-Mer. 'Oppy', as he was known to his friends, was a prolific writer of crime fiction, with over 150 works to his name, and was the inventor of the genre of the 'gentleman crook', much later to be personified by Cary Grant in the film *To Catch a Thief*.

It is not recorded whether or not Oppenheim was even aware of it, but he would have enjoyed the impressive literary compliment paid to him by F. Scott Fitzgerald in a letter to his publisher in 1934, about the marketing of *Tender is the Night*. 'Please do not use the phrase "Riviera" ... ,' he wrote. 'Not only does it sound like the triviality of which I am so often accused, but also the Riviera has been thoroughly exploited by E. Phillips Oppenheim and a whole generation of writers.'

Although he did not live in Cannes, Oppenheim was a regular visitor to the Locke family at their villa, Les Arcades, in Cannes. 'During those days, it was the centre of literary hospitality upon the Riviera and the rendezvous of many notable visitors. That was in the days before Hollywood had begun to exercise its devastating effect upon its disciples and before divorce had become their afternoon amusement.'

He also frequented the Bay of Cannes in his yacht *Echo* (which has been called by contemporaries 'a floating double bed'). In his memoirs, he wrote nostalgically of the bay as seen from *Echo*:

> I never expect to see a more wonderful sight than the Mediterranean coast from the deck of a yacht on a summer night. From partly hidden Cannes there was an unbroken line of lights tracing with a fiery finger the outline of the Golfe, shorewards past Juan les Pins and out to the Cap.
>
> Those were nights of peace and joy and happiness. The throbbing of music from a dozen dance orchestras of the smaller cafés, even from the casinos themselves, seemed to fill the air with a sort of quivering background of vague yet concerted melody ... Nearer, one could almost pick up the rhythm of the dance music and follow the movements of hundreds of swaying figures. Here and there, behind the alluring lights of the Casino at Juan, one could catch an even clearer glimpse of the dancers themselves.

The Hôtel Carlton was also the setting of a dramatic event during the Second World War. In the summer of 1940, with the French expected to capitulate at any moment, Oppenheim, having driven all over France in an unsuccessful attempt to leave by the northern or western ports, returned with his family to the Carlton, where consular officials were trying to charter some ships to evacuate the British residents ahead of the advancing German troops.

Finally, two coal hulks, having dropped their shipments, were commandeered and passage offered to the non-French civilians waiting in the Carlton and other hotels. The ships were black with coal dust, there was no water, food, or cabin accommodation, there were only two toilets on each ship, and no convoy or other protection was available.

Knowing that Somerset Maugham was one of the 3,000 or so people hoping to travel in them, Oppenheim thought seriously about boarding, but then decided that he did not wish to subject his family to such risks, and that they would stick out the war in Roquefort-les-Pins.

He was to regret his decision: conditions during the Occupation were little better than on board ship, but whereas Maugham was soon comfortably housed in the USA until the end of the war, it took Oppenheim more than a year to get back to England.

Scott and Zelda Fitzgerald, although more closely linked in the early to mid-1920s with Antibes and Juan-les-Pins, did choose Cannes for their final stay in 1929.

By this time, Scott was looking for a workplace rather than an escape. He was, he thought, in the final stages of his masterpiece, *Tender is the Night*, which, mainly because of Zelda's illness, he was not to publish until 1934.

This time they stayed in a less fashionable part of town, renting the villa Fleurs des Bois in the boulevard Gazagnaire and, while Scott wrote, Zelda – now in her 30s and hoping to become a dancer – took ballet lessons. But the Wall Street crash in November marked the beginning of a world-wide depression, and the end of an era that the French were to call *les années fitzgeraldiennes* – the Fitzgerald Years.

For Fitzgerald, it was also the end of hope. Three years later, Zelda had her first breakdown, and two years later was permanently confined. Fitzgerald said, 'I left my capacity for hoping on the roads that led to Zelda's sanatorium.' He remarried, but never won his battle with alcoholism, and died of a heart attack at 44.

*

From the old port of Cannes it is just a 15-minute ferry trip to the Îles de Lérins. The larger of the two main islands, St-Honorat, is just two miles long by half a mile across. The islands were Roman strongholds in the first century, and, in the fourth century were discovered by St Honorat, who established a Christian monastery there, while his sister, Ste Marguerite, founded a convent on the other, smaller, island.

In the late seventeenth century, the island of Ste Marguerite became a state prison, and received its most mysterious guest on 30 April 1687: the Man in the Iron Mask.

The prisoner had made the 12-day journey from an Alpine prison seated in a sedan chair wrapped in waxed cloth, completely hidden from view. The chair was placed aboard a boat in Cannes, and accompanied by an armed escort to the island prison.

The bare, damp, vaulted cell in which he lived is today the islands' main tourist attraction. Its sole light source is a high window which permits no sunshine, and the atmosphere is so claustrophobic that one can barely stay there for a few minutes. The Man stayed there for 11 years.

In 1698, he was taken from the cell and moved to the Bastille prison in Paris, where, still masked, he died five years later. The chief jailer, de Saint-Mars, wrote to the minister Louvois, 'You have my complete assurance, Monseigneur, that no one in the world saw the prisoner, or could have guessed his (or her) identity'. (The French personal pronoun was abbreviated, so could be translated as either male or female.)

Alexandre Dumas used the theme in his book *The Man in the Iron Mask*, the final episode in his series *The Three Musketeers*, in which he embellishes the theory that the prisoner was the brother of King Louis XIV. The musketeers were attempting to release the prisoner and replace him with the real king.

The question 'Who was the Man in the Iron Mask?' has fascinated writers and historians even to the present day.

There are as many theories as there are special interest groups. There is even a literary Man in the Iron Mask (MITIM) theory – that the death of the French actor and playwright Molière from consumption in 1673 had been faked, and that he had been imprisoned in the iron mask because his plays offended the Church. Voltaire, himself imprisoned in the Bastille, knew one of the MITIM's jailers, who claimed that, although the prisoner was treated with the utmost deference, he could not have been related to Louis XIV because he was almost twice as tall as any contemporary royal.

There is the Matthioli premise: that he was an Italian diplomat at the court of Louis XIV. There is an Anglo-Saxon MITIM speculation – that he was an illegitimate son of Charles II – and for feminists, a lawyer, Maître Bouche, supports the WITIM theory: the Woman in the Iron Mask. A variant of this is the WITVM hypothesis: the assumption that, in the interests of *bonne couture*, her mask would have had to be made, not of iron, but of black velvet.

We will never know – only the king, his Interior minister and de Saint-Mars ever knew, and they aren't talking any more. But any supposition based on foreigners would seem dubious – the diplomatic repercussions would probably have been too embarrassing. The two strongest contending theories are that he was possibly a brother of Louis XIV, despite the height question, or the favoured choice, Eustache Dauger, a friend of Louis XIV who had helped the king to poison a former mistress in return for a promise of immunity from execution.

There is unanimous agreement on one point: that the prisoner was of noble birth. As Lord Brougham recorded following an investigation in 1857:

> At the same time, all accounts agree that the prisoner was treated as if of the blood-royal – waited upon by the governors of his different prisons, treated with the greatest respect, clothed in the finest linen, and served upon silver.

The island still shelters a few Cistercian monks, who tend their vines and distil a traditional liqueur called la lérina. One wonders if they realize that their eleventh-century monastery owes its survival to another writer: its ancient cloisters were restored in the nineteenth century through the efforts of the French Admiralty's Inspector of Historic Monuments, Prosper Mérimée.

Six miles west of Cannes, the resorts of Mandelieu and La Napoule have now sprawled into one.

The old Château of La Napoule sits on the water's edge between the two communities. During its 2,000-year history, its prominence has made it a ready target. Successive restorations have revealed first-century Roman and tenth-century Saracen traces, but most of the structure dates from the eighteenth century.

It was a glassworks when, in 1918, it was discovered by the American sculptor Henry Clews and his wife Marie.

Independently wealthy, they dedicated the rest of their lives to its restoration, and – if you can accustom yourself to Clews's idiosyncratic sculptures everywhere you look – they succeeded. Henry brought with him his huge *God of Humormystics*, a wedding gift to his bride, which still stands in the courtyard.

Clews saw himself as Don Quixote: he named the house – and his first son – Mancha, and called his valet Sancho. (Mancha, when he grew up, changed his name to Madison.)

For special meals, the couple would dress in what they believed were medieval Arthurian costumes, which they designed themselves, and promenade its cloisters and gardens among the doves and peacocks – some of which, having strayed on to the nearby rail track, had the misfortune to be culled by vehicles of the French National Railways.

The Château of La Napoule probably makes a more important contribution to literature today than it did in the era of the Clews: after Marie died in 1957, having survived her husband by 20 years, it became the Franco-American Arts Foundation of La Napoule, a resident academy for the international exchange of writers and artists.

La Napoule must have made a strong impression on Ernest Hemingway. His last novel, *Garden of Eden*, begun 40 years after he left the Riviera, describes its topography in detail.

It was while staying on the Cap d'Antibes with the wealthy Boston couple Sara and Gerald Murphy that Hemingway came to know La Napoule, from cycling there with his first wife, Hadley, and their son. La Napoule was the setting for *The Garden of Eden*. Its main characters, Catherine and David, rent an apartment in the pines at the western end of the town and are joined by another woman, the bisexual Marita.

This *ménage à trois* is clearly an evocation of the period when Hemingway lived in Juan-les-Pins with Hadley and his second-wife-to-be, Pauline, in the summer of 1926 – which he describes in his last book, the autobiographical *A Moveable Feast*:

> The husband has two attractive girls around when he has finished work. One is new and strange and if he has bad luck he gets to love them both.

> Then, instead of two of them and their child, there are three of them. All things truly wicked start from an innocence. First it is stimulating and fun and it goes that way for a while ... You lie and hate it and it destroys you and every day is more dangerous, but you live day to day as in a war.

It was to La Napoule that the Irish author of *My Life and Loves*, Frank Harris, brought Oscar Wilde after Wilde's release from Reading Gaol.

They were long-time friends – Wilde had dedicated his play *The Ideal Husband* to 'Frank Harris: a slight tribute to his power and distinction as an artist, his chivalry and nobility as a friend' – and Harris was one of the few who remained loyal to Wilde after his dramatic downfall and imprisonment in Reading Gaol.

The public attitude to his 'crime' was at the time exemplified by the words of the judge at his trial: 'You, Wilde, have been the centre of a circle of extensive corruption of the most hideous kind among young men' (despite the fact that there had been no allegations of this nature).

Harris's public support and private generosity to Wilde went unappreciated as far as Wilde's grandson, Merlin Holland, was concerned: when he wrote an introduction to the 1997 reprint of Harris's eulogistic biography of Wilde, he began it, 'Frank Harris was a rogue: he was also a braggart and a liar.'

After losing his widely publicized libel suit against the Marquis of Queensberry, father of Lord Alfred Douglas, in 1895, Wilde had been sentenced to two years' hard labour for his homosexual activities. After his release from Reading, he moved to Paris, where, instead of writing more plays, as Harris had hoped, he began to frequent the same society as before his arrest.

After being told by Wilde that he 'would write as naturally as the bird sings in a warmer climate', Harris went to Paris and invited

Wilde to come to the Riviera, in the hope of encouraging him to resume his work. Harris agreed to cover all of Wilde's expenses for the first three months, but what he did not know was the amount of upfront debt that Wilde had to settle before he could leave Paris – not to mention the farewell gifts, such as a new bicycle for his lover, Maurice Gilbert.

On the train south in that autumn of 1898, the two discussed the choice of location. Harris favoured some back country hideaway in the Esterel mountains or in the hills behind Nice, where Wilde could write undistracted; but Wilde, having spent the time since his release in Paris, demurred. Although he feared Nice because of the risk of meeting people who knew him, he was reluctant to give up the amusements of the city.

La Napoule was the compromise. There, thought Harris, Wilde could work in peace, and visit Cannes for occasional recreation. They both went there, for instance, to meet Sarah Bernhardt, who was performing *La Tosca*, and were greeted warmly. She was to have performed Wilde's *Salomé* in London in 1892, but it was banned because the play included biblical characters. It did not help with the censors to point out that most great art featured biblical characters.

In the end, the diversions won: Wilde did not write anything significant. He wrote to a friend, 'Even in Napoule there is romance: it comes in boats and takes the form of fisher-lads ... they are strangely perfect.' He preferred to sip absinthe in quayside cafés, chatting with young fishermen, than to write. One evening, they hired a boat to take them back across the bay to the Hôtel des Bains, and Harris was amazed to find that Wilde called the boat boy by name. 'When we landed I went up from the boat to the hotel, leaving Oscar and the boy together.'

Although Wilde would occasionally quote stanzas of unwritten poetry, he insisted that he could write no more. 'The intense energy of creation has been kicked out of me,' he said. Harris, realizing that his sponsorship was unlikely to bear fruit, would keep to his bargain, but on his own terms: since most of his business ventures were in Nice, he would move Wilde to the Hôtel Terminus there, where he could keep an eye on him.

In Nice, Wilde's worst fears were confirmed: he was recognized in a restaurant by English tourists, and he was asked to leave his hotel.

Harris's attempt at patronage had failed. Wilde returned to the more tolerant milieu of Paris, where he died in poverty two years later.

Cannes was born out of a cholera epidemic and a Scotsman's meanness. When Lord Brougham was prevented by the quarantine from entering Nice, he turned back and looked first at Antibes, but thought the only accommodation there was too expensive. The other godfather of Cannes was Lord Brougham's next-door neighbour, Stephen Liégeard, the man who invented the term Côte d'Azur, who died in Cannes at the age of 95. In 1887, Liégeard published a guide to the region, which he called *La Côte d'Azur* in an allusion to the *La Côte d'Or* of his native Burgundy. Liégeard's florid style, as seen in the description of Cannes that follows, helps to explain why author and book are largely forgotten, even if the title survives:

> Yes, the favourite daughter of the sun is Cannes, a patrician of supreme distinction, reserved in its welcome, a trifle proud at first, whose good graces can be gained only by elegance or conquered by merit.

– whereas 150 years of travel brochures have scarcely improved on Lady Margaret Brewster's description of winter in this Festival City:

> The sea here is certainly at times bluer than the bluest of other seas, but it is not its loveliest phase; on the contrary, the greatest charm of the Mediterranean seems to me to be its exquisite variety; there is the lilac, the stony grey, the *bleu foncé*, the pale blue flushed with rose, the milkiness, as if it were a milky way, the sheet of silver, – and that I think is the most beautiful, for the sky is then silvered blue also, and yet the sun so bright and clear that you can scarcely believe the colour is not the usual sky blue.

CHAPTER THREE

I sat on the mole ... to look at Antibes in the setting sun.
I have never seen anything so spectacular or so beautiful.

(Guy de Maupassant)

Antibes: The City Opposite

Antibes wears its history in its name. 2,300 years ago the Greeks called it 'anti polis' – the city opposite – because it was across the bay from their original settlement, Nice.

It is still a little 'opposite'. Although it lies half-way between trendy Cannes and busy Nice, the *autoroute* passes it by five miles to the north and the Route Nationale that connects to it is permanently traffic-jammed, leaving the town slightly off the beaten track for land travellers. Its non-chic is reflected in its property prices.

This landward polarization seems to unite it more closely with the sea: its yachting industry – its pleasure-boat harbour is Europe's biggest – keeps it buzzing all the year round, so that, unlike many of the Riviera's smaller coastal towns, it does not close its shutters for the winter.

Antibes was once a stop-over for Phoenician traders, and a Roman encampment. Its church and chateau – where Picasso worked, and left his output behind as a museum – date from the twelfth century, the fortifications around its old port are seventeenth century, and its bus station is classic 1930s art deco. And if its land approaches are a pustulation of modern apartment blocks (Graham Greene lived in one of them), at least the old town – *la vielle ville* – survives almost intact.

South of the town, the Cap d'Antibes reaches out into the Mediterranean like a basking dolphin, with old Antibes as its tail, the boulevard du Cap stretching along its dorsum, the lighthouse its blinking eye, and at its nose the fabled Eden Roc Hotel – host to the fabulously rich.

Antibes is also rich in literary association. Here, Jules Verne wrote his scenario for *Around the World in 80 Days*, Guy de Maupassant wrote *Mont Oriol*, F. Scott Fitzgerald wrote *Tender is the Night* and Graham Greene his last seven novels, among them *Monsignor Quixote.*

However appealing Antibes may be to migrant authors, indigenous ones are relatively scarce. A notable exception is Jacques Audiberti, Antibes-born novelist and prolific playwright who wrote in the turn-of-the-century surrealist style, with titles that translate as *Slaughter*, or *In Favour of Infanticide.* Even though, like most French artists, he had to move to Paris in his early 20s to pursue his career, his name is commemorated by the town with an annual prize for a literary career based wholly or in part in the Mediterranean region. (In 1989, the first year of the award, it was won by the India-born British author Lawrence Durrell.)

The town's first recorded writer-traveller was the English diarist and art historian John Evelyn. On 12 October 1644, he 'coasted within 2 leagues of Antibo which is the utmost towne of France', on his way to Italy. He wrote of the coastal hills of Provence as 'sweetely declining to the ... Coasts, full of Vine-yards, and Olive-yards, Orange trees, Myrtils, Pomegranads and the like sweete Plantations'.

In 1763, a more famous visitor arrived by sea from Genoa – Giacomo Casanova. His journal says that he made love to 23 women on the trip, convincing him that 'the only women as indiscriminately passionate as Venetians are those of Provence' – and giving a whole new meaning to the term 'all-inclusive tour'.

On the evening of 13 July 1867, a cruise ship, the *Quaker City*, sailed past the Cap d'Antibes bound for Genoa. On board was Mark Twain. He had just visited the Château d'If in Marseilles harbour, from which the fictional hero of Alexandre Dumas's *Le Comte de Monte Cristo* (*The Count of Monte Cristo*), Edmond Dantès, escaped to take revenge on his accusers. As a budding journalist, Twain knew that nothing sells like xenophobia, and his reports home centred on such odd French characteristics as their inadequate plumbing and aversion to soap. Yet, some impressions of Twain's journey must have left their mark: years later, in *Huckleberry Finn*, Tom Sawyer was to tell Huck about a man imprisoned for 37 years in the 'Castle Deef'.

On the ancient ramparts of the old town, a bust of Victor Hugo gazes out to sea, the inscription on its base his tribute to the town:

'Here everything shines, everything sings. Sunshine, women, and love are all resplendent here.' Hugo set the opening of Les Misérables, in which Valjean steals the bishop's silver candle-sticks, in the nearby market town of Dignes.

But in 1838, Hugo was there on a pilgrimage. Twenty-four years earlier, when Napoleon had escaped from Elba, it was in this region that he first landed before making his way to Cannes.

Napoleon sent an officer to Antibes with 20 men and orders to capture its fortress. In fact, the fortress captured them, as it did the party that was sent to find them. Said the public-relations-conscious Napoleon, 'We must travel faster than the news', and marched on, leaving the captives behind.

Victor Hugo's awe had obviously not been tarnished by the defeat at Waterloo and Napoleon's imprisonment on St Helena: 'I walked for two hours where Napoleon walked,' he wrote, 'and left the beach in a state of religious fervour: the ebb and flow of tide had failed to erase his penultimate steps.'

Many other French authors have itinerant associations with the town. Its museums boast sculptures of the parents and sister, Caroline, of Gustave Flaubert, the author of Madame Bovary: the 24-year-old Flaubert was here with them all in 1845. They must have been a close-knit family – Caroline was on her honeymoon.

The marriage was a brief one. Caroline was widowed young, remarried, and came to live in Antibes, where she died giving birth to a daughter, also called Caroline. Having been orphaned at an early age, the younger Caroline was to Flaubert the daughter he never had, and he wrote to her affectionately for the rest of his life. She became a talented painter, whose works can be found in the town's Picasso Museum – which also houses a picture of the poet Louise Colet, who, from 1846 on, was Flaubert's mistress, and his inspiration for Madame Bovary.

In his journal, the 24-year-old Flaubert complained throughout the trip: about hotels and food, about how long it took to check passports at the Italian border, and of how family obligations hindered his romantic pursuits. But there is an important literary relic of the journey: he was so struck by Brueghel's painting of The Temptation of Saint Anthony in the Balbi palace in Genoa that he wrote the novel of that name.

*

In *Wild Swans*, an autobiographical account of the Maoist revolution in China, author Jung Chang tells of her mother's arranged marriage. When the mother finally met the suitor, she turned him down – because she could never marry a man who thought that Guy de Maupassant wrote *Madame Bovary*.

If he had lived long enough to hear the story, de Maupassant would have liked it: he was an admirer of Flaubert, who taught him much about style and observation. 'He taught me,' says de Maupassant in his preface to *Pierre et Jean* – also written in Antibes – 'that talent is long patience – a way of looking at something long enough to discover in it some aspect that no-one else has yet seen'.

De Maupassant found Antibes inspirational, and praised it lavishly. 'In Antibes I am in a dream,' he wrote. 'The first traces of spring here tug at my nature and pull out literary fruits that I didn't know were there.' It was also his favourite port:

> I have never seen anything so spectacular or so beautiful as this little town, jutting into the immense bay of Nice. The waves break against its walls, surrounding it with a bouquet of foam, while, above the ramparts, houses cluster on top of one another around the two towers, like the horns on an old helmet.

His first visits to the area had been to see his mother, who lived in the Villa Bellevue in La Fontonne, on the western outskirts of the town. He was to spend much of the last seven years of his life in the area.

In a side street at the northern end of the boulevard du Cap stands La Bastide du Bosquet, where, in 'the yellow room', which he rented in 1886 at the age of 36, de Maupassant wrote *Mont Oriol*. He wrote of this period, 'I sail, I work, and I live in total solitude.' It was not quite *total* solitude: his assignations in Cannes with the mysterious 'woman in grey' became so demanding that he eventually moved there, and it was in Cannes on 1 January 1892 that he tried to cut his own throat and was transferred to an asylum.

Today, the Villa Bellevue is the site of the cardiology department of the La Fontonne hospital, and La Bastide du Bosquet is a delightful bed-and-breakfast run by Christian and Sylvie Aussel. La Fontonne has come down in the world: what was once the great Roman road linking Arles with Rome along the Mediterranean coastline – the Aurelian Way – is now the traffic-congested, hoarding-infested Route Nationale 7, and the only writing done there today is with spray cans.

But a trace of de Maupassant remains: hewn into the ancient walls of medieval Antibes is a tiny restaurant, Le Sucrier – the Sugar Bowl – whose owner, Marc Estrada, is his great-great-nephew.

Just behind the bust of Victor Hugo is a square so tiny that it is called a *placette*. It is named after Nikos Kazantzakis, the Cretan author of *Zorba the Greek* and *The Last Temptation of Christ*, who was exiled from Greece for his political views, and made his home in the old town of Antibes. Kazantzakis, a playwright and translator of Dante into Greek, did not publish a novel until he was in his 50s, but such was the influence of his work that in the year in which he died, 1957, he failed by only one vote to win the Nobel Prize for Literature.

Zorba the Greek is the story of the relationship between an academic studying Greek culture and the earthy Zorba, whose interests are rather more basic. It was made into a film in 1964 featuring Anthony Quinn in the title role. In the end, the intellectual leaves in frustration – but not before asking Zorba to teach him the Greek male dance. Kazantzakis once summed up the message of the film as 'How simple and frugal a thing is happiness: a glass of wine, a roast chestnut, a wretched little brazier, and the sound of the sea.' His philosophy of life is engraved in French on the commemorative plaque in the little *placette* off the place Safranier: 'I fear nothing, I want nothing, I am free.'

Marcel Proust did not share the wanderlust of his fellow writers – chronically asthmatic for most of his life, he found that smoky trains aggravated his condition. But while Proustian associations are rare outside of his native Paris and Normandy, Antibes has a mysterious link with his most famous character.

In La Fontonne before the First World War, near the home of de Maupassant's mother, the brothers Garbero ran a flying school. In March 1914, a year after the publication of À *la Recherche du temps perdu* (*Remembrance of Things Past*), a man registered for training there under the name 'Marcel Swann'. On 30 May, he took off over the

Bay of Antibes on his first solo flight. It was also his last: the aircraft immediately plunged into the sea. Eye-witnesses said that the plane floated for a few minutes with 'Swann' clinging to the fuselage and shouting for help, then disappeared.

A literature-minded investigator would soon have deduced that 'Marcel Swann' – a combination of the names of the author and his most famous character – was a member of the Proust household. He was in fact Proust's secretary and former chauffeur, Alfred Agostinelli. Immediately after the accident, his half-brother travelled from Nice to Paris to beg Proust for money so that he could recover the aircraft and give Alfred a less humid resting-place. As Agostinelli had left Proust without warning the previous December, it seemed an unusual request.

When the plane was lifted, Alfred was not in it. His decomposed body was netted by a fisherman some time later, raising many unanswered questions. Why had Agostinelli used a false name, especially one so famously associated with Proust? And why were the pockets of his flying jacket stuffed with banknotes? Had Agostinelli taken them from Proust, and, if so, did his half-brother know?

The only person who could have said was Proust himself, and he never mentioned it. His journals record his grief at the loss of Alfred; he sent a wreath to the funeral and on each anniversary thereafter until his own death in 1922. But the fact that not one single letter has survived from what is known to have been a copious correspondence between the two seems to confirm the view that their relationship was rather more intimate than that of employer and secretary.

If you stand by the old port with your back to the bay in which Agostinelli crashed his plane and look through the arched entrance to the old town, you will see the Café Félix, formerly Chez Félix, the unassuming restaurant where for many years Graham Greene, the author of *The Third Man* and *Brighton Rock*, was a regular client. He even had his mail delivered there, and the chef's wife was his cleaner. Lunch was almost invariably preceded by a dry Martini – without lemon – and accompanied by a local Château des Garcinières. 'I go there,' he told his friend and confessor Father Duran, 'because Félix saves any wine that I leave in the bottle for my next visit.'

Greene set much of his writing in Antibes. Like most Riviera towns, its true character is revealed only when the holiday crowds have left, and in this opening paragraph of *Chagrin in Three Parts*, Greene captures that ambience exactly – and manages to slip in a commercial for Félix:

> It was February in Antibes. Gusts of rain blew along the ramparts, and the emaciated statues on the terrace of the Château Grimaldi dripped with wet, and there was a sound absent during the flat blue days of summer, the continual rustle below the ramparts of the small surf. All along the Côte the summer restaurants were closed, but lights shone in Félix Au Port and one Peugeot of the latest model stood in the parking-rank. The bare masts of the abandoned yachts stuck up like tooth-picks and the last plane in the winter-service dropped, in a flicker of green, red and yellow lights, like Christmas-tree baubles, towards the airport of Nice. This was the Antibes I always enjoyed; and I was disappointed to find I was not alone in the restaurant as I was most nights of the week.

Antibes was also the setting for Greene's *May We Borrow Your Husband?* in which Félix became 'Lou-Lou'. The sub-title of the book is *And Other Comedies of the Sexual Life*. The narrator of the story – about two male homosexuals on a business trip in Antibes who set out to break up an English honeymoon couple by 'borrowing' the vulnerable husband – is a famous writer, William Harris, who is working on a historical biography of the Earl of Rochester. It was a shrewd piece of marketing: Greene had already completed a biography of Lord Rochester for which he was trying to find a publisher. Again, he sets the novel in wintry Antibes:

> It was the time of year I liked best, when Juan les Pins becomes as squalid as a closed fun-fair with Lunar Park boarded up and cards marked *Fermeture annuelle* outside the Pam-Pam and Maxim's, and the Concours International Amateur de Striptease at the Vieux Colombiers is over for another season. Then Antibes comes into its own as a small country town with the Auberge de Provence full of local people and old men sit indoors drinking beer or pastis at the *glacier* in the Place de Gaulle. The small garden, which forms a roundabout on the ramparts, looks a little sad with the short stout palms bowing their brown fronds; the sun in the morning shines without any glare, and the few white sails move gently on the unblinding sea.

You can always trust the English to stay on longer than others into the autumn. We have a blind faith in the southern sun and we are taken by surprise when the wind blows icily over the Mediterranean. Then a bickering war develops with the hotel-keeper over the heating on the third floor, and the tiles strike cold underfoot. For a man who has reached the age when all he wants is some good wine and some good cheese and a little work, it is the best season of all.

When the actor-turned-writer Dirk Bogarde was asked to play the part of Harris in the film version, he turned it down, but he eventually accepted on condition that he be allowed to write the script. He wrote it as the story of Harris's love affair with the spurned wife, so he got a juicier part, his first screenplay and a romantic lunch scene with Charlotte Attenborough – at Chez Félix.

In the avenue Pasteur, a short walk out of the old town, stands the Residence des Fleurs, the modest apartment block where Greene lived alone in a one-bedroom apartment. Beside the rear entrance a tiny plaque – its size and discreet placement a manifestation of his many disagreements with local authorities – reads: 'Graham Greene lived here from 1966 to 1990'. For the novelist whose publications spanned a period of 67 years, and who had more of his works adapted into films than any other writer, it seems a subdued tribute.

Yet the restraint seems appropriate: the low profile helped him to compartmentalize his twin careers – author and part-time spy. Exotic settings derived from his subsidized travels often featured as backdrops to his novels, from corrupt post-war Vienna in *The Third Man* to cloak-and-dagger Cuba in *Our Man in Havana*.

His partitioning skill also proved helpful in his voracious love life. At the beginning of the Second World War, he 'evacuated' his wife Vivien and their children to Oxford – ostensibly to avoid the German bombs – while he stayed in London and began a nine-year affair with his landlady's daughter, Dorothy Glover.

While still in this relationship, Greene, a convert to Roman Catholicism at 23, was asked to be godfather to Catherine Walston, a 30-year-old married woman, at her own conversion. Her entry into the faith was celebrated at Rules restaurant in Covent Garden, and consummated that same evening.

Four years into the Walston affair (and, ironically, while proof-reading *The End of the Affair*) he began a torrid relationship with

Australian painter Jocelyn Rickards. In addition, over this period, this highly numerate author who cast himself as the meticulous accountant in *Loser Takes All* recalled transactions with precisely 47 prostitutes.

The main motivation for Greene's move to the south of France was provided by the Inland Revenue. In an attempt to reduce his tax bill, he had got involved with a Brighton solicitor, Theodore Lowe, who specialized in relieving the Hollywood famous of their wealth on the pretext of investing it in Switzerland (his client list included Charlie Chaplin and Laurel and Hardy). Their money did in fact go to Switzerland, but it got no further than Lowe's bank account. Lowe's client list came to light when he was caught with $100,000 in forged notes in his car.

In 1965, reluctant to prosecute Greene (possibly for fear of revealing the secret tax-free payments from MI6), the Inland Revenue gave him until the end of the year to leave the country. He chose Antibes, which he had discovered 20 years earlier as a guest aboard the yacht of Sir Alexander Korda, who produced the first films of his novels.

Once there, he bought his apartment in the Residence des Fleurs, and lost no time in rekindling a liaison with a Frenchwoman, Yvonne Cloetta, whom he had met six years earlier, and who lived with her husband in nearby Juan-les-Pins. It was to be his longest relationship, lasting until his death 25 years later.

Despite his self-imposed seclusion, his public profile was raised irrevocably in 1982, when he published *J'Accuse: The Dark Side of Nice*, a 33-page diatribe in English and French which accused the city of Nice, its police and legal system, of collusion with the Mafia.

It all started as a result of the marital misfortunes of the Cloettas' daughter, Martine. The failure of her attempts to get a satisfactory divorce settlement from her French husband, Daniel Guy – and the fact that he was able to abuse her without the police offering any protection – convinced Greene that Guy was mixed up with the Mafia and that the police were shielding him.

In protest, Greene returned to the government the insignia of the Chevalier de la Légion d'Honneur that he had been awarded under President Pompidou, and published *J'Accuse* in an attempt to highlight local Mafia activities.

Like the script-writer that he was, Greene set the scene:

> Twenty-three years ago I met and made friends with M. and Mme.
> Jacques Cloetta at Douala in the Cameroons, and their daughter
> Martine, a child of seven ... Later when I settled in Antibes they be-
> came my near neighbours, as they had a house in Juan-les-Pins, and
> my close friends.

He fails to mention his relationship with Yvonne, by then in its 17th year. Typical accusations were:

> I accuse certain police officers in Nice of protecting criminals, of en-
> couraging them in their crimes by guaranteeing them immunity
> whether for the sake of the information they provide or for money
> or favours ...
>
> By ensuring the impunity of some criminals (suppressing evidence
> and abandoning the pursuit) they are enabled to lay their hands with
> little trouble on unimportant delinquents and ensure that at year's
> end they can show satisfactory statistics.

In publishing *J'Accuse* he must have known that he would also be publicizing his affair with Mme Cloetta. For one so secretive, knowingly to put himself in the public spotlight – and possibly risk physical danger from the Mafia which he was sure held unassailable power in the city – must have been a difficult and brave decision.

It was also a futile one. Guy sued for libel and won, the book was banned in France and Jacques Médecin, the then mayor of Nice, claiming that *J'Accuse* was a pun on Jacquou, his nickname in the Nice patois, received an out-of-court settlement. Fortunately, Greene's costs were more than covered by his profits from *J'Accuse*, and the incoming president, François Mitterand, returned his Chevalier de la Légion d'Honneur.

Despite threats on his life following the publication of *J'Accuse*, Greene remained in Antibes until he left in 1990 for treatment in Switzerland, where he died in hospital on Easter Saturday 1991.

Today, the old town of Antibes seems populated by (mostly British) yachtsmen, who carouse in pubs with names like The Hop Store, Comic Strips and Le Yacht. And the books in the town's only bookshop, Heidi's, are all in English.

The terrace of Le Yacht was directly beneath Greene's balcony. He used to complain to them about the noise, and the drinkers used to complain about his complaints. But despite the noise, he managed to publish seven more novels during his time there, including *Travels with My Aunt*, *A Sort of Life*, *The Honorary Consul*, *The Human Factor* and his light-hearted confrontation between a Marxist mayor and a Catholic priest, *Monsignor Quixote* (the film of which starred Alec Guinness and Leo McKern).

Greene never divorced Vivien, whom he had married 63 years earlier, and Yvonne never divorced her husband – wife and mistress met for the first time at his graveside. His friend and confessor – and his inspiration for *Monsignor Quixote* – Father Duran, read 'Goodnight sweet prince' from *Hamlet* (which, since he had previously recorded Greene's extreme dislike of the play, seems to have carried a hint of retribution).

Sadly, Greene did not live long enough to savour the vindication of his Quixotic gesture in publishing *J'Accuse*: three years after his death, Jacques Médecin was convicted of fiscal fraud and, after serving a jail sentence in France, died in exile in Uruguay.

A near neighbour and contemporary of Greene in Antibes was the American writer Paul Gallico. Born in New York in 1897, he served in the US Navy in the First World War. Gallico had the rare distinction – for an author – of having been knocked out by the world heavyweight boxing champion, Jack Dempsey. It was part of a stunt aimed at raising his profile as a budding sports writer.

He moved to South Devon in 1936, wrote a symbolic *Farewell to Sport* and was a war correspondent in the Second World War. In 1941 he became famous with *The Snow Goose*, the story of a reclusive misfit who reveals his true worth in the war by rescuing British troops during the evacuation of Dunkirk. With its message that everyone has a valuable role to play, the story made ideal cinema for those dark days, and its success enabled him to become a full-time author. He wrote over 40 books, among them *The Poseidon Adventure*. The last of his four wives, Virginia, was lady-in-waiting to Princess Grace of Monaco, where he lived for a time before settling for his last years in Antibes. He died there in July 1976, a few days short of his 79th birthday.

*

At the southern end of Antibes town, the road divides into two. The road on the right goes to brassy Juan-les-Pins, where, despite its name, pine trees are scarce. The one on the left, the boulevard du Cap, leads to the leafy Cap d'Antibes, a plethora of pine. Even the junction between the two roads has literary links, for it was near this roundabout, on the 'painters' seat', that writer, historian, painter and former prime minister Winston Churchill sat while painting the view of the old town previously depicted by Monet. (When he had finished the painting, Churchill gave it to his bodyguard, who sold it for $25,000.)

From the beginning of the Cap, it is an easy walk south along the boulevard du Cap to a mansion called Les Chênes Vertes (Evergreen Oaks). To the left along the way is the chemin de l'Ermitage, where, in 1938, the Russian novelist Vladimir Nabokov lived at No. 18.

Antibes had been yet another stopping place in the Nabokovs' peregrinations along the coast in search of healthy – and suitably priced – locations. They had been staying in the back country village of Moulinet, but their sojourn in the mountains had been less than idyllic and they had missed the amenities and comforts of the coastal towns.

Although he was already accomplished in English, it was in Antibes that Nabokov wrote his last works in Russian. It was also their last port of call on the Riviera before leaving for the United States, and the fame and fortune that followed the success of *Lolita*.

Les Chênes Vertes was the occasional residence between 1874 and 1879 of the doyen of science fiction writers. Twelve years before de Maupassant sailed into the port, Jules Verne had moored his own yacht off the Cap. Like de Maupassant, he had named it after one of his profitable works. It was called *Saint Michel*, after his *Michel Strogoff*.

Verne came here to work on the stage adaptation of his novel, *Around the World in 80 Days*. He must have found the greenhouse in the grounds of Les Chênes Vertes conducive to work: *Around the World* opened in Paris on 7 November 1874 to enthusiastic reviews, and Verne was to return over the next six years to write novels and scenarios, among them *Twenty Thousand Leagues under the Sea* and *From the Earth to the Moon*.

Les Chênes Vertes is now 152 boulevard President Kennedy, but it still carries its original name on one gatepost, with a plaque saying that Jules Verne wrote some of his works there. On the other gatepost a sign says 'Irish Consulate', for it is now the residence of Pierre Joannon, the Irish Consul – and author of a number of historical works about the region. As an ambassador for Antibes, Verne was less than enthusiastic. He wrote to his publisher: 'I have paid for this magnificent climate. I've been here three times and each time I've had neuralgia, sore throats and ear abscesses.'

If Verne's house on the Cap was the cradle of space fiction, it also has a link with space fact. A frequent guest at Les Chênes Vertes during the occupancy of its next owner was one Abram Spanel, founder of the International Latex Corporation, the company that made the space suits worn by Neil Armstrong, 'Buzz' Aldrin and Mike Collins on the lunar landing in July 1969 – which Jules Verne had described 100 years earlier.

Across the boulevard du Cap from Les Chênes Vertes stands the Hôtel Eden Roc, the jewel of the Cap d'Antibes for almost 100 years. Its guest list reads like a world *Who's Who* of royalty, statesmen and stars of film and rock.

It was at this hotel, with the nearby plage de La Garoupe, the 'bright tan prayer-rug beach' as Fitzgerald called it, and in the sumptuous villas that surround it, that the legend of the 'Jazz-Age' Riviera was born.

No other writer has encapsulated this era as powerfully as did F. Scott Fitzgerald in his *Tender is the Night*, which, although it was not published until 1934, remains the essential history of the 1920s Côte d'Azur. Strangely, as we saw in Chapter 2, he advised his publisher not to use the word 'Riviera' when promoting the book, lest it 'sound like the triviality of which I am often accused' – although Fitzgerald himself uses it in the first line.

Scott Fitzgerald and his wife Zelda spent much of the 1920s on the Côte d'Azur. When they arrived, he had just published *The Great Gatsby*, to critical acclaim; they were young, glamorous, well off if not fabulously rich, and ready to enjoy the high life, sunshine and favourable exchange rate. When they left at the end of the decade, Zelda was showing the first signs of madness and Scott was fighting the battle against alcoholism which he eventually lost.

A literary guest during their 1924 stay was the American humorist and short-story writer Ring Lardner, a drinking buddy of Hemingway and Fitzgerald, and the latter's near neighbour on New York's Long Island. The *New York Daily News* called Lardner 'America's foremost humorist of the 1920s'. He became Abe North in *Tender is the Night.*

It took Fitzgerald eight years to finish *Tender is the Night*, delayed by the need to write short stories and film scripts to pay for Zelda's illness, but it remains a faithful fictional record of between-wars expatriate American life. Although the Fitzgeralds lived in many hotels and villas in the region, their strongest association will always be with the Hôtel Eden Roc, and it is appropriate that we are introduced to the hotel – known as Gausse's Hotel in the book – in the first paragraph:

> On the pleasant shore of the French Riviera, about half way between Marseilles and the Italian border, stands a large, proud, rose-colored hotel. Deferential palms cool its flushed façade, and before it stretches a short dazzling beach. Lately it has become a summer resort of notable and fashionable people; a decade ago it was almost deserted after its English clientele went north in April. Now, many bungalows cluster near it, but when this story begins only the cupolas of a dozen old villas rotted like water lilies among the massed pines between Gausse's Hôtel des Étrangers and Cannes, five miles away.

Fitzgerald took his title from Keats's 'Ode to a Nightingale', which, with its 'Provençal song and sunburnt mirth' must have recalled those heady nights on the Cap, but whose reference to 'the dull brain' that 'perplexes and retards', carried such ominous overtones.

> Tender is the night,
> And haply the Queen-Moon is on her throne
> Clustered around by all her starry Fays;
> But here there is no light,
> Save what from heaven is with the breezes blown
> Through verdurous glooms and winding mossy ways.

At least one such 'winding mossy way' remains: at the entrance to the chemin des Mougins, just off the boulevard du Cap, a fragment of a sign remains nailed to a post. The sign used to direct visitors to the Villa America, the home of wealthy Bostonian couple Gerald and Sara Murphy, who lived there in the 1920s.

The villa has another name now, but it still looks out on the rocky western coast of the Cap, where the Murphys extended hospitality – and sometimes money – to galaxies of contemporary artists, writers and hangers-on. The artists included Picasso and Matisse; among the writers, in addition to Fitzgerald and his friend Ernest Hemingway, were Gertrude Stein, John Dos Passos, Anita Loos (who wrote *Gentlemen Prefer Blondes*), Dorothy Parker and Robert Benchley.

The last two were members of the group of writers who regularly lunched at the Round Table in New York's Algonquin Hotel, for marathons of gossip and drink – although according to Harpo Marx, it only became a Round Table 'when everybody was getting nostalgic about the twenties'. Until then it was just a table, 'with people drifting in and out, eating, arguing, gossiping, telling jokes, talking shop and having brainstorms'.

Harpo brought a unique talent to the Round Table. As a professional mute:

> I had absolutely nothing to contribute ... The dining room corner was a hotbed of raconteurs and conversationalists. But until I came along, there wasn't a full-time listener in the crowd. I couldn't have been more welcome if I had had the power to repeal Prohibition.

The Murphys had been introduced to the Cap d'Antibes in 1922 by Gerald's former Yale college-mate, the song-writer Cole Porter, who invited them to the Château de la Garoupe – at various times home to the Duke and Duchess of Windsor and ship owners Onassis and Niarchos. Porter, having managed, to quote one of his own songs, to 'wive it wealthily', made a hobby of discovering such unknown gems.

Porter never came back, but the Murphys did, in turn inviting the Fitzgeralds. Scott and Zelda came first in 1924 and decided to stay on the coast, renting the Villa Paquita in Juan-les-Pins and spending much of the rest of the decade in or near the Cap.

The Murphys' lifestyle was lavish and their parties notorious. They were the models for Dick and Nicole Diver in *Tender is the Night*: in the book, when someone asks the Divers if they like the Côte d'Azur, another character says, 'They have to – they invented it.' As the drink flowed, the egos of the literary legends could be piqued. Upset when Hemingway was given a bigger welcome party than himself, Fitzgerald started to throw ashtrays, and even threw Sara's Venetian glasses over the garden wall, earning himself a three-week banishment from the villa. But in the end Fitzgerald showed his gratitude: *Tender is the Night* is dedicated 'To Gerald and Sara – many fêtes'.

Ernest Hemingway brought his first wife, Hadley, to the Villa America in June 1926, but because their son had whooping cough, they did not stay with the Murphys. As the Fitzgeralds were away, they went into quarantine in the Villa Paquita, but the quarantine did not prevent their friend Pauline Pfeiffer from coming from Paris to join them. The result of this *ménage à trois* was that when the Hemingways returned to Paris at the end of the summer, they lived apart.

The next year he appeared at the Cap d'Antibes with a different wife – Pauline.

As we saw in the previous chapter, Hemingway, in the autobiographical *A Moveable Feast*, published after his death, saw himself as the helpless bystander.

It was the Murphys who, having persuaded the exclusive Hôtel Eden Roc to retain a skeleton staff so that they might stay there for the summer of 1923, are most often credited with the transformation of the Côte d'Azur from a winter to a summer resort.

There is no doubt that, with the advent of paid holidays and cheap air travel, it would have happened anyway, but in the 1920s, only Americans would have made such a request. As the writer friend of Fitzgerald and Hemingway, John Dos Passos, put it:

> The upper-class French and British would not be seen dead on the Riviera in summer … but for Americans the temperature was ideal, the water delicious, and Antibes was the sort of little virgin port we dreamed of discovering.

For the British at least, it was not just a matter of temperature. The main reason for their summer exodus was that, to the gentry of the day, attendance at the London 'Season' – Ascot, Henley, Wimbledon, Goodwood, Lords – was a virtual royal command, not to mention the annual charade of 'Coming Out': the presentation to the reigning monarch, and subsequent auctioning-off, of marriageable daughters. There were other, equally grave, concerns: the social stigma, for instance, of one's absence from Ascot being interpreted as having failed to be accepted into the Royal Enclosure. (Divorcees were not admitted.) And, further down the list, there was cholera, which was thought to be more prevalent in summer.

Thus it was that Fitzgerald came to be the first writer in English to capture summer on the Cap d'Antibes:

> the distant image of Cannes, the pink and cream of old fortifications, the purple Alp that bounded Italy, were cast across the water and lay quivering in the ripples and rings sent up by the sea-plants through the clear shallows.

The clear, calm waters off the Eden Roc still offer the best diving to be found off the Cap, and La Garoupe is still its best beach. It lies, sandy and shaded by umbrella pines, not, as Fitzgerald says, 'as one with the hotel', but on the eastern shore of the Cap, and it is much more crowded today than was Fitzgerald's 'bright tan prayer-rug'.

Hemingway was convinced that Zelda, herself a would-be writer, was jealous of Scott's success, and that she set out to destroy him. As evidence, in A Moveable Feast, written after Scott's death, Hemingway records a conversation in Michaud's restaurant, in which Fitzgerald tells him that Zelda has questioned the adequacy of his genitalia, and he asks Hemingway for his opinion. Following a visit to the men's room and the exposure of the equipment in question, Hemingway tries to assure Fitzgerald of its sufficiency and, failing, offers to take him to the Louvre, so that he may compare it with those of the ancient Greeks.

Whether or not that particular incident took place, there were many recorded incidences of Zelda's attention seeking: jumping down the stairwell at a restaurant in St-Paul-de-Vence, diving from the rocks in La Garoupe. Fitzgerald's own view was poignantly expressed in a letter to his daughter Scottie, many years later:

> When I was young, I lived with a great dream. The dream grew and I learned how to speak of it and make people listen. Then the dream divided one day when I decided to marry your mother after all, even though I knew she was spoilt and meant me no good ...

> But I was a man divided. She wanted me to work too much for her and not enough for my dream. She realised too late that work was

dignity and the only dignity, and tried to atone for it by working herself, but it was too late and she broke and is broken forever.

Robert Benchley – whose CV proclaimed his skill at 'society drunk' roles, and who, sent on assignment to Venice, famously cabled back 'Streets flooded, please advise' – introduced Fitzgerald to the author and journalist Sheilah Graham. She was celebrating her engagement to the Marquess of Donegal at the time, but she married Fitzgerald instead. He remained in the grip of alcoholism, and died at the age of 44, while Hemingway, who was only three years younger, survived him by 20 years.

Gertrude Stein, author and critic, who was a great help to Hemingway in his early attempts to move from journalist to novelist, once upset him by saying that Fitzgerald's books would be read 'when many of his well-known contemporaries are forgotten'.

It was at La Garoupe in 1935, the year after the publication of *Tender is the Night*, that the English essayist and critic Cyril Connolly wrote his only novel, *The Rock Pool*, its title a metaphor for the human flotsam who, like sea life stranded by the tide, inhabit the coastal resorts. For its main character, Naylor:

> It was his favourite beach: for him the white sand, the pale translucent water, the cicadas' jigging away at their perpetual rumba, the smell of rosemary and cistus; the corrugations of sunshine on the bright Aleppo pines, held the whole classic essence of the Mediterranean.

As children are engrossed looking into rock pools, Naylor is initially fascinated by the debauchery of the expatriates' lifestyle, but he is eventually seduced by it.

> The intolerable melancholy, the dinginess, the corruption of that tainted inland sea overcame him. He felt the breath of centuries of wickedness and disillusion; how many civilizations had staled on that bright promontory.

Today the likes of Clint Eastwood, Bruce Willis and Madonna adorn the striped sun-beds of the Hôtel Eden Roc, and one wonders if they think of the cravatted ghosts who capered there so long ago. The title of Calvin Tomkins' book about the Murphys sums up those Jazz-Age summers on the Cap d'Antibes: *Living Well is the Best Revenge*. But there was no revenge for Fitzgerald. Alcoholic and in declining health, and with the pressing need for ready cash preventing him from completing his last novel, appropriately called *The Last Tycoon*, Fitzgerald was to regret the fortune he squandered on the Riviera.

Contrary to the Riviera's vaunted curative effect on tuberculosis, the Murphys' son Patrick contracted it there, and it was the need to remove him to a Swiss sanatorium in 1929 that caused the closure of the Villa America and their departure from the coast.

The 'Swiss Family Murphy', as Dorothy Parker called them, invited her to join them in the sanatorium, to help look after the children and dogs. It was the month of the Wall Street crash, and Parker must have been even more than usually short of cash to exchange the Côte d'Azur for a winter on the top of a 'God damn Alp' with all the windows open and wine the main alcoholic beverage. But she stayed, and with the exception of a brief trip to New York to pick up an award cheque, she did not see the Algonquin for more than a year.

A fellow 'Gonk' – as the Algonquin bootleg drinkers called themselves – was James Thurber, the American humorist and illustrator. Although a friend of Parker and Benchley and a drinking member of the Algonquin clan until his last cirrhotic days, Thurber was not a member of its Round Table – or, as some called it, the Vicious Circle. Not only did he consider himself of a younger age group, but he found their humour forced and rehearsed. (Example: Ask me to give you a sentence using the word 'punctilious'; Answer: A guy has two daughters, Lizzie and Tillie. Lizzie is all right, but you have no idea how punctilious.) Thurber sat in on only one of its famous luncheons.

He was the author of *The Secret Life of Walter Mitty* – the story of a shy incompetent, who in his daydreams acts out incredibly skilful and heroic exploits. When asked who was his model for Mitty – whose frailty is so universally recognized that it has put Thurber's hero into the *Oxford English Dictionary* – he said, 'Every other man I've ever known'.

When Thurber and his wife rented the Villa Tamisier on the Cap d'Antibes in 1937, the Thurbers were relative late-comers to the Cap and most of their compatriots had returned.

Thurber himself was returning to a Riviera that he had known ten years earlier, when, as we shall see in Chapter 5, he had worked in the Nice office of the *Chicago Tribune*. In the late 1920s, when the *Tribune*, like many of its American expatriate readers, packed up and left, Thurber went back to New York, broke and alone – his wife having left him for a colleague.

But when he got back to the USA, he found that his fame had preceded him, and he was better known at home than he was in France. When he returned to the Riviera in the spring of 1937, he was rich and famous both as writer and illustrator, and on the permanent staff of *New Yorker* magazine – and he had a new wife.

But the clouds of another war were looming. Many writers were involved in the Spanish Civil War, and Hitler and Mussolini were in power in their respective countries.

After visiting Paris, London (where he had the distinction of being the first American since Mark Twain to be invited to lunch at *Punch* magazine) and Scotland, Thurber and Helen, his second wife, drove south. He was delighted to be back on the Riviera. He wrote to a friend:

> Nobody could do justice to this blue, purple, warm, snowy mélange
> of sea, mountains, and valleys. God, what a place to drive a car in!
> You're always either a mile high, looking down at the sea, or on a
> valley floor looking up at a town a mile above you.

The Murphys and their entourage may have been long gone, but the British invasion had only just begun. At one afternoon tea party the Thurbers met the recently abdicated King Edward VIII – by now the newly married Duke of Windsor – and Winston Churchill. Thurber was unimpressed by the future prime minister's paintings, possibly because he had heard that Royal Academician Churchill had called him 'that insane and depraved American artist'.

They arrived back in New York on 1 September 1938. Thurber's stay on the Cap had been a fruitful one, resulting in dozens of drawings and articles, many evoking 'some bright cherished memory of the France which so many of us will always love'. A year later the major powers of Europe were at war.

This series of articles seemed to be Thurber's farewell tribute to a France on the eve of defeat and occupation – a France that he thought he would never see again. In this he was correct, for although he and Helen were to return 20 years later, by that time he was blind.

In 1928, another Cap d'Antibes villa was occupied by American writers. The *New Yorker* columnist and critic Alexander Woollcott rented the seaside Villa Galanon for the summer and invited his fellow Algonquinian Harpo Marx, to join him. Marx called it his literary period: he visited Somerset Maugham on Cap Ferrat a number of times and the unlikely friendship lasted for some years. One luncheon guest at the Villa Galanon was the 72-year-old George Bernard Shaw and his wife – for whom Harpo acted as chauffeur for the rest of their stay. Three years earlier, Shaw had refused the Nobel Prize for Literature, calling it 'a lifebelt thrown to a swimmer who has already reached the shore'.

Harpo was also introduced to H.G. Wells. 'I've heard a lot about your company, Mr. Wells,' he said. 'Especially out west. Every town has a Wells-Fargo office.' He later summed up his literary adventure: 'Passed my Maugham, flunked my Wells.'

There is yet another literary villa near the Hôtel Eden Roc: a fictional one. Although Somerset Maugham is more often associated with Cap Ferrat, one of his stories that was dramatized by BBC Television, *Three Fat Women of Antibes*, is set there. It tells of three fat, rich, middle-aged women guests at the hotel. They are trying desperately to lose weight, but they realize that they will never do so if they stay at the hotel because the food is irresistible. So they rent a villa nearby and hire a chef who claims to specialize in non-fattening meals.

The scheme works well until, desperate for a fourth for bridge, they invite a relative of one of the women to come to stay. The string-bean-shaped and aptly named Lena likes to eat, and the chef enjoys her appreciation, but her ability to indulge her gluttonous appetite for French cuisine without putting on any weight has a dramatic impact on the fat women's lives.

In 1931, Georges Simenon, who wrote over 400 books in his career, wrote three of his 86 Maigret mysteries at the Villa Les Roches

Grises in the boulevard James Wyllie – presumably in an afternoon or two. An even bigger mystery is how he managed to achieve this phenomenal output while claiming to have bedded more than 10,000 women.

During the Second World War, the old town of Antibes was a warren of artists, some of them writers who chose not to work for German propaganda in Paris, others fleeing the hardships of occupied France. In the rue de l'Orme, a few metres from where Victor Hugo's bust now contemplates the Mediterranean, lived the poet Jacques Prévert, with his wife, daughter and dog Hergé (named after the creator of Tintin). In an adjacent cul-de-sac barely wide enough for two people to walk side by side, René Laporte's 'Chateau René' was host to a galaxy of celebrities that included Maurice Chevalier and Man Ray. So many writers settled in the area that after the war Sartre came to try to recruit well-known intellectuals to his left-wing Socialisme et Liberté group.

Although they enjoyed separate careers, the names of Sartre and Simone de Beauvoir are often said in one breath. They met as students at the Sorbonne and remained together – despite extra-marital dalliances by both – until Sartre's death in 1980. Although they both worked in many parts of the Riviera – in the mountains, on islands and in seaside towns – they each retained their own long-standing links with Antibes. De Beauvoir first hitch-hiked there from Paris in 1937, and the couple visited friends and former students in the area over three decades. In 1962, Sartre and de Beauvoir, Cubanophiles and communists both, were in Antibes celebrating the failure of the Bay of Pigs 'invasion' to overthrow Castro.

With their long association with the town, they must have had some views on what drew so many artists to Antibes. De Beauvoir once wrote to the American writer Nelson Algren: 'I'm just leaving for Antibes. I am dreaming of sun, silence, and time to work.' With its suburban sprawl at one end and dreamy Cap at the other, the medieval heart of Antibes remains unspoiled – and unspoilable. As Graham Greene, its most prolific author, put it: 'I was very happy in Antibes. It was the only town where I found it possible to live.'

CHAPTER FOUR

Grasse is better than all the places I've yet seen!

(Henry Miller)

The Back Country: The Balcony
of the Mediterranean

I f the boundaries of the Côte d'Azur are vague, those of the Arrière-Pays are mysterious. Its literal translation, 'Back Country', means – like Humpty Dumpty's 'word' – just what you choose it to mean.

For the purpose of this book, it means the foot-hills of the Alpes-Maritimes: that 30-mile-wide stretch of undulating terrain that lies between the coastal towns of Cannes, Nice and Monaco and the beginning of the Maritime Alps. It is a scented landscape of olive groves, pine forests, vineyards and domes of lavender; of perched villages that look as if they sprouted from their hilltops, and of country towns; a place of gently rolling hills, rivers, rocks and waterfalls.

Although the region takes in historic market towns like Grasse and Vence, almost every village in the area has some artistic heritage, which makes the task of selection an idiosyncratic, but fascinating one.

In the Arrière-Pays, you are more likely to hear the unadulterated twangy patois of Provence than in the more cosmopolitan cites: if the plumber says he'll be there *demang matang*, he means tomorrow morning.

But, above all, it is a place of tranquillity – hence its appeal to writers.

If the Arrière-Pays is the Riviera's balcony, Grasse is its royal box: it was Queen Victoria's retreat from the summer heat of the coast. Seemingly balanced precariously on a limestone ridge, from which it seems likely to slide off at any moment, Grasse has what the Brooklyn-born writer Henry Miller once called 'a superb decrepitude'.

It has been the heart of the perfume industry for more than four centuries. The town got into scent by accident; it was primarily a tanning centre specializing in soft pelts. If you have ever been near a tannery, you will know that anything that can disguise the smell is an improvement. Thus the makers decided that they would sell more pairs of women's gloves if they could use the aromas of the abundant local flowers to make their smell more appealing.

Today, most of its basic fragrances are imported: farmers around Grasse can make much more money selling their property to real-estate developers than growing lavender and jasmine.

Grasse looks like an unsuccessful attempt to graft a new town on to an old one. You can still see the joins. If anything happens in Grasse, it happens in the old town or not at all – and probably not at all. Cultural highlights of this summer's festival include an exhibition of woods used in boat building, and the main library is closed for six months for computerization. At 9 pm on Saturday evening in Grasse, with the exception of high summer, the restaurants are closed and the waiters are stacking chairs. It has to boast about things that happened somewhere else.

The statue in the middle of the new town, for example, has a dedication: 'Witness of the Revolution', honouring the contribution of François-Joseph Paul (1722–88), the Admiral of Grasse, to the American War of Independence. One might wonder why the only victory the town feels it appropriate to celebrate took place 3,000 miles away, or why, some 11 miles from the sea, the town should need an admiral at all, and have the only maritime museum on the Riviera.

Napoleon, after his escape from Elba in 1815, came through the town on his way to Paris to reclaim his throne, but he felt that the townsfolk would be hostile to his troops, and wisely carried on into the mountains.

Despite – or because of – its innocuousness, the town has attracted literary expatriates both fictional and real. In Victor Hugo's *Les Misérables*, Jean Valjean, after his release from the prison in Toulon, gets a job in a perfume factory in Grasse.

A plaque in the appropriately named chemin du Vieux-Logis tells that the road leads to the old Villa Belvedere, in which lived the Russian poet and novelist – and in 1933 the first Russian winner of the Nobel Prize for Literature – Ivan Bunin, for 15 years. He left Russia after the Revolution and settled in Grasse in 1923. He found its scenery conducive to creative thought, and remained there until 1945, when he moved to Paris.

André Gide came to see him in Grasse in the autumn of 1941, but the visit was a disappointing one: 'because despite our attempts at cordiality, we did not make true contact. His worship of Tolstoi annoyed me as much as his scorn for Dostoievski ... We do not even have the same saints, let alone the same gods.'

Among mundane details of his move from the Park Palace to the Grand Hotel, Gide's journal records his emotions while looking at the clear skies of Grasse on that September night:

> A half moon hovered in the cloudless sky. Neither sound nor movement stirred the supernatural quiet of the night. And suddenly the beauty of the sky, the serenity of the sleeping world, my presence there, the little shadow that I made on the ground; everything seemed to merge into one great unanswered question which gripped my soul with grief and despair. Oh yes! – and love and adoration too.

Another French writer who passed through Grasse was the novelist and playwright Stendhal. His most famous work was *The Red and the Black*, published in 1830, but he achieved much of his fame late in life and from posthumous publications. He reached Grasse in 1838 at the age of 65, when he was on extended leave from his job as consul to the Vatican States. His visit started inauspiciously: as the stagecoach from Draguignan drew near to the town, he was struck by the stench of resin from the perfume factories, which gave him a headache.

From this, things ought to have improved, but his journal entry for 20 May was:

> As I got nearer to Grasse, the colour of the olive leaves became a darker green ... because Grasse is sheltered on the north side by a barren mountain. Finally I saw whole fields of cultivated roses.

> The town has an appearance that is totally Genoese. The streets are as narrow as those on the Genoese coast, and one would think one was in Sestri [Levante] or Nervi ... The best spot, the one in which, in Italy, there would be cafés, is occupied by the general hospital. It

is all very well to have a hospital, but it should be built outside the town. If the inhabitants had any sense this would be a place for getting together and having fun. And the Paris papers arrive five days late.

No one took up Stendhal's suggestion: 160 years later, the hospital still stands on the top of the hill – but at least the Paris papers arrive the same day.

Henry Miller, the American-born author of *Tropic of Cancer*, *Tropic of Capricorn* and many other novels, was more enthusiastic about the town, and mentioned it often in his long and copious correspondence with the French writer Anaïs Nin and the English writer Lawrence Durrell. Miller wrote to Nin from Grasse in June 1939, 'Grasse is better than all the places I've yet seen! You must go – after I leave. Explore it thoroughly. The old town lies on one side of the main street, in descending layers of labyrinthian coils. Superb decrepitude and very much alive.'

Miller's early writing was better known in Europe than at home, having appeared in Cyril Connolly's *Horizon* magazine, and even more so after the European publication of his *Tropic* books, which were viewed in the USA as obscene. Later, his anarchical style was also viewed as anti-American, particularly after his *The Air-Conditioned Nightmare*, which was published in 1945 after an extensive tour of the USA in 1938 and 1939.

During and just after the Second World War, his style suited the turbulent times. He returned to the USA in 1942 and settled on the Californian coast, where he was hailed by the 1950s 'beat' generation and enjoyed a renewed period of fame. He remained in California until his death in 1980, aged 88 – three years after the death in Los Angeles of his lifelong friend Anaïs Nin.

During the German occupation in the Second World War, a number of writers came south in the hope of greater freedom from the censorship of the Germans and the constraints of the Vichy government. Jean-Paul Sartre was in Grasse in 1941 in the hope of recruiting André Gide to his left-wing action group. He never found him, because, whether by accident or design, the address that Gide wrote for him – in nearby Cabris – was illegible.

The two did eventually meet in Cabris in 1950, during the filming of a documentary on Gide's life. Photographs of the event show the two giants of modern French literature, aged 81 and 45 respectively, sitting solemnly in adjacent armchairs, as unaware of each other as if they were in a doctor's waiting room.

If nothing much happens in Grasse itself, even less goes on in its surrounding countryside - which seems to be part of its allure, particularly for English writers. One of the advantages that Kipling quotes of spending the spring in Cannes was the fact that 'we can climb by car into the hills behind Grasse and smell the pines as the spring snow melts from beneath them, and the anemones begin to come out.'

Herbert George (H.G.) Wells had three residences on the fringes of the town during what he called 'the vociferous transit of Odette Keun', which began in 1923. (While keeping a wife and family in suburban Essex, Wells changed his foreground mistresses in ten-year cycles, usually in years ending in the figure '3'. The background was replete with 'women I had only a brief and simple use for'.)

He met Odette Keun in a hotel in Geneva. Wells said she pursued him there: his son Anthony West - the fruit of his decade with the writer Rebecca West from 1913 to 1923 - said they met by written appointment. That they became lovers instantly is not in dispute, and the affair lasted until Wells left Grasse in 1933.

Their first home was in nearby Magagnosc; the second, Lou Bastidon, was in Malbosc - it is the villa Jasmin in *The World of William Clissold*; and the third was a villa that they built to their own requirements in the Grasse countryside. They called it Lou Pidou - a Provençal corruption of 'the treasure'. Over the fireplace Wells had the builder erect a shield bearing the words, 'Two Lovers Built This House'.

Wells wanted, he said, 'hidden away in the sunshine, a home to which I could retreat from England and work in peace ... I wanted a mistress to tranquilize me and companion me.' What he got was a Grasse widow of his own making. He may well have wanted peace, but Keun, after long periods alone in the bucolic *pays grassois*, was usually ready for war. The stormy relationship lasted until 1933, when Wells assigned her the lifetime use of Lou Pidou, and walked out – this time never to return. In the autobiographical *The World of William Clissold*, Wells says, 'I told her that now at last we had come to the end of our relationship.' Wells's son Anthony put it rather differently: 'That was not quite how it had been. He had been sent packing. Odette had thrown him out.'

Keun liked to shock Wells's friends – the more distinguished and stuffy the better. When one eminent guest was indiscreet enough to ask what Casanova did, Keun told him in a word. It was, wrote Wells in 1935 – an era when the f-word was not printable – 'the vulgarest and most indecent of English bad words'. He was to fictionalize the impetuous Keun in his *Apropos of Dolores* in 1938: 'she was pseudo-oriental and addicted to every extremity of emotional exaggeration'.

Wells's many works written in Lou Pidou include *Meanwhile*, a novel set in the Hanbury Gardens, just across the Italian border in La Mortola; *The Book of Catherine Wells*, a tribute to his first wife; his *Collected Short Stories*; and much of *The Work, Wealth and Happiness of Mankind*. Among his many essays was an obituary commissioned by some far-sighted editor on George Bernard Shaw – who lived to the age of 94, surviving his obituary writer by four years.

Derek Jules Gaspard Ulric Niven van den Bogaerde – Dirk Bogarde – was another writer who lived on the Grasse verges. As a film actor, he was one of Britain's most popular leading men in the 1950s, making his name in light comedies like the 'Doctor' series, mostly written by Richard Gordon, and later in more complex roles like von Aschenbach in *Death in Venice* and the title role in *The Servant*. The taut screenplay written by Harold Pinter turned a modest book by Robin Maugham – nephew of another long-term Riviera resident – into a tense Oscar-winning drama.

Bogarde discovered Le Pigeonnier, his Provençal home, in November 1968. It was an isolated farmhouse near St-Sulpice, a tiny village five miles east of Grasse, and he stayed there for 20 years. The village has a bar and a restaurant and a monument to its liberation by the Allies on 21 August 1944 – but seemingly no people, as if some Marie-Celeste-like tragedy had purged it of every living thing except the cats.

At Le Pigeonnier, Bogarde's writing followed the pattern of his film career: after the fairly lightweight memoir *Backcloth* in 1985, he decided to make writing his career, graduating to serious autobiographical works, novels and press articles. He finally wrote 11 books, six of them autobiographies. His *A Short Walk from Harrods* is 'a tribute to the patch of [France] which I was privileged to own and which I greatly loved', and the book tells of his discovery of the dilapidated *mas* and its transformation into Le Pigeonnier.

In about 1986, one of Bogarde's newspaper articles told of his planting a *figuier*. Fig trees take many years to bear fruit, so to plant one is a metaphor for the intention to stay a long time. The article was followed a few months later by another, saying that he was returning to London. The reason was the illness of his long-term partner and manager, who died shortly after their return to England.

Although André Gide spent some time in Grasse during the Second World War, he is more often associated with a tiny village some three miles to the west of the town. Cabris stands on its own 1,800-feet-high peak and claims the tallest palm tree in the Alpes-Maritimes. The view from the terrace of its ruined tenth-century chateau is one of the most spectacular on the Côte d'Azur: from the Cap Ferrat in the east, by way of Cannes and the Lérins Islands to Toulon in the west. And on those increasingly rare, clear, crisp winter days, one can even see the mountains of Corsica 100 miles away to the south.

The history of the village goes back to the Romans, and later the *Templiers* – the Knights Templar founded early in the twelfth century. It was so badly impacted by the plague in the fifteenth century that it remained uninhabited for 150 years.

But perhaps the village's most surprising feature is that the ratio of writers – and certainly of Nobel Literature Prize winners – to its 1,300 residents is one of the highest in the world.

The proportion is reflected in its street names, which celebrate Camus, Saint-Exupéry, the poet Mistral and, of course, André Gide.

Gide's early distinction as a publisher was a dubious one: he rejected the first volume of Proust's masterpiece, *À la Recherche du temps perdu* (*Remembrance of Things Past*). Gide became a regular visitor to Cabris over two decades, first for inspiration and quiet and later for some relief from the constraints of German-occupied Paris.

The original reason for this preponderance of laureates was the desire of a wealthy Luxembourg industrialist, Émile Mayrisch, and his wife Aline to create environments where artists and intellectuals could meet and work. One of these retreats, La Messuguière, was purpose-built by Aline after her husband's death, and became a winter Mecca for French authors.

In addition to Gide, many other distinguished authors visited what its architect called a 'home for tired intellectuals', including Albert Camus, Roger Martin du Gard and Bunin (all Nobel Prize winners), Paul Valéry, Antoine de Saint-Exupéry, Marcel Pagnol and Jean-Paul Sartre (who refused the Nobel Prize in 1964 on the grounds that no writer is qualified to assess the value of another's work). Pagnol made his home in the village throughout the Second World War.

Looking at La Messuguière – now a private residence – through the iron gates in the chemin des Laurents on the outskirts of the village, it is not difficult to imagine how its immaculate gardens and Tuscan tower could have inspired some of France's greatest post-war literature. In addition to Gide's contribution, it was in Cabris that Albert Camus wrote much of *L'Homme Révolté* (*The Rebel*); Colette, Saint-Exupery and Pagnol all completed major works there in the 1940s and 1950s; and Sartre completed his *Huis Clos* (*No Exit*) and *Les Chemins de la liberté* (*The Roads to Freedom*) there.

La Messuguière was not the only writers' retreat in Cabris. Camus also wrote at another, smaller, house, closer to the centre of the village – the home of Pierre and Elizabeth Herbart – called Les Audides. Herbart was a close friend of Gide – so close indeed that when he married Elizabeth in 1932, he adopted her daughter (who was the mystery child fathered by Gide on the beach of the island of Porquerolles on that summer day in 1922.)

Albert Camus came to Cabris for the first time in the winter of 1949–50 hoping for some alleviation from tuberculosis. He had been consumptive for a long time: newspaper reports from his high school days in his native Algeria, when he had shown great promise as a goalkeeper, refer to his absences through illness. At 17, while staying with relatives in Algiers, he had begun to cough and vomit blood, and been ordered complete rest – even from reading.

He nevertheless achieved considerable success in Paris, both as a playwright and novelist, but in late 1949, his doctor advised that, if he wanted to live to write more, he would have to find a higher, drier, place.

Cabris not only met both criteria, it offered refuge. His room at Les Audides looks out across groves of olives to the village, with its sixteenth-century chapels and the ruins of its tenth-century castle. It was in that room that he wrote:

> In the afternoon, the sun and light flood into my room, the sky blue and veiled, cries of children rising from the village, the song of the garden fountain ... and the hours of Algiers come back to me.

Camus worked well in Cabris, spending ten hours a day at his desk while trying to improve his general health. He wrote a number of political articles and essays, but mainly he saw his confinement as the opportunity to embody his personal and political philosophy in *L'Homme Révolté*.

The abundant mimosa heralded the spring, and as peach, cherry and almond trees blossomed, so did the work, and his euphoria shows in his journal:

> From everywhere the song of birds explodes, with a force, a jubilation, a joyous dissonance, an infinite joy. The day trickles and sparkles.

As so often happens when creative thoughts are flowing, his notes are full of ideas for future projects. He even felt well enough to return to Paris in April 1950, but within weeks had been ordered back, discouraged and, according to his journal, suicidal. He spent most of the year in Cabris, returning the following winter determined to finish *L'Homme Révolté* by mid-March. He sent it to the publisher in July.

In 1957, at the age of only 44, he was awarded the Nobel Prize for Literature, but just three years later, in what seems a wry comment on the injustice of life, having taken such pains to cure his medical condition and thought so seriously of suicide as the ultimate cure, he was killed in a car accident. He is buried at Lourmarin in western Provence.

*

Antoine de Saint-Exupéry was a French author whose life, and most of his writing, were dedicated to flying. Yet his most translated work was *Le Petit Prince* (*The Little Prince*), a morality tale for children, whose message is that it is better to give than to receive. His many links with the Côte d'Azur include his marriage in Agay, near St-Raphaël, in 1931, and his stay in Cabris in 1939, when he worked on the autobiographical *Terre des hommes* (*Wind, Sand and Stars*) and *Pilote de guerre* (*Flight to Arras*).

He joined the French Air Force in North Africa during the Second World War. On 31 July 1944 he dipped the wings of his P38 fighter over his sister's house in Agay as he headed south over the Mediterranean – and was never heard of again.

Seillans, a medieval village in the mountains 22 miles west of Grasse, is well fortified. It even gets its name from *Seilhanso*, the Provençal word for the vessels in which the oil was boiled before being decanted over the heads of Saracen invaders. The village is further protected by three Roman portals, and the ancient two-storeyed houses that cluster around its feudal chateau form an impenetrable wall.

It was in the chateau that the English travel writer and novelist (Charles) Bruce Chatwin spent his last years. He was born in Sheffield, Yorkshire, and had first achieved fame with the account of his travels *In Patagonia*, which won awards on both sides of the Atlantic. Before becoming a writer he had worked as an appraiser of impressionist art for the London auctioneers Sotheby's, and until the success of *In Patagonia* had been planning a career as an art historian.

He developed a new style of travel writing, blending fact, fantasy and impressions, the search for which took him to remote places. The use of this technique in his *Songlines*, which speculated on Australian Aboriginal myth and legend, offended many Australian historians. Chatwin also provided much of the photography for his travel books and was a successful novelist, with poignant works like *On the Black Hill*, a story of the lives of reclusive twin brothers who farm in the Welsh borders.

While some mountain villages were wiped out by the plague in the fifteenth century, everyone in Seillans was spared, reputedly because of its healthy climate and the fact that the fortifications kept the residents in and potential disease carriers out. This should have made it the ideal spot for Chatwin, who had been sent south on medical recommendation and had been staying in the chateau since December 1986. It was on its vast south-facing terrace that he wrote his novel *Utz*, a story about the obsession of collecting, set in Vienna. It was his last book.

He described his illness as 'unidentified'. Despite having tested HIV positive at least four years earlier, he preferred to blame his condition on something more exotic, claiming that it was the result of having eaten a 1,000-year-old egg in China.

Like Lawrence with his tuberculosis, Chatwin staunchly refused to acknowledge the nature of his illness. He complained that French doctors were not interested in his problem, and although he had blood transfusions in the hospital at Draguignan – some 15 miles away – and the Anglo-American Sunny Bank hospital in Cannes, he refused any specifically AIDS-related treatment.

His condition worsened until he was finally rushed by ambulance to Les Archets, a public hospital in Nice, where he died two days later.

Five miles to the south of Grasse is the medieval village of Auribeau-sur-Siagne, where, in March 1932, P.G. Wodehouse took a one-year rental on the Domaine de la Freyère. He described it as 'a sort of Provençal country house, with a hundred acres of hillside and large grounds and a huge swimming pool'.

'We have a German butler, an Alsatian footman, a Serbian cook, a French chauffeur, an Italian maid, and an English odd-job man,' he wrote. 'Good material for the next war.'

While at Auribeau, Wodehouse wrote a collection of short stories, *Pearls, Girls and Monty Bodkin*. He also found time to read, but couldn't manage Aldous Huxley's *Brave New World*, complaining that 'the whole point about Huxley is that he can write better about modern life than anybody else, so off he goes and writes about the future'. It says something about Wodehouse that, while every other writer of English was in awe of his effortless use of the language, he could not handle allegory: *Brave New World* was no more about 'the future' than was *1984*.

By the time they got to Auribeau, the Wodehouses seem to have overcome their aversion to 'foreign countries', so vividly expressed in 1925: 'we hate their ways, their architecture, their language and their food'. Seven years later, he had become almost cosmopolitan and was a regular visitor to the tables of local restaurants – and those of the Cannes casino.

His hatred of the French language seems now to have been a manifestation of the fear that afflicts us all: of being seen to be less dextrous in another language than in our own. By the time he settled in Auribeau he was boasting, 'A woman comes to me for two hours a day and we talk French to each other. I am really getting darned good, but the strain is awful and lays me out for the rest of the day.'

Eight miles east of Grasse is the village of Valbonne. Much enlarged in the last 20 years because of its proximity to the international high-tech science park, Sophia-Antipolis – which local dignitaries like to call the 'French Silicon Valley' – its Roman origins are evident from the perfect square grid of the narrow streets in the old town.

It was a perfect compromise for the English playwright John Osborne, because it was remote enough for him to find a secluded farmhouse in which to write, while near enough to Cannes to enjoy its high life and lobby the judges at the film festival.

Of the two, his writing was the more successful venture: he won an Oscar for his screenplay of *Tom Jones*, but his attempts to get the film of his *Look Back in Anger*, with Richard Burton and Sarah Miles, selected as the British entry for the Palme d'Or competition in May 1959 failed when it was beaten by *Room at the Top*. (It was not a surprising choice: although both films were British, *Room at the Top* had a French lead, Simone Signoret.)

Vence is a small cathedral town – and a town with a small cathedral. Its eleventh-century church is among the smallest in France. The old town is a vaguely concentric maze of narrow streets protected on one side by monumental gates of Roman origin, and on the other by medieval ramparts. Elegant, urn-shaped fountains play in sheltered squares, of which one served as the Romans' forum, and another housed the town guillotine in Revolutionary times. The old town is now the traveller's reward for having negotiated the suppuration of hotels and ugly apartment blocks that surround it.

Vence stands almost a thousand feet up in the hills, about ten miles inland: two features that, in January 1930, caused the English novelist and travel and short-story writer David Herbert (D.H.) Lawrence to move there. In Bandol, he had been examined by Dr Morland, an English chest specialist on holiday in the area, who had told him that he should move to a higher altitude, away from the coast.

Lawrence finally, and belatedly, accepted Dr Morland's diagnosis: that he had had tuberculosis for many years. As Katherine Mansfield had done 13 years earlier, he left coastal Bandol for the last time.

He had hoped that his ranch in Taos, New Mexico, might better meet the doctor's requirements, but, apart from his visa problems, the doctor was sure that Lawrence was in no condition for such a long journey.

So he moved into what he called 'a sort of sanatorium' in Vence. When he got there he weighed just over six stone – 85 pounds – and was close to death. The building had formerly been the home of a local astronomer, and both its name, Ad Astra (To the Stars), and its location – just across the road from the cemetery – now took on a grisly significance. Frieda checked into the nearby Hôtel Nouvel.

It was not really a sanatorium. As Lawrence wrote on a postcard to Aldous Huxley's wife Maria, it was just 'an hotel where a nurse takes your temperature and two doctors look after you once a week'. H.G. Wells, who was living near Grasse at the time, came to see him there, as did the Aga Khan. On 27 February, after only two weeks, he wrote to the Huxleys again; this time with a P.S. 'This place no good.'

The next day Frieda took him away from the home to a villa she had rented: the Villa Rochermond (later the Villa Aurelia) near the great 2,400-foot cylindrical rock of St-Jeannet.

Optimistically, she took a six-month lease starting on 1 March, and moved her bed into his room because he wanted to be able to see her. He was writing a book review when the Huxleys arrived, and he grasped Maria Huxley's hands and said, 'Maria, don't let me die.'

At 9 pm the next day, a doctor came from the 'sanatorium' and gave Lawrence morphine for his pain. He said, 'I am better now', and fell asleep. He died at 10.15 pm.

Lawrence was buried beside a south-facing wall in the Vence cemetery. In addition to Frieda and Barby, her daughter by her previous marriage, the small group of mourners included the Huxleys and their friend Robert Nichols, an English poet living in Villefranche.

At the time, no one thought that, exactly five years later, another small group would gather in *carré* 7 of Vence cemetery to witness Lawrence's exhumation.

In the time between burial and disinterment, Leonard and Virginia Woolf, on their way home from a holiday in Italy, had made a side trip to Vence to visit the grave – and, it being 1933, found him in. In the meantime, Frieda had been comforted by a number of lovers, at least two of whom had shared her with Lawrence while he was still alive.

One was John Middleton Murry, with whom she had had a torrid affair immediately following the death of his wife Katherine Mansfield in 1923. By the time Lawrence died, Murry had acquired another consumptive wife, whom he left with their children in his haste to fulfil his urgent mission to Vence, to fill the void left by Lawrence's death. It is uncertain who comforted whom: Frieda at 50 was still alluring enough for him to write later, 'You don't know what you did for me in Vence ... you recreated me.'

The next to console her was Angelo Ravagli, the Fascist Italian army officer who had served as her occasional extra-curricular lover during her marriage, and was the reason for her late arrival at Port Cros. By 1935, he and Frieda had moved to Taos. He had built a small mausoleum chapel there – a friend called it a 'station toilet' – in Lawrence's memory, and had been charged with exhuming Lawrence's remains in Vence and shipping them to Taos to complete the shrine.

Deterred by French bureaucracy from exporting a long-dead body, Ravagli had the remains burned and urned in preparation for their 5,000-mile journey. At the docks in New York, the ashes – just as the live Lawrence had done – suffered immigration difficulties, but they were finally accepted as unlikely to have subversive intent or communist sympathies, and permitted to board the train to New Mexico.

The anarchic Lawrence would probably have enjoyed the rest of the story, as researched by biographer Brenda Maddox. Distracted by the enthusiasm of Frieda's welcome, Ravagli left the urn and its incinerated contents on the train, after which the fate of the ashes becomes confused. Either Ravagli went back to the railway station and collected them, or he was unable to find them at the station and bought another urn, which he filled with some similar substance.

The disposal of the ashes has raised even more conspiracy theories. Some, including Maria Huxley, believe that the anti-Ravagli school suspected that he had built the Lawrence mausoleum in Taos with a view to charging admission to tourists, and they planned to thwart him by stealing the ashes and casting them to the desert winds. Frieda, hearing of this plan, tipped them into the mixer that was making the concrete altar stone for the chapel.

Twenty years later, a drunken Ravagli revealed that, immediately after the cremation of Lawrence's body in 1935, afraid of hassles with the French authorities over the export of the remains, he had tipped the original ashes out in Vence and replaced them with cindered wood.

Although this contradicted his earlier, already conflicting, statements, it seems to leave only three possible fates for the true ashes: they are either in Vence, or in a block of concrete in Taos, or in a left luggage office somewhere in New Mexico. And the only true tomb of David Herbert Lawrence is the one in *carré* 7 in Vence cemetery, over which a plaque reads, 'David Herbert Lawrence reposed here from March 1930 to March 1935'.

Murry (without mentioning his relationship to Frieda) swore on oath that he had seen a will in which Lawrence bequeathed all the rights in his works to her, and none to his family, and Frieda and Angelo lived on in New Mexico, getting ever richer on the royalties. They married there in 1950, his Italian wife having given her consent for them to marry.

It was convenient that Italian law had not recognized Angelo's American divorce and marriage, because after Frieda died in New Mexico at the age of 77, Ravagli's wife was able to accept him back as her legal husband without further ceremony.

*

Towards the end of the Second World War, the artist Matisse moved to Vence, fearful that the south coast would be bombarded by the liberating Allied troops. While there, he designed and decorated the Chapel du Rosaire at the upper end of the town, in what is now, appropriately, the avenue Henri Matisse. The chapel is administered by the order of the Dominican Sisters, and Matisse reflected the Dominican theme in his frescoes, painting the Stations of the Cross in black on the white ceramic walls in his minimalist style of the time.

He said later, 'What I have done in the Chapel is to create a religious space ... to give it, solely by the play of colours and lines, the dimensions of infinity.'

A visitor to the chapel on 6 January 1956, was the American poet Sylvia Plath. She had made the train journey south on New Year's Eve of 1955 with her lover of the time, Richard Sassoon, and her journal records her anticipation:

> Off into the night, with the blackness of a strange land knifing past. In my mind, a map of France, irregularly squarish ... and a line of railway tracks, like a zipper, speeding open to the south, to Marseille, to Nice and the Côte d'Azur where perhaps in the realm of absolute fact the sun is shining and the sky is turquoise.

Anyone who has made that train journey will recognize her evocation of the first sight of the Mediterranean:

> Then, lifting my head sleepily once, suddenly the moon shining incredibly on water. Marseille. The Mediterranean. At last, unbelievable, the moon on that sea, that azure sea I dreamed about on maps in the sixth grade.

> The Mediterranean. Sleep again, and at last the pink vin rosé light of dawn along the back of the hills in a strange country. Red earth, orange tiled villas in yellow and peach and aqua, and the blast, the blue blast of the sea on the right. The Côte d'Azur. A new country, a new year: spiked with a green explosion of palms, cacti sprouting vegetable octopuses with spiky tentacles, and the red sun rising like the eye of God out of a screaming blue sea.

And, on arrival, her first impressions of Nice:

There is the sea, heaving blue against the roundly pebbled shore, and the white gulls planing and crying in the quiet air, like the breath from a glass of iced champagne. Everywhere little black-clad people walk along the sparkling Sunday morning pavement, sitting in the turquoise-painted deck chairs along the Promenade des Anglais and facing the rising sun: painted bleached blondes pass by in high heels, black slacks, fur coats and sun glasses.

Plath was 23 at the time, on a Fulbright scholarship at Cambridge University. From Place Garibaldi in Nice, she posted a word-packed postcard to her mother in the USA on 7 January:

Yesterday was about the most lovely of my life ...

How can I describe the beauty of the country? Everything is so small, close, exquisite and fertile. Terraced gardens on steep slopes of rich red earth, orange and lemon trees, olive orchards, tiny pink and peach houses. To Vence – small, on a sun-warmed hill, uncommercial, slow, peaceful. Walked to Matisse cathedral – small, pure, clean-cut. White, with blue tile roof sparkling in the sun ... I just knelt in the heart of sun and the colors of sky, sea, and sun, in the pure white heart of the Chapel.

(Evelyn Waugh called it 'the Matisse public lavatory cocktail bar chapel'!)

In early March, she told her mother she was 'very much in love with Richard', and was dreaming of going to live in Vence to write and learn French. On 17 April she wrote that 'in the last two months I have fallen terribly in love' with the poet – later Poet Laureate – Ted Hughes, and on 16 June she and Hughes were married.

After a honeymoon in Benidorm, Spain, they spent the next two years in Boston before returning to England in December 1958, but the couple separated in October 1962. Four months later she gassed herself in her London apartment.

St-Paul-de-Vence, just two miles south of Vence, meets all the criteria for the classic perched village. It sits along the jagged skyline of a mile-long ridge, as if the village and the rock on which it stands were carved out as one. It has a winding medieval *rue grande* – main street – twelfth-century arched gates and sixteenth-century fortifications. One of its less desirable features is that, as the most convenient *village perché* to the main tourist centres, it is on the itinerary of every coach tour.

The interesting restaurants that used to line its winding streets have long ago given way to higher profit margins: art shops sell mass-produced 'originals', craft shops show dried herbs, scented candles and olive-wood anything, and the rest is fast food and ice-cream. There is a 500-space underground car park where, not 20 years ago, the road used to be blocked twice a day by farmers moving their sheep.

Fortunately, 95 per cent of the visitors are only there to look, photograph and move on, so that in the evenings it becomes almost a Provençal village again. And, just outside the gates, the auberge du Colombe d'Or has not changed its management, staff or menu in 25 years.

The floral terraces of the Colombe d'Or - the Golden Dove - used to be the haunt of artists like Modigliani, Picasso, Chagall, Dubuffet and Miró, who, the story goes, paid their bills with the paintings that now adorn its walls. It has also hosted many writers. The French poet Jacques Prévert once published a poem in its praise, in which he names H.G. Wells as a regular client 'who parked his time machine in the wash house'. At the Colombe one 1920s night, when Zelda Fitzgerald felt that Scott was paying too much attention to the dancer Isadora Duncan, she regained his attention by throwing herself down its stone staircase.

Here Simone Signoret met Yves Montand in 1949 while he was on tour. 'We were struck by lightning,' she said. They never returned to their respective spouses: they were married in St-Paul, and the owner of the Colombe d'Or - 'our third home' - was a witness. They stayed together for 28 years - and now share a marble tomb in the Père Lachaise cemetery in Paris.

St-Paul attracts the rich and famous: a single day there will provide enough ammunition, in terms of rock, and film stars, for a month of name dropping. Dirk Bogarde was staying there when he found Le Pigeonnier, and hurried back to tell Simone Signoret. She always sat in the same seat: against the left-hand wall nearest the kitchen. There was no 'Reserved' card on it; one just didn't sit there. Signoret had once had her memoirs ghost-written, but decided that they were unreadable and hid them away. Years later she decided to write them herself, without reference to the earlier work – and began her writing career with the autobiographical *Nostalgia Isn't What It Used to Be*.

In those days Signoret's husband Yves Montand would be playing *boules* with the locals – over whom he towered – outside the Café de la Paix, of which he was part owner. The village people, who could not get by for the camera-clicking crowds, called it his 'court'.

In the Colombe's tiny granite-paved bar, where stands *the* Colombe, but wrought in iron rather than gold, James Baldwin, the black American novelist and playwright, used to drink – and drink.

Baldwin lived in a Provençal villa just half a mile down the road from the hotel for the last 18 years of his life, at times commuting to and from the USA to take part in political protests.

Baldwin's work was noted for its passionate condemnation of racial discrimination in America. Twin themes in a number of his works were the conflicts of race and homosexuality.

He could be scathing about his fellow Americans: 'In the US I can distinguish types and accents. Here they all look as if they just arrived from Nebraska.'

His stay in St-Paul did not do much for Baldwin's writing career – his first novel *Go Tell It on the Mountain* and his early plays were his most successful – but his time on the Côte d'Azur was beneficial for him in other ways:

> I think exile saved my life, for it inexorably confirmed something which Americans appear to have great difficulty accepting. Which, simply, is this: a man is not a man until he is able and willing to accept his own vision of the world, no matter how radically that vision departs from that of others ... What Europe gives an American ... is the sanction to become oneself.

About 30 miles north of the coast, the Alpes-Maritimes villages become more sparse and the mountains higher. Here are the ski resorts to which enthusiasts of Nice and Cannes flock each weekend from December to March. The roads are narrow, often icy, and subject to minor avalanches; but the biggest hazard on the 90-minute journey are the drivers – high on pre-ski adrenalin or après-ski stimulants. More people are injured on the Route Nationale 202 and its tributaries than on the ski slopes.

In the summer, however, these resorts are havens of peace, soundless except for the chirping of crickets, the friendly trill of the time-share salesmen and the clicking of word processors. In 5,000-foot-high St-Martin-Vésubie, Marcel Pagnol dodged the coastal hordes to write the script for *Jean de Florette* in 1951. (Pagnol wrote his scripts first, made the films, and only then wrote the books.)

In the summer of 1937, Vladimir Nabokov and his wife and son moved from Menton to Moulinet, a remote village 15 miles north, some 4,000 feet up in the Maritime Alps. Whether they went there for isolation or, now that the Riviera was a summer resort, to avoid the coastal prices is not known, but their stay was brief even by Nabokov standards. It was memorable only for its wealth of butter-flies – Nabokov found many rare and some previously unrecorded species there – and for the cockroaches that finally drove them out of their hotel. They moved on to the House of the Union of the St George Cross for Disabled Veterans in Antibes.

Still further north, and higher, in the Vallée de Tinée, Jean-Paul Sartre fled the distractions of the boulevard St Germain and barri-caded himself into the popular weekend ski resort Auron to write *Le Diable et le Bon Dieu (Lucifer and the Lord)*.

Despite its isolation, the back country is also changing, as can be seen from contemporary writing.

J.G. Ballard, author of *Empire of the Sun* and *Crash!*, set his *Super-Cannes* in Sophia-Antipolis – although he calls it the libel-avoiding 'Eden-Olympia' – between Valbonne and the coast. Appropriately for a writer who began his career writing science fiction, Sophia-Antipolis is a science park: not the traditional Mediterranean back-drop of Provençal villas and *Belle Époque* mansions, but a less well-known terrain of autoroutes, mirror-walled office blocks and man-made landscapes, with artificial lakes and manicured lawns.

The book's main character discovers that the veneer of corporate efficiency conceals a culture of depravity. For relaxation after a stressful day at the park, senior managers don black uniforms and embark on nocturnal escapades of racist violence and paedophilia – a therapy enthusiastically endorsed by the park's resident psychia-trist.

As the park authorities start to plan an even bigger complex, one has to ask if this is Ballard's vision of the future for the Riviera's back country – one vast science park where moralities are reversed? As the psychiatrist puts it:

> A titanic battle is about to begin, a Darwinian struggle between competing psychopathies. Everything is for sale now – even the human soul has a barcode.

It is a frightening prospect – or it would be if it were credible. These are, after all, high-tech expatriates who live with their families in mock Provençal villas with swimming pools. It is difficult to imagine a group of gung-ho corporate executives planning their next frenzy of mass carnage without one of them looking at his electronic organizer and saying, 'Sorry chaps, not Friday – that's our bridge night.'

CHAPTER FIVE

And the colours of Nice! I wish I could take
them down and send them to you.

(Friedrich Nietzsche)

Nice: The Heart of the Riviera

Nice is the capital city – and cradle – of the Riviera. In the centuries before the birth of Christ, it was a trading centre for Greek merchantmen, who called it Nikaïa, after their god of victory. When the Romans crossed the Alps in the first century BC, they founded a hilltop city there whose ruins can still be seen in what is now the elegant residential suburb of Cimiez. The ancient stones of Cimiez still bear the traces of chariot wheels, but its streets have incongruous names: Duke Ellington Alley and Dizzy Gillespie Way – for today it is the home of the Nice Jazz Festival.

The ten days of the festival apart, Cimiez is a quiet backwater of undulating roads lined with *Belle Époque* villas and museums. The former Hôtel Regina – named after Queen Victoria, and her preferred summer retreat in her last years – dominates its skyline, and its cemetery houses artists of the calibre of Raoul Dufy and Henri Matisse and writers like Roger Martin du Gard, winner of the Nobel Prize for Literature in 1937.

Writers were relatively late in discovering Nice. The spearhead of the invasion was the Scottish surgeon and author Tobias Smollett. He was already known as a translator of Cervantes and Voltaire, and as a prolific novelist in his own right. He was publishing epic novels with alliterative titles like *Peregrine Pickle* and *Roderick Random* more than a century before Dickens wrote *Nicholas Nickleby*: his *Humphrey Clinker* was the blueprint for *Oliver Twist*. Asthmatic, consumptive and jaundiced, he came to Nice with his wife in 1763 at the age of 42, hoping that the Mediterranean climate would ease his respiratory problems, and stayed for two years, using the city as a base for his journeys in Provence and northern Italy.

The publication of Smollett's *Travels through France and Italy* is acknowledged by Nice as its metamorphosis from an interesting side

trip to destination. The book was published in 1766, ten years before
the American Declaration of Independence, when British eyes were
turning towards Europe and the Enlightenment. The Scottish
biographer James Boswell, who had visited Corsica the previous year
and met its progressive president, Pasquale Paoli, was completing his
exhaustively titled *An Account of Corsica, the Journal of a Tour to that
Island and Memoirs of Pasquale Paoli*.

Before Smollett, the accepted route to Nice was by felucca – a
sail-assisted rowing boat – along the coast from Marseilles. This was
how John Milton, John Evelyn and Joseph Addison reached it in the
seventeenth century.

But not only did Smollett suffer from chronic seasickness; he also
had a dread of being kidnapped by pirates after the misfortunes of
an earlier writer-traveller, the French comic author and dramatist
Jean-François Regnard. Regnard might have become more famous
had he not had the misfortune to be a contemporary of Molière. As
it was, he often survived by ghost writing works for other authors.
His adventures were more bizarre than his most outrageous plots. As
we saw in the Introduction, Regnard had tried to reach Nice by sea a
hundred years earlier, but his travel plans were foiled by pirates and
he finished up as a slave to the Sultan of Algiers.

For these reasons, Smollett chose to make his way by land, where
the only brigands were the innkeepers and the only ransom the price
of being carried across bridgeless rivers. Finding that the bridge
across the river Var, on the western outskirts of Nice, had been
destroyed, Smollett had to have his coach manhandled across the
stony river bed by six brawny locals. (Even this was less hazardous
than the crossing made by the Abbé Papon some 20 years earlier. He
had had to be carried across on the shoulders of two farmers, and on
reaching the other bank gave them a blessing in payment.)

A self-confessed malcontent, with, to use his own words, 'a
meagre wrinkled countenance', he hated the 'garlic-smelling workers,
who spent all their time sitting in the sun', the food, the 'cold,
dismal and dirty' inns; the 'lazy, greedy, and impertinent' coachmen;
and the women, 'most of them pot-bellied', in their 'hideous painted
masks'. The inns, he thought, 'are cold, damp, dark, dismal, and
dirty; the landlords equally disobliging and rapacious; the servants
aukward, sluttish, and slothful'.

Even the English did not escape the Scottish Smollett scorn.
When he was on his way home in 1764, he heard of 'an English
gentleman' who had broken his arm, and sent his servant to offer his
services. The gentleman said 'he did not choose to see any company'.
Wrote Smollett:

> This sort of reserve seems peculiar to the English disposition. When
> two natives of any other country chance to meet abroad, they run
> into each other's embrace like old friends, even though they have
> never heard of one another till that moment; whereas two English-
> men in the same situation maintain a mutual reserve and diffidence
> ... like two bodies endowed with a repulsive power.

But, just like the travellers of today, he came to appreciate the climate of Provence, the scenery and even the food. His ultimate
accolade was to rate the local Provençal wines 'very near as good as
Burgundy'. So much did his impressions mellow over the two years
that, after his return to Scotland, he tried hard to get himself appointed British consul to Nice, but the British foreign minister of
the time feared that, after his earlier invective, he might face a hostile
reception. So he went to Tuscany instead, where he died in 1771.

As if to confirm the words of the French poet Jean Lorrain –
'The Riviera is the land of legend where a bad reputation has done
no one any harm' – Nice acclaims Smollett, despite his criticisms, as
its first tourist: the fact that he was also a writer was even more
fortuitous.

The British were to follow in droves. The hotels were given solid
English names, like Westminster and Windsor, and, since the word
'tourist' did not yet exist in the Provençal language, the locals used
what they saw as its nearest equivalent: 'Anglais'. The synonymity of
the two words was confirmed by Alexandre Dumas, who was staying
at the Hôtel d'York in Nice in 1835 when a coach pulled up at the
front door. When Dumas asked the manager who the guests were,
he replied, 'They are certainly English, but whether they are French
or German I don't know!'

Dumas was not impressed by English women. In his *Impressions of
Travels*, he describes *les Anglaises* as 'pale, frail women without the
strength to live elsewhere, who come to Nice each winter to die'.

*

Whether you arrive in Nice by air, rail or road, your first glimpse of the city is likely to be the spectacular crescent of the Baie des Anges (Bay of Angels), and the Promenade des Anglais that follows its sweeping seven-kilometre arc. On one side, a succession of gleaming villas and luxury hotels, in styles ranging from turn-of-the-century *Belle Époque*, through art deco, to mirror-walled twentieth-century cubes, and on the other a panorama of gardens, palm trees, aquamarine seas and azure skies.

The Promenade des Anglais was so named because its construction was financed by the British community. Following the failure of the citrus crop during the heavy frosts of the winter of 1821–22, members of the newly established Anglican Church collected money for a project to provide employment for local workers – and to indulge the congregation's nostalgia for the seaside resorts of home. But it has developed in a Mediterranean way: far from the candy floss and sideshows of the British seaside, it is a busy thoroughfare, with pavements wide enough to accommodate joggers, cyclists and skateboarders. It is also a mine of literary heritage.

Louisa May Alcott, the American author of *Little Women*, walked the Promenade in 1865. She came to Nice at the age of 33 with an invalid friend, Anna Weld. Alcott was still recovering from typhoid pneumonia contracted while a nurse in the American Civil War. The two women spent the winter of 1865–66 here, Alcott returning alone via Paris and London on 1 May 1866. Parts of *Little Women*, published two years later, are set in Nice, and although it was written almost 140 years ago, her description of the Promenade des Anglais is just as vivid and authentic today:

> At three o'clock in the afternoon, all the fashionable world at Nice may be seen on the Promenade des Anglais – a charming place; for the wide walk, bordered with palms, flowers, and tropical shrubs, is bounded on one side by the sea, on the other by the grand drive, lined with hôtels and villas, while beyond lie orange orchards and the hills. Many nations are represented, many languages spoken, many costumes worn, and on a sunny day the spectacle is as gay and brilliant as a carnival.

No. 343, at the western end of the promenade, was where Isadora Duncan had her dance studios in the 1920s. It was here, on 14

September 1926, that Jean Cocteau, the multi-talented French author, artist and poet, visited the dancer. They were rehearsing a joint performance in Nice, and Cocteau asked her to dance for him. She danced, as was her custom, barefoot, and used as a prop a long pink and white scarf, which became by turns a banner, a veil and a reptile.

One year later to the day, on the same promenade, the scarf was to end her life. She had seen a torpedo-shaped Bugatti sports car in Juan-les-Pins in the afternoon and was eager to buy one, so she asked a friend who owned a garage to take her for a drive in one. Her friend, the American writer Mary Desta, who had given her the scarf, watched as they drove off. They had only travelled a few yards when the end of the scarf became entangled in the rear left brake drum, pulling her head to one side and strangling her. It seemed a bizarrely appropriate ending to a life filled with incident and tragedy: 14 years earlier, her two young children had been drowned in the River Seine when the brakes on their governess's car failed.

Just inland from the scene of Isadora Duncan's accident, in the suburb of l'Archet, is the public hospital to which, on 16 January 1989, an ambulance brought the Yorkshire-born novelist and travel writer, Bruce Chatwin.

He had been brought from Seillans, a medieval village in the mountains west of Grasse, and two days later, at 1.30 in the afternoon, he died of AIDS. The doctors said that, if he had gone into a dedicated AIDS hospital, he might well have survived to write more.

If Chatwin's denial of the nature of his illness had been intended to keep his homosexuality from the general public, at least it had a temporary success: the myth of the 'rare Chinese killer disease' was repeated by the BBC when it announced his death. *Utz*, his last novel, was published posthumously and nominated for the Booker literary prize.

But for all Chatwin's skills as a novelist, he is likely to be best remembered as a travel writer – in particular for his *In Patagonia*, published in 1977.

Next door to where No. 63 now stands was the villa of Marie Bash-kirtseff, the precocious Russian writer, dancer, singer and painter who came to Nice with her aristocratic parents in 1872 at the age of

12, and made it her home. 'I love Nice,' she wrote in her journal. 'It is like being in a nest, surrounded on three sides by mountains ... Nice is my country. I grow here.'

An enthusiast of the works of Guy de Maupassant, she first wrote to him at his Chalet de l'Isère in Cannes when she was 18. Knowing his reputation – he claimed to have had intimate relations with 'two or three hundred' women – she cautiously signed herself 'Miss Hastings'. Intrigued, de Maupassant wrote back to her Poste Restante address. The correspondence continued for some years, but Bashkirtseff retained her anonymity, not identifying herself until she invited him to her villa on the Promenade shortly before her early death at 24 from tuberculosis. De Maupassant never commented on the relationship, but his valet, François Tassart, described it as 'very serious'.

De Maupassant's mother lived in the Villa Ravenelles at 140 rue de France – the first street back from, and parallel to, the promenade. It was here on 1 January 1892 that de Maupassant came to celebrate the New Year with his mother, sister-in-law and little niece. It was a sunny day and they lunched in the garden, after which de Maupassant returned to Cannes, saying that he had arranged to go sailing.

That night, as we saw in Chapter 2, he slit his own throat.

A few doors to the east of Marie Bashkirtseff's house is No. 57 Promenade des Anglais, where Vladimir Nabokov and his wife rented an apartment in the winter of 1960–61.

It was by no means Nabokov's first visit to the Côte d'Azur or to Nice. Born in St Petersburg in April 1899, son of a liberal party leader and former justice minister, and grandson of a minister to the Tsar, he had spent a holiday in Beaulieu in 1904, at the age of five, with his wealthy parents. In 1924, at the age of 25, in severe depression following the murder of his father by Russian Fascists (a bungled political assassination in which his father was killed in mistake for a government minister), and rejection by his fiancée, he came south to find solace – and found work in a Nice vineyard.

Nabokov, a compulsive lepidopterist throughout his life – and later Professor of Entomology – was working in the fields one day when an English gentleman asked him to hold his horse while he chased a butterfly. The Englishman was somewhat taken aback to find a farm hand who not only spoke English - having graduated with Firsts from Trinity College Cambridge two years earlier - but who knew the Latin names of indigenous species of butterflies.

In 1937 and 1938, Nabokov, with his wife Vera and son Dmitri, lived in Cannes, Menton and Antibes. They had been living in Berlin, where Vera was employed by the German High Command as a simultaneous translator. When she decided to tell the head of her department that, despite her blonde hair and perfect German, she was Jewish, he replied, 'Oh, that doesn't make any difference to us. We pay no attention to such things.' Such was her trust in this promise that the Nabokovs always claimed that their departure was precipitated not by fear of Nazi persecution, but by the fact that one of his father's killers had been released from prison and been appointed to a senior post in the Nazi party.

It was during this stay on the Riviera that Nabokov recorded 'the first stirrings' of his controversial work *Lolita* - and then lost track of his notes for a number of years.

Years later, another Riviera writer was to play an important role in Nabokov's career, when Graham Greene inadvertently set him on the road to fame and wealth. In 1955, in a year-end book review for the *Sunday Times*, Greene named *Lolita* as one of the three best novels of the year. The review prompted the editor of the *New York Times Book Review* to read it, and he immediately accused the *Sunday Times* of promoting paedophilia. The rest is hysteria: the book was a runaway hit and Hollywood could not wait to film it. Despite its publisher's fears, *Lolita* was never banned (except in New Zealand, where everything is banned that is not compulsory) and, as with *Lady Chatterley's Lover* five years later, the furore guaranteed its future.

Thus it was that, by the time that Nabokov and Vera returned to Nice for the winter of 1960-61, he was, thanks to the success of *Lolita* - and the consequent interest in his other books - a wealthy American citizen living on the shores of Lake Geneva. In the apartment overlooking the Promenade des Anglais, he completed what many critics believe to be his finest work, the poetic novel *Pale Fire* - a semi-autobiographical story about a couple looking back over more than 50 years of marriage. It was to be their last visit to the coast.

Although all of Nabokov's later works were financially successful, none achieved the fame or notoriety of *Lolita*. He died in Lausanne, Switzerland, in July 1977.

In his autobiography, *Speak Memory*, Nabokov gives an idea of the awe in which Nice was held in his Russian childhood. His grandfather, lying dying in St Petersburg, got the idea that if only he were in Nice, all would be well. The long train journey being out of the question, his family transformed his bedroom into the one he had in Nice to convince him that he was there – even to the extent of having items of furniture shipped from Nice, and painting the visible outside walls like the ones in Nice. The grandfather died, but contentedly, thankful for having escaped the Russian winter.

At No. 37 Promenade des Anglais stands the legendary Negresco Hotel – host to royalty, statesmen and rock stars, from Queen Elizabeth II and Presidents Truman and Chirac to Elton John and Michael Jackson. More than 30 films have been shot in this classic turn-of-the-century Riviera hotel, where liveried flunkies dressed as Napoleonic soldiers wear white gloves to open the doors of Rolls and Bentleys, and where the toilets are replicas of Napoleonic field posts – complete with swords as towel rails.

Jean Cocteau used to stay here when filming at the nearby Victorine studios, and was made an Honoured Citizen of Nice in the magnificent neo-classical Palais Masséna next door. Here Ernest Hemingway and F. Scott Fitzgerald cavorted, and H.G. Wells conducted an affair with a wealthy but anonymous American widow in the spring of 1935. He had met her when, with his erstwhile concubine Moura Budberg, he was a guest of Somerset Maugham at his Villa Mauresque on the Cap Ferrat. Wells was staying at the Hermitage Hotel at the time, while Budberg was away and his long-suffering wife Jane was at home in England. Wells would work in the mornings, and in the afternoon a chauffeured Hispano-Suiza would arrive to take him to the Negresco.

Wells had a long association with the Côte d'Azur. Some years earlier, as we saw in the previous chapter, he had built a house near Grasse, where he had lived with his previous mistress, Odette Keun, until their break-up in 1933.

Wells used Hanbury Gardens at La Mortola, just across the Italian border, as a setting for his novel *Meanwhile*. In it he expounds what he believed were his liberal views on marital fidelity. The wife of a philandering husband is reminded that 'the role of a wife is not to compete and be jealous, but to understand and serve. Through him you may do great things in the world, and in no other way will you personally ever do great things.'

The eastern continuation of the Promenade is called the quai des Etats-Unis. The quay and its beach are overlooked from the old town by the house of Matisse, and are the background of many of his sunlit fenestrate paintings. Like the Promenade des Anglais, the quay is a garden of remembrance for literary historians. No. 107, at its western end, is an art nouveau apartment block containing the now ultra-modern Hôtel Beau Rivage. A plaque on the wall attests that Anton Tchekhov stayed there on his first visit to Nice in 1891. It was to be the first of at least three visits to Nice between then and his death in 1901. (An adjacent plaque says that Henri Matisse stayed there in 1916.)

The completion of the railway in 1864 and the visit of Emperor Alexander II and the Empress a week later had signalled the beginning of the Riviera's 'Russian' period. In 1900 there were two Russian libraries in Nice, a Russian sanatorium in Menton and a Russian zoological research centre in Villefranche-sur-Mer; and the most striking building in Nice is the Russian Orthodox Church, built by Nicholas II, with its gleaming gold-and-turquoise onion-shaped domes.

As with the later American 'invasion' of the 1920s, there were plenty of wealthy Russian exiles with luxurious villas who liked to entertain impoverished intellectuals. Tchekhov was a frequent visitor between 1898 and 1901 to the Villa Batava in Beaulieu, the home of Maxim Kovalevsky, a professor of history at the University of Moscow. He had been assigned by his government to study French law and sociology, and became an outspoken advocate of the rights of Russian women and serfs. Like Leo Tolstoi's brother Nicolas – who also lived in Beaulieu – the consumptive Tchekhov came there primarily for his health.

But in leaner times, for Tchekhov and other expatriates, the heart of impecunious Russia was the Pension Russe, at 9 rue Gounod (now the Hôtel Oasis) in what is known as the *Musiciens* quarter of Nice.

Tchekhov wrote at length to his brother Ivan about life in Nice. His letter written in December 1900 – 'It is hot, the sun is shining, and the windows of my room are wide open – as are those of my soul' – was a cut above the average holiday postcard. He rarely mentioned Nice in his stories or plays, but, according to his biographer, Ludmilla Nalegatskaia, the separation enabled him to view and write about Russia from a distance.

Although Tchekhov's time in Nice was productive, deadlines were his ultimate motivation: he finished Acts III and IV of *The Three Sisters* at the Pension Russe – while the actors in Moscow were already rehearsing Acts I and II.

This was his last visit to Nice. After his return to Moscow in 1901, he married the actress Olga Knipper, but their time together was short: after his critical success with *The Cherry Orchard*, he died of tuberculosis in 1904, aged 44. The French sometimes call him 'le Maupassant Russe' because of his skill as a writer of short stories.

(Nalegatskaia, who came to Nice to research the biography, never left the city. She married a Frenchman and died there in 1973. She is buried in the same cemetery in Vence in which the remains of D.H. Lawrence rested between 1930 and 1935.)

Scott Fitzgerald recorded the falling numbers of Russian visitors following the Revolution in 1917:

> Most of all, there was the scent of Russians along the coast – their closed book shops and grocery stores. Ten years ago, when the season ended in April, the doors of the Orthodox Church were locked, and the sweet champagnes they favoured were put away until their return. 'We'll be back next season,' they said, but this was premature, for they were never coming back any more.

In the late autumn of 1869, the Danish storyteller Hans Christian Andersen toured the Côte d'Azur at the age of 64, and spent Christmas at the Pension Suisse. Although known at home for a range of works including short stories and travel writing, he built his international reputation as a teller of fairy tales.

Rarely the Pollyanna depicted in the film of his life by Danny Kaye, Andersen had been more than usually miserable in Toulon: 'I have never felt so lonely and depressed.' But in Nice things looked better: on Christmas Eve his fellow guests presented him with a laurel wreath with ribbons in the colours of his national flag, and in February he was able to write, 'I have now been in Nice six weeks and am feeling quite at home. I am living nicely and comfortably at the Pension Suisse, hard by the open ocean.'

James Joyce, the Irish author of *Ulysses* and *Finnegans Wake*, and his wife Nora had planned to spend the winter of 1922–23 in Nice with their daughter Lucia – their son Giorgio was to join them later. But their departure from Paris was delayed because of Joyce's serious eye problems, and he had to wait for his ophthalmologist to return from holiday. The doctor's advice – weird by today's standards but seemingly accepted without question at the time – was to have his teeth removed in Nice, so that his eye could be operated on when they returned to Paris.

After four days in Marseilles, the Joyces arrived in Nice on 17 October 1922 and stayed at the Hôtel Suisse at the western end of the quai des Etats-Unis with a view to renting something more permanent.

It did not work out in that way. As can sometimes happen in late autumn, the weather changed for the worse, and the wind and rainstorms worsened the eye condition to such an extent that a local doctor was called. His treatment was even more eccentric: he applied leeches to the eye and advised Joyce to drink red wine rather than white – measures which did not fill Joyce with confidence.

In addition, Joyce's latest novel *Ulysses*, published in Paris because it was ruled obscene at home, had proved an instant success, and Joyce felt pressed to return to Paris for the marketing operations that he felt were lacking from Sylvia Beach, its publisher. Finally Nora, possibly missing the cultural and social life of Paris, proved to be less than enthusiastic about Nice. She wrote to a friend in November: 'the weather is fine today and people are walking about in cotton. But when all's said and done, I find the place uninteresting. You may think I'm being difficult, but one can't live solely on sunshine and the blue of the Mediterranean.'

All of these factors, but mainly the problem of Joyce's eye, combined to hasten the family's return to Paris, and they left on 12

November. But there could well be at least one literary legacy of their visit. Did the crescented view of the Baie des Anges from their hotel – a scene so often painted from that very spot by the impressionist Raoul Dufy – inspire the opening sentence of *Finnegans Wake*: 'from swerve of shore to bend of bay'?

Until 1860, Nice was the Italian city of Nizza, birthplace of Garibaldi, and the border with France was the Var river, near the present airport. The *rattachement* to France in 1860 followed a referendum in which the city voted overwhelmingly (for: 6,810 votes; against: 11) to become French, ratifying a deal already struck between Napoleon III, Bonaparte's nephew, and Victor Emmanuel II, king of Piedmont-Sardinia – and later Italy. Church leaders helped to influence the vote: Napoleon III promised the clergy better pay as French clerics than they would get if they remained Italian.

Although much of the modern city's architecture dates from its French period, the old town, huddled below the Castle Hill, between the boulevards and the sea, still retains its Italian flavour, with its narrow, meandering streets and baroque churches. The old port of Nice, at the eastern end of the quai des États-Unis, is bordered on three sides by pink and terracotta buildings with turquoise shutters, which still give it an Italian air.

French writer Jean Lorrain described the port of Nice at the turn of the century:

> Nice and its tiered circus of mountains, the fleeting line of the Esterel far away on the horizon, a mauve arabesque hovering on the line of the sea, while in the foreground, at the mouth of the valley, the dark maze of the castle alive with the lights of the port, huddled like a crouching animal in the immense yellow halo of the city lights.

In 1939, the American writer Henry Miller, who had cycled there from Grasse, wrote to his lover Anaïs Nin:

> It's just what I like – the old port which is quite big, or seems so at first sight. I could kick myself for not having been here sooner. Why don't people talk about these places?

In the late nineteenth century, the streets around the old port provided cheap accommodation for exiles arriving by sea. It was here, at No. 38 rue Catherine Ségurane, that the German philosopher Friedrich Nietzsche rented a small unheated, uncarpeted room in December 1883. He wrote *The Will to Power* and *Beyond Good and Evil*, and began *Thus Spake Zarathustra* in the area. He found the Riviera climate conducive to work – 'Like a plant, I grow in the sunshine' – and he was to return, staying in a number of different residences, for the next five winters. In January 1888, he wrote home: 'I should not fail to mention that this period has been rich in sweeping insights and inspirations for me, and that I have summoned up my courage to undertake the unimaginable and commit [it] to writing.'

Nietzsche hated what he called 'French Nice' – it was 'a blot on the splendour of the town', he said. In the old town, however, 'one must speak Italian – it is like being in a suburb of Genoa'.

The house in rue Catherine Ségurane (named, Nice legend says, after a sixteenth-century peasant leader who put Turkish invaders to flight when she turned her back on them and bared her buttocks) has a plaque outside it bearing a bas-relief of Nietzsche's head. It does not, fortunately, show a bas-relief of Ségurane – nor does it record that Nietzsche was evicted without refund when a longer-staying lodger came along.

Like Nietzsche, Niccolò Paganini, the violinist and composer, was asthmatic, and came to Nice by sea. He hoped to escape the mists of Genoa – as well as a number of creditors – and chose to live in the Italian quarter until his death in 1840. His biography was written by the English writer and historian John Sugden.

But extraordinary though Paganini's life was, it was not nearly as strange as the peregrinations of his corpse after his death. Nice was still part of Piedmontese Italy at the time, but for some reason the Genoese public administration concluded that it was French, and ruled that Paganini had died outside of Italy. The power of the Church was bolstered by political uncertainty in the wake of Napoleon's departure, and the Bishop of Nice, because Paganini had carelessly died without submitting to the formalities of absolution, refused to allow him to be buried in consecrated ground. (The body of the French novelist Colette suffered a similar indignity, despite the fact that the French government had honoured her with a state funeral.)

While his son and friends appealed against this judgement, Paganini's embalmed body waited – for the first two months on his deathbed, and then for a year in the basement of the house in which he died. Then his friends, having failed to persuade the Pope to reverse the decision of the bigoted bishop, were ordered to remove the body from the cellar. There began a ghoulish game of 'hide-the-corpse', in which Paganini's friend the Count of Cessole personally moved the body from cellar to cellar in the Nice area – first to a former leper house in Antibes, from which it had to be moved because passing fishermen complained about the macabre music of violins emanating from the cellar. It was then transferred to an old olive-mill, and finally to the garden of the house of a friend of Cessole on the Cap Ferrat peninsula.

In all, it took four years for Paganini's body to reach the port of Genoa, and thence to his family home – but its journey was still not over, because the Piedmontese church leaders then refused to accept the unabsolved body for burial. It was not until 1876, 36 years after Paganini's death, that the bishop's decision was overturned and the travel-weary corpse transferred to the cemetery in Parma where it now lies.

The continuation of the rue Paganini is the rue Alphonse Karr, in which the Bistro Alphonse Karr was for many years one of the best down-market eating places in Nice. The food was excellent, the prices low, and if dining alone, there was a back room where one could watch television while eating. Karr's name, although not famous on an international scale, appears in most dictionaries of quotations. He was the writer who originated the second most quoted French phrase after 'Let them eat cake': 'Plus ça change, plus c'est la même chose' (the more things change, the more they stay the same).

Alphonse Karr was a Parisian author and journalist, and editor of the magazine *Les Guêpes* (*The Wasps*) in which he used to publish stinging criticisms of anything he did not like. He especially did not like Napoleon's nephew Louis-Napoleon, and was violently opposed to the latter's ascent to power, a sentiment he shared with his friend Alexandre Dumas. When in fact Louis-Napoleon did become the Emperor Napoleon III, Karr thought it prudent to emigrate.

His 'emigration' took him only as far as Nice, which was still part of Italy but, as we have seen, in 1860, with the encouragement of the Church, became French – under Napoleon III.

Thus vilified by both the Church and the politicians, Karr took the advice of Voltaire's Candide and became a gardener – a very successful one. He found that the nearest florist was in Genoa, 120 miles away, so he concentrated on growing flowers. He built many greenhouses – one of them in the street now known as the rue Alphonse Karr – and was soon shipping flowers all over Europe. He wrote to a Parisian friend, 'Leave Paris, where the sun never shines, and come and work here. If you stick your walking-stick in the ground, the next morning you'll find roses growing on it.'

He had a unique way of publicizing his own name. In French, the name Karr lends itself easily to puns. Graffiti started to appear around the town with phrases like 'Karr nage', 'Karr n'avale', even 'Karr avance et raille'. The written phrases are innocuous enough: Karr swims; Karr doesn't swallow; Karr steps forward and jeers. But when spoken, each is a single word: carnage, carnival, caravanserai.

His dress also was calculated to attract attention: he wore black silk from head to toe and had a mulatto manservant, whom he dressed completely in scarlet. He was reputed to have a knife in a frame on his wall, a souvenir of a disagreement with a lover. It was inscribed: 'Given to me by Mme. Collet (in the back)'.

Karr eventually pulled out of the flower business because it was preventing him from writing, and moved to St-Raphaël, at the time a small port to the west of Cannes, where he wrote and painted until his death in 1890.

The little bistro in the rue Alphonse Karr is now no longer a neighbourhood restaurant. The zinc bar has gone, it is furnished in black wood and chromium and there are chopsticks on the tables. It is called, simply, Karr, and its culinary theme is Japanese. But last summer, the little room at the back was packed: staff and customers were watching the World Cup on television.

Plus ça change …

Just south of the rue Alphonse Karr, the rue da la Buffa runs parallel with the promenade. In it stands the English Protestant church, in whose graveyard is buried a writer whose work is celebrated at every

FA Cup final. The Rev. Henry Francis Lyte came here after 25 years as minister to the parish of Lower Brixham in Devon, and wrote 'Abide with Me'.

Next door to the church, at No. 9, lived the Irish-born novelist, biographer and publisher Frank Harris. He wrote 30 books, including the notorious *My Life and Loves* (which was banned in Britain and was the subject of a lawsuit by that serial litigant, the Marquis of Queensberry) and biographies of Oscar Wilde and George Bernard Shaw, the last published a month after Harris's death.

His own life was also the stuff of novels. He was born in Ireland, moved to England, then emigrated to the United States, where he was groom, hotelier and cowboy, before being attracted to literature. Returning to England, he edited a literary review and published two magazines. A committed Francophile for most of his life, with business interests in Monaco and Cannes, he moved permanently to Nice in 1922.

He remarried in 1927, aged 71, to the former Nellie O'Hara, 31 years his junior, and died on 26 August 1931. Nellie survived him by 24 more years. They are both buried in a modest grave in the Caudace cemetery, just inland from the western end of the promenade. The memorial plaque outside Harris's apartment building reads, 'Frank Harris, Irish journalist and writer and faithful guest of the Côte d'Azur, died in this house'.

It was Harris who brought Oscar Wilde to the Côte d'Azur after his release from Reading Gaol. As we saw in Chapter 2, Harris's attempts to encourage Wilde to produce more plays failed, and he moved him to the Hôtel Terminus – 'a tenth-rate hotel near the station' – in Nice.

Shortly after Wilde's arrival in Nice, Harris met him for lunch at the La Reserve in Beaulieu, where a group of English guests recognized him and ostentatiously walked out of the restaurant. He was finally asked to leave his hotel because of further complaints from guests, and was probably relieved to return to the more tolerant milieu of Paris, where he died a pauper just over a year later.

Wilde's disgrace followed him to the grave: Jacob Epstein's art deco statue on his tomb in the Père Lachaise cemetery in Paris still bears the scars of its castration.

*

The American humorist and cartoonist James Thurber, author of *The Secret Life of Walter Mitty*, came to Nice in the wake of the American invasion of the 1920s.

The manner of his original arrival in France had been suitably Mitty-esque. At the end of the First World War, a US Army colonel who was comfortably based in Paris sent a coded message to the USA requesting a dozen coding books for his office. He certainly had coding problems: because the code word for 'book' was similar to that for 'clerk', and he was sent 12 coding clerks. Thus, in November 1918, a 23-year-old James Grover Thurber found himself ensconced in the sumptuous Crillon Hotel overlooking the Place de la Concorde, with not a great deal of work to do. He made the most of this opportunity to see Paris at his government's expense.

At the end of this gruelling tour of duty, the war duly won, the bemedalled hero returned to his home town of Columbus, Ohio, where he scratched a modest living as a freelance journalist. But in May 1925 he returned to Paris with his bride Althea, confident that in bohemian Paris, he would be following in the footsteps of Hemingway and Scott Fitzgerald, and would become a famous novelist.

Unfortunately, he found his novel-writing career blighted by the fact that he had a disturbing tendency to lose interest in his own characters after 5,000 words. But he was lucky enough to get a job with the French bureau of the *Chicago Tribune*. It was a sign of the times that there were enough Americans on the Riviera to justify a local edition of the *Tribune*, and Thurber was transferred to its Nice office to help produce it.

It was mostly a society supplement, and none too arduous, and, since his copy was written in the evenings, he had the daytime free to enjoy the Riviera. The main part of the job was to 'stop in at the [Hôtels] Ruhl and the Negresco each day and pick up the list of guests who had just registered'. They would then invent the rest of the 'gay and romantic cavalcade':

'Lieutenant General and Mrs Pendleton Gray Winslow have arrived at their villa, *Heart's Desire*, on the Cap d'Antibes, bringing with them their prize Burmese monkey, Thibault ...' Then, our four or five hours of drudgery ending, the late Frank Harris would drop in.

Septuagenarian Harris would regale Thurber and his fellow coun-
trymen with tales of his friends Oscar Wilde, Walt Whitman and
George Bernard Shaw.

The undemanding work of reporting on - or improvising - the
social life of expatriate Anglo-Saxons on the Côte d'Azur left him
plenty of time to submit articles to American magazines, their content changing gradually from the oddities of the French to the
brashness of American tourists.

By then committed Francophiles, the Thurbers enjoyed what he
called 'the languorous somnolence of our life': able to get to know
the French Riviera and its Arrière-Pays, to enjoy tennis in the sun -
which included reporting on the Helen Wills Moody versus Suzanne
Lenglen match in Cannes - or to drink with contemporary expatriates.

Sent to interview Isadora Duncan for her reactions to the suicide
in Moscow of her ex-husband Serge Yessenin, Thurber failed to
confirm beforehand that she had already been informed. As she had
not, her 'No, no, no, no' was almost as shattering to him as it was to
her.

But the days of the mighty dollar were drawing to a close. The
depression was beginning to bite, the exchange rate was declining
and life in the sun, although pleasant, was becoming expensive.
Having pawned his return ticket to pay the rent, he had to borrow
enough money to buy it back and, exactly a year after he arrived,
Thurber sailed for New York. At least he needed only the fare for
one - Althea was involved in an affair with one of his colleagues and
had decided to stay.

Walter Mitty became a bestseller and a successful film, and on his
subsequent visits to the Riviera - to Antibes in the winter of 1937 to
1938 and again in the late 1950s - he was hailed as the great international humorist. But he never recaptured that 'languorous
somnolence' of those early years.

The western continuation of the rue de la Buffa is the rue Dante,
where, at No. 4, lived William Boyd, the English novelist and scenarist, when a student at the University of Nice. Boyd, who was born in
Accra, Ghana, of British parents, spent his first 20 years in Africa,
and now lives in London. Africa is the setting for many of his early

works. After graduating from Nice, he continued his studies at Oxford, where he became professor of literature.

Boyd has said that he likes to write 'fiction that doesn't look like fiction', and his recent books have included a fake autobiography, *The New Confessions*, a fake biography, *Nat Tate: An American Artist*, and a fake journal, *Any Human Heart*, complete with index. Among his credits as a scenarist was the script for the Richard Attenborough film *Chaplin*.

Charles Dickens came with his family and staff - 11 people in all - by sea in a steamer from Marseilles in July 1844, on their way to Genoa. His first sight of the Mediterranean Sea reminded him of Turner's *War - the Exile and the Rock Limpet*: 'Lofty emotions rise within me when I see the sun set on the blue Mediterranean. I am the limpet on the rock; my father's name is Turner, and my boots are green.' They arrived in Genoa on 16 July 1844 and settled at the Villa Bagnello in nearby Albaro. On 9 September, he went to Marseilles to collect his brother Frederick and, unable to enter Nice because of quarantine, stayed overnight on the Corniche, 'in an inn which is not entitled, as it ought to be, "The House of Fleas and Vermin", but *La Grande Hôtel de la Poste*'. He embellished the quarantine incident in *Little Dorrit*.

At the end of January 1845, he made a trip to Rome, and went some distance out of his way to visit the grave of Tobias Smollett in the little English cemetery in Leghorn. Dickens has named Smollett as one of his early influences, and there are many echoes of him in Dickens's work. It was a touching homage to the pioneer novelist who had been buried there 74 years earlier.

The year before Louisa M. Alcott's visit, the English artist, poet and indefatigable traveller Edward Lear spent the winter of 1864–65 in Nice. (For the following two winters, as we have seen in Chapter 2, he switched his allegiance to Cannes - probably because of his friendship with the French writer Prosper Mérimée, who was the government's Inspector of Historic Monuments there at the time.) Lear's *The Owl and the Pussycat* was written in Cannes in 1867, but his only literary tribute to Nice was one of his anthropomorphic limericks:

There was an old person of Nice,
Whose associates were usually geese.
They walked out together,
In all sorts of weather.
That affable person of Nice!

Fortunately Lear's is not the only Nice-inspired limerick. In Nice
with his family in 1921 on a day trip from Cannes, Kipling, like Lear
60 years earlier, was moved to compose one:

There were two young ladies of Nice,
Who drank seven cocktails apiece
Then they tried to undress
In the Paris express,
But were stopped by the local police.

Robert Louis Stevenson had first visited Nice with his parents at the
age of 12 in January 1863. They stayed at the Hôtel Chauvain at the
start of a family tour of Italy, Austria and Germany. He returned at
the end of the year and joined his mother, seeking respiratory relief a
little further along the coast in Menton, the town that de Maupassant called 'the pulmonary capital of Europe'. (In 1867, the Scottish
writer and historian Thomas Carlyle noted that there were almost
800 *pulmonaires* – consumptives – in the town.)

Ten years later, the consumptive Stevenson returned to Nice, this
time for his own health. (One of his first publications was an essay
called *Ordered South*.) He settled at the Hôtel Mirabeau on the eastern bay of Menton, facing the Italian border.

Between this and his next visit, ten more years later, he had met
and fallen in love with a married Californian, Fanny Osbourne. At
first he was convinced that marriage would be incompatible with his
career as a writer. It was a problem over which he agonized during
the gruelling mountain walk in 1879 that was to result in the soul-
searching *Travels with a Donkey in the Cévennes*: 'Should he [the writer]
be living and working on his own, celibate ... or should he commit
himself emotionally?' His solitary journey must have helped him to
decide, because on the next trip to the Riviera, Fanny, too, was
ordered south, and, with her son Lloyd, joined Stevenson in Nice.

In October 1882 he set off in search of a home in Provence, and
rented a house in an industrial suburb of Marseilles, which turned

out to be totally unsuitable, and at the end of the year, with his condition deteriorating daily, his wife sent him urgently to Nice, staying behind to pack up. Because none of his letters or telegrams were delivered, she thought he had died on the way to Nice, and after four distraught days she went to Nice and tried every hotel until she found him.

This time he was staying at the Grand Hôtel, but he made a pilgrimage to the old Hôtel Chauvain – by then called the Cosmopolitain – where he had stayed with his parents as a child, 20 years earlier.

He wrote a nostalgic letter to his mother:

> What a change from twenty years ago! The river is now bridged over, and gardens and casinos and the like occupy its place. The old Chauvain I looked into: gone was the gardened court, gone, of course, all the travelling carriages I used to play among with the little Italian girl ... Only the place Masséna still has its arcades and the identical café still remains where I remember seeing my father ... sitting in the moonlight.

This time the weather was unkind, and after not seeing the sun for two days, he wrote to a friend that he was in what they called 'Nice' but which they should call 'Nasty'.

Despite the weather, after three weeks in Nice his health had improved sufficiently for him to renew his search for a permanent home, which they eventually found in Hyères, at the western limits of the Côte d'Azur.

As we saw in Chapter 1, their 18-month stay in Hyères was idyllic, and one of Stevenson's most productive periods, and they returned to England only because of a suspected cholera outbreak.

It was to be his last stay in France. In 1889, after wandering in the South Pacific, he died in Samoa in December 1894, aged only 44.

Seven years before the young Stevenson and his parents had been guests at the Hôtel Chauvain, another visitor from Edinburgh stayed there, Lady Margaret Maria Brewster, who wrote *Letters from Cannes and Nice* (1857). At the time, Nice was still Italian, and she describes her excitement on crossing the Var river into a strange country:

> The view from the bridge, looking up the Var to the Alps, is quite magnificent. One of the mountains is in the form of a fortress; that

is to say, it is crowned by natural rocks, taking a rampart-like and castellated form. A few steps further we had crossed the river. We were in Italy!

Her letter from Nice talks of 'the strange sounds of another language', but she also noticed that, in anticipation of the coming *rattachement* with France, the streets already had their names in both French and English. Her 'democratic feelings received a shock' when her carriage was directed to one side so that a Russian princess could go by. But she liked the surrounding scenery – perhaps there were fewer tall buildings blocking the view than there are today:

> During my drive to-day I was constrained to acknowledge the exceeding beauty and pictorialness of the mountain scenery around Nice, and far far away in the blue misty distance, I caught a peep of an *Esterel*, which seemed quite home-like.

In recent years, one of the city's most controversial critics was Graham Greene. Annoyed at the failure of the Nice police to prevent his girlfriend's daughter from being harassed by her ex-husband, Greene assumed that the husband had Mafia connections, and that the city authorities were protecting him.

He gallantly published *J'Accuse* (1982), a pamphlet in English and French accusing the city chiefs of being run by the Mafia. It began:

> Let me issue a warning to anyone who is tempted to settle for a simple life on what is called the Côte d'Azur. Avoid the region of Nice which is the preserve of some of the most criminal organisations in the south of France: they deal in drugs; they have attempted with the connivance of high authorities to take over the casinos.

As we saw in Chapter 3, Greene did not live long enough to see at least some of his allegations confirmed: three years after his death, the mayor, Jacques Médecin, was jailed for fiscal fraud.

Every year, in the weeks before Lent, the Nice Carnival takes place. It has its roots in a merrymaking event first recorded in 1294, but is now a huge festival in which bands, 20 or more decorated floats, hundreds of marchers and *grosses têtes* – big heads – parade, first along the Promenade des Anglais and through the main squares, then, on successive nights, in the different neighbourhoods of the city, the festivities culminating in a huge bonfire on the beach on mardi gras – Shrove Tuesday.

It seems to have been a less impressive function in 1765, for the diary of the great biographer James Boswell dismissed the whole city in 16 words: 'went on to Nice, where I walked about a little but saw nothing but a procession.'

But by 1903, the French poet Jean Lorrain was able to write:

> Confetti was being thrown by the handful, making a multi-coloured halo, through which carriage after carriage went by, *masques* passing and repassing, shouting and prancing to the deafening music.

La Promenade des Anglais is the title of the last volume of a bestselling trilogy, *La Baie des Anges*, set in Nice, by Max Gallo, the best-known contemporary Niçois writer.

Originally famous as an historian, Gallo's first nationally acclaimed work was *Mussolini's Italy*. In a country that accords national acclaim to its artists, he was able to switch to politics and became parliamentary deputy in 1981 and Euro-MP in 1984.

Gallo was the first writer to enshrine the city of Nice in fiction on an epic scale. *La Baie des Anges* tells the story of a family of Italian immigrants through the twentieth century, against a fresco of the developing city. At the end of the third volume in the series, its hero, Dante Revelli, goes to meet his granddaughter on the Promenade:

> As he was early, he sat on one of the benches on the *Promenade des Anglais*, facing the sea. He started to read, but the seagulls wheeling above the eddying tide drew his eye towards the hills of Mont Boron, and the curve of the bay on which his whole life was inscribed.

But it was surely Naylor, Cyril Connolly's leading character in *The Rock Pool*, who best sums up the variety and charm of this capital of the Riviera:

> It was customary, in the circles in which Naylor moved, or used to move, to disapprove of Nice – such a horrible trippery place, like Brighton; but he realized that evening how delightful it was; the pink Italian piazzas, the derelict casinos, the Russian churches, the Gothic taverns, the *déclassé* yacht harbour, the musical-comedy palms, the little sea-food restaurants along the front, the Genoese

atmosphere of the old town. It was all charmingly dowdy and romantic.

CHAPTER SIX

In the sylvan paths of the nearby mountains or on the peninsula of Saint Jean, one has the most exquisite things that nature can offer, all to oneself.

(Friedrich Nietzsche)

Cap Ferrat: Almost an Island

With its breathtaking coastal scenery and benign temperatures, it is hard to believe that the Cap Ferrat gets its name from the Latin word for 'fierce'. Its climate is blessed, even by pampered Côte d'Azur standards: it is backed by precipitous white cliffs on its north side, whose three levels – the beach resort of Eze Bord de Mer, the village of Eze clinging to the rock face high above it and, towering over both, the 1,500-foot-high peak, the Col d'Eze – both shield it from northerly breezes, and reflect the southern sun like a satellite dish.

The Cap Ferrat peninsula (the French call it a *presqu'île* – almost an island – which sounds much more romantic) dangles like an earring into the Mediterranean between the bays of Villefranche and Beaulieu, its clasp the tiny sub-peninsula of St-Hospice, its jewel the coconut-ice Ephrussi Palace perched along its skyline.

Since the Cap's main road follows a former goat track, cars are a nuisance and buses sporadic, so the best way to see its literary landmarks is on foot: most of them are either on, or within a stone's throw of, the path that traces the coastline around the Cap.

It is an undemanding three-hour walk that older locals call the Sentier des Douanes, because it was originally created to help customs officers to catch smugglers – or, in wartime, spies. There are maps posted helpfully along the path, but, less helpfully, they do not have 'You are here' dots on them; thus you know where you want to go, but you don't know where you are. It's better to pick up your own map from the tourist office in the avenue Denis Seméria.

One writer who found this walk so inspiring that he trekked it many times in the years between 1883 and 1889 – often after having already walked the seven kilometres from his home in Nice – was the German philosopher Friedrich Nietzsche. He called it 'an ideal spot for calm and reflection'.

Location played a vital role in the well-being and the writing of the often depressive Nietzsche, and he found the area highly conducive to work. He completed *Thus Spake Zarathustra* and many other works in the area. 'The richness of the light on a tortured, sometimes suicidal, soul like me is almost miraculous,' he said. 'Like a plant, I grow in the sunshine.'

He liked especially to climb from the beach to the medieval village of Eze, perched precariously on its granite crest, and has said that the solution to the decisive third part of *Zarathustra* came to him while clambering up the escarpment. It is an easier path today, but Nietzsche would probably not choose to climb it – certainly not in summer. The village is on the itinerary of every Riviera excursion, and in the holiday season the narrow alleyways that spiral up to its peak can barely cope with the hordes. But at least he would probably be honoured to find that his vertiginous, winding footpath is now called the Sentier Friedrich Nietzsche.

Around the coastal path of the Cap, the recommended direction is clockwise, starting from the intriguingly named Baie des Fourmis (Bay of Ants) in Beaulieu. That way the sun follows you around. The bay is dominated by a gleaming white *Belle Époque* building, an apartment block that was once the Hôtel Bristol. In its heyday, the early years of the twentieth century, the hotel welcomed Europe's crowned heads, like Queen Marguerite of Italy and Queen Victoria, and those soon to be crowned, like Victoria's son, the future Edward VII. During the First World War it was a military hospital.

In February 1921, Winston Churchill's wife Clementine stayed there, and proudly took four games off seven-times Wimbledon champion Dorothea Douglas, while the French tennis star Suzanne Lenglen looked on.

A guest of the hotel in the winter of 1904 – long before the Riviera became a summer resort – was a five-year-old boy from St Petersburg whose parents had brought him for his first glimpse of the Mediterranean. Young Vladimir Nabokov must have cherished his memories of the Côte d'Azur: as we have already seen, he was to return many times over the next six decades.

The former Hôtel Bristol has another literary – or at least journalistic

– memento. In its gardens stands a rusty anchor that came from the motor yacht *Lysistrata*, the floating home and office of peripatetic publisher James Gordon Bennett. In 1867, Bennett inherited ownership of the newspaper the *New York Herald*, which his father had founded, and proceeded to improve its circulation by pioneering photographic journalism and sensational stunts – one of which was to send reporter Henry Morton Stanley on the quest for the missionary Dr David Livingstone, who had been missing for three years in Central Africa.

Stanley did, of course, find Livingstone, adding a new cliché to the English language in the process, but the Royal Geographic Society would not believe him. (Its president called the whole exercise 'a vast and immoral humbug'.) It was not until Stanley started to receive letters from the reclusive doctor that Stanley – and Bennett – were vindicated.

(It was suggested by Joseph Conrad's biographer Frederick Karl that it was Stanley's triumphant return to Marseilles in January 1878 that motivated the 21-year-old Conrad, who was there at the time, to go to the Congo.)

Bennett's move to France in 1877 was precipitated by a scandal. At a New Year's Eve party at the home of his fiancée's parents, a drunken Bennett, complaining that the toilet was too far away from the lounge, urinated in the fireplace. The ensuing remonstrations resulted in Bennett finding himself in a duel with his fiancée's brother Frederick, and after a number of shots were fired into the air, Bennett left, his formerly exalted position in New York society in tatters and his engagement to socialite Caroline May at an end.

After a stay in Paris, during which time he founded the European edition of the *Herald*, eventually to become what is today the *International Herald Tribune* (now managed jointly by the *New York Times* and the *Washington Post*, and still headquartered in Paris), Bennett, a keen sailor, found the Mediterranean more to his taste. He continued to run the paper from either his new yacht, the *Namouna*, or from his luxurious villa of the same name in the Petite Afrique quarter of Beaulieu, for almost the next 40 years.

He was well known for his lavish lifestyle, and he is reputed, when he was unable to get a table at his favourite Monaco restaurant, to have bought it – and to have given it to the waiter as a tip.

Two days after his 77th birthday, in May 1918, Bennett, on reading in his own newspaper that he was ill, said to his wife, 'Cable the paper and tell them that I'm in perfect health.' Two days later he died of pneumonia.

The mayor and civic fathers of Nice were at the station to bid farewell to his remains on their way to the Passy cemetery in Paris, and messages of condolence came from the presidents of the USA and France, the latter calling Bennett 'a great journalist and pioneer of the *entente* between our two great republics'.

On the eastern shoreline of the Cap, a few hundred metres south of Beaulieu, stands a sumptuous Italianate mansion called the Villa Lo Scoglietto, with its own private harbour at the water's edge and its front door in the Square David Niven. Formerly the residence of another actor-turned-writer Charlie Chaplin, it was Niven's home until his death in 1983.

Niven, who starred in films over a period of 40 years, from *The Prisoner of Zenda* in 1937 to *Candleshoe* in 1977, began his writing career with autobiographical works about the film industry, such as *The Moon's a Balloon* and *Bring on the Empty Horses*. The first of these was dictated to a retired English secretary whom he had found in Nice, but either her shorthand, or her modesty, baulked at the number of four-letter words, and thereafter he had to write in long-hand.

The port of St-Jean, the Cap's only town, enjoys a panoramic view that stretches north and east from Eze to Monaco and the Italian Riviera. Until the closing decades of the nineteenth century, the population of the Cap Ferrat was numbered in the hundreds. The main industries of St-Jean were the harvesting of olives and figs, and fishing for tuna and anchovies – a fairly non-stressful job that consisted of stretching a huge net, a *madrague*, 400 metres long and 40 metres deep, across the harbour and watching it fill up. So abundant were the fish that the net virtually filled itself. When it looked full enough, but not so full that it was a chore to lift, the bells of the little eleventh-century Church of St John the Baptist – not surprisingly the town's patron saint – would peal, everyone would give thanks, and the fishermen would then go out and collect their 'catch' – usually as many as a thousand large tuna at one haul.

Today, the port – overlooked by a pink town hall with *trompe l'oeil* flowers around its entrance, and internal frescoes by Cap resident, writer and painter Jean Cocteau – is a pleasure-boat marina. Where once fishermen sold their catch, blazered weekend mariners sit on the after decks of their floating gin palaces and gaze at the inviting bars and restaurants just an olive-stone's throw away, hoping to catch a glimpse of Andrew Lloyd Webber or Michael Winner.

The Cap Ferrat is the upmarket end of the Côte d'Azur, with an unmistakable air of old money: none of your freshly laundered Marbella millions here. Its transformation from bucolic backwater to millionaires' retreat began at the turn of the century, when financial heavyweights like King Leopold II of Belgium and banker Baron de Rothschild built summer homes there.

It was the Cap's golden age. Leopold made it his summer retreat from Belgian respectability, and, from 1895, used the fabulous wealth he had accumulated from the Congo's mineral deposits and slavery to buy slices of the Cap. No one knows how many properties he owned – he often bought under false names to keep the price down – but the accepted figure is 'dozens'.

One of these properties, the Villa Mauresque, housed Leopold's personal priest. (The king's profligate lifestyle – he was known locally as *le noceur*, the night person – necessitated ready access to a doctor and a confessional.) In 1926, the villa was bought by the English novelist and playwright W. (Willie) Somerset Maugham, who had moved to France following the arrest for gross indecency, and subsequent deportation from England, of his American companion, Gerald Haxton. The villa cost Maugham £16,000, and he lived in it – with the exception of the years of the Second World War occupation – for almost 40 years.

When he came to the Cap, Maugham had already achieved fame as a dramatist (in 1908, at the age of 34, he had four hit plays running simultaneously in London's West End) and was well into his 'storytelling' phase, with novels of the calibre of *Of Human Bondage* and *The Moon and Sixpence*. In his early years in Cap Ferrat, he produced the novel *Cakes and Ale*, in addition to a prolific output of short stories.

Although the Riviera was outside the borders of German-occupied France, during the Second World War it was occupied by Italian troops as a token defence against an Allied invasion. As the Italians arrived, the British left, Maugham having to leave on the last coal ship to sail from Cannes, the *Saltersgate*, with one suitcase, a blanket and three days' provisions. This time there was no first class: there were 500 passengers and toilet facilities for only the 38-man crew.

The ship travelled via Marseilles, Oran in Algeria, and Gibraltar, Maugham sleeping on its iron, coal-dust-covered deck. As he put it later in a talk on British radio: 'We had been in the ship for twenty days without taking our clothes off. From beginning to end, with few exceptions, this crowd of refugees behaved with coolness and courage. Social distinctions went by the board. Our common dirt did that.' Seven people died on the voyage.

Maugham finally reached London via Lisbon, but spent the rest of the war in Parker's Ferry, South Carolina, in a house provided by his publishers, sometimes working for the British government (he had previously worked for MI5) in providing propaganda aimed at bringing the USA into the war. It was, he admitted later, a waste of time: 'only facts counted. The first information to impress the Americans was of our victories in the North African desert.' But the most important literary product of his sojourn in the United States was the novel *The Razor's Edge*.

He returned to France to find his beloved villa 'looking like a patient who had barely survived a deadly disease'. It had suffered abuse at the hands of three nations' forces. The Italians had pillaged his renowned wine cellar and smashed the porcelain lining of his swimming pool. After Italy surrendered, the Cap – and Maugham's villa – were occupied by Germans, who wrecked his boat, removed his art and book collections, and mined the street; and the Allied fleet, in its attempts to destroy the lighthouse, had wrecked his garden and left an unexploded shell lodged in his bedroom. Until the restoration work was complete, Maugham and his staff had to camp out in the exclusive Hôtel Voile d'Or, with its private beach, at the southern end of the harbour of St-Jean.

For most of Maugham's long reign there, the Villa Mauresque was a writers' Mecca, its pampered pilgrims including Noël Coward,

Godfrey Winn, Cyril Connolly, Evelyn Waugh, H.G. Wells, Rudyard Kipling, T.S. Eliot, Arnold Bennett and near neighbour Jean Cocteau. Crime writer E. Phillips Oppenheim wrote, 'Everyone on the Riviera accepts an invitation from Maugham at any time they are lucky enough to receive it, for they are always sure of being entertained.' Maugham called the Riviera 'a sunny place for shady people', which was hardly flattering to his guests.

The lavish hospitality was Maugham's way of combining the Riviera with the London literary scene he missed so much and, as the travel that had for so long been his inspiration became increasingly difficult for him, he turned to his guests for characters and plot. Cynics saw the possibility of being pilloried in some future book as part of their accommodation fee, like unpaid Shakespearian 'fools'. But not everyone agreed: Maugham's friend Sir Hugh Walpole, who was cruelly lampooned as the pushy, self-important Kear character in *Cakes and Ale*, was deeply offended, and it was some years before the two were reconciled.

Being writers, many recorded their own accounts of their visits to Maugham – not always complimentary to their host. To Raymond Chandler he was 'a lonely old eagle'; Frieda, D.H. Lawrence's wife, thought him 'an unhappy and acid man'; Virginia Woolf found him 'like a dead man'; Dorothy Parker, who had accepted his hospitality in South Carolina for three weeks when she was hard up, now called him 'a crashing bore'; and Noël Coward capped them all with 'the lizard of Oz'. Although Coward quarrelled with Maugham about his treatment of his first wife, they too later made up, and Coward was one of his last visitors.

Another guest with whom relations were less than cordial was Ian Fleming, creator of James Bond. In 1953, the Villa Mauresque was, for Fleming, a convenient place to leave his wife while he went about the main purpose of his visit: to work with the amphibious Jacques Cousteau in raising a sunken ship off Marseilles. When Fleming asked Maugham if he could make public relations use of some flattering words that Maugham had used about his work, Maugham said that he wouldn't do it for the author of the Book of Genesis – and after the Flemings had left he complained about the number of towels they had used.

Although there is extensive evidence of Maugham's kindness to other writers – especially beginners – his irascibility was legendary, particularly towards his own family. When his lawyer suggested that, to avoid estate duties, he should put the villa in the name of his daughter, he said, 'Thank you, I've read King Lear.'

Harpo Marx, who was a guest in 1928, was astonished at Maugham's art collection: 'French Impressionists and Moderns – such paintings I had never seen in a private collection before.' Six years later, Harpo noticed Maugham in the audience at a theatre in New York, and clambered, monkey-fashion, across several rows of seat backs to greet him. Maugham said, 'Terribly sorry, I didn't bring a banana.'

Other guests at the Villa Mauresque, although sometimes occasional writers, had found their fame in other fields. They included Maugham's contemporary, Winston Churchill (born in the same year, 1874), the Duke and Duchess of Windsor, Cecil Beaton, press baron Lord Beaverbrook, who lived on nearby Cap d'Ail, musician Artur Rubinstein, dancer Isadora Duncan, painters Matisse, Picasso and Marc Chagall, and art historian Kenneth – later Lord – Clark.

Maugham's writing schedule was strict, and he seldom allowed visitors – even his own family – to disrupt it. His fortress-like study was accessible only by a narrow gangway on the roof of the villa. André Cane, now 92 years old and son of a local builder, remembers his father being called out to brick up the window of Maugham's study, because he found the panoramic view across the Bay of Villefranche distracting.

He socialized on his own terms, and his guests knew the rules. 'Willie' would condescend from his eyrie for a brief lunch, and meet them again for cocktails and dinner. He almost invariably went to bed before 11 pm, after which his guests would be free to stay up and drink or have the chauffeur drive them to the casinos and night clubs of Nice or Monaco. Nothing was too much trouble: Maugham's nephew Robin, himself a moderately successful author whose story The Servant became – with the help of a Harold Pinter screenplay – an Oscar-winning film, said in his Conversations with Willie that the chauffeur was qualified to advise on brothels to suit all preferences.

Maugham in his later years often said that he wanted to die, but he went to considerable lengths to stay alive. In his late 70s he started to visit a Swiss clinic for an anti-ageing treatment involving injections of animal foetuses – as a doctor, he presumably knew what he was doing. He was certainly in illustrious company: 'graduates' of the treatment included Marlene Dietrich, Charlie Chaplin, Gloria Swanson, General de Gaulle and Pope Pius XII – a random selection whose life spans averaged more than 84 years. (Which could simply mean that anyone willing to undergo such treatment must already have a powerful life-wish.)

In his later years, it seemed that the measures he had taken to ensure longevity were now merely keeping him alive when most of his faculties had left him. On the day of Churchill's death in January 1965, a shocked André Cane found Maugham wandering the narrow lanes of the Cap, completely disoriented.

In December of that year he was admitted to the Anglo-American hospital in Nice, and a few days later, comatose and close to death, was taken by Alan Searle, his loyal companion for almost 40 years, back to his bedroom on the Cap Ferrat, where he had said that he wanted to die.

In 1895, after the trial of Oscar Wilde, many young homosexual men who could afford to leave Britain had gone in search of more tolerant regimes. Maugham, aged 21 at the time, went to Capri. He used to say, of his first sight of the Mediterranean, that that was when his life began. Seventy years later, in the early hours of 16 December 1965, at the Villa Mauresque – still within sight of his beloved Mediterranean – his life ended.

Today much rebuilt and painted the colour of scrambled eggs, the villa stands facing the boulevard Somerset Maugham. On its wall is that universal icon of American occupancy, a basketball net. But one Maugham icon has also survived: the gate post bears Maugham's personal talisman, the mystical Moorish sign – said to be a representation of the hand of Fatima warding off the evil eye – that appeared on all his books.

About 200 yards south of the Villa Mauresque, almost next to the lighthouse and sharing its spectacular seascape, stands the former home of the multi-talented French author Jean Cocteau – the Villa

Santo-Sospir, at 14 rue Jean Cocteau. The villa's name is derived from the legend that it was from this point that sailors' loved ones waved their farewells and prayed for their menfolk's safe return. Here Cocteau lived from 1950 until his death. Painter, poet, sculptor, composer, dramatist and film-maker, Cocteau lived there *en famille*, and paid his rent by painting ('tattooing', he called it – which is perhaps more descriptive of the technique) frescoes throughout the house.

The theme of the frescoes is Etruscan, and he made frequent trips to Tuscany during the painting process – although it seems that these visits were less in the pursuit of artistic authenticity than to replenish his supplies of opium, which he had smoked regularly since 1924.

From time to time he would visit his near neighbour Somerset Maugham, of whom he noted in his journal in September 1952, 'his success comes from the fact that he writes on the level of the public. Nothing underneath. Nothing behind.' On other occasions he could be more indulgent: 'Maugham was in fine form today.'

Cocteau's friends came from all levels of society, from stonemasons to statesmen, from fishermen to Princess Grace of Monaco, but mostly they came from the arts: ballet dancers and choreographers such as Diaghilev, Nijinski and Isadora Duncan, musicians like Stravinsky and Milhaud, artists such as Matisse and Picasso (with whom he would regularly boat from the port of Villefranche to lunch at the Plage de Passable on the west coast of the Cap), and a whole galaxy of Hollywood stars that included Orson Welles, Marlene Dietrich and Chaplin. And, of course, the writers: he enjoyed many a *fluide amicale* with Marcel Pagnol and Georges Simenon, and thought Sartre 'the most noble soul I know'.

He described his art technique as 'spontaneous'. 'My method of drawing is like improvisation in jazz,' he said. 'I improvise with lines or colours in the same way that Charlie Parker improvises with the saxophone. When I paint, I am writing, and when I am writing, I paint.'

Like Maugham, Cocteau was Mediterranean by adoption – Monique Lange wrote that 'the Mediterranean was the only woman in his life' – but, unlike Maugham, he never achieved mass popularity outside his own country. He has been accused of having missed the fame and wealth his talents deserved through having spread them too thinly across too many disciplines.

It was certainly not through indolence: during his 13 years at Santo-Sospir, the tireless Cocteau decorated a number of public buildings and chapels in the area, including the town hall of St-Jean-Cap-Ferrat and the chapel of St Pierre – the fisherman's church – in Villefranche. (This despite the fact that the work was almost stopped when the macho fishermen realized that he had painted his angels male.) He also wrote operas and ballets, for which he sometimes painted the scenery and designed the costumes, he published volumes of poetry, wrote film scenarios, and was three times president of the Cannes Film Festival, of which he was honorary life president. 'Il faut que je travaille' – I have to work – was his mantra.

He died in 1963 at his house on Milly-le-Fôret in the Île de France, at the age of 64, and is buried in the grounds of the nearby chapel, which he had also decorated. His epitaph reads 'Je reste avec vous' – I am still with you.

On the other side of the lighthouse, overlooking the tip of the peninsula, are the sun-drenched terraces of the five-star, 14-acre Grand Hôtel du Cap, where the guest book has included such notables as Queen Victoria, Charlie Chaplin and Winston Churchill, and whose swimming coach taught the children of Frank Sinatra and Paul McCartney. A suite with sea view would cost £1,700 a night.

In the late 1930s a writer called Murray Burnett sat in the lounge of the Grand Hôtel du Cap watching a black pianist play on its multi-coloured piano, and was inspired to write (in collaboration with another writer, Joan Alison) a play called *Everybody Comes to Rick's*. He sold it to Warner Brothers for $20,000 – a record for an unproduced play at the time. Warners employed six more writers on the screenplay, changed the ending and gave the film version a much catchier title: *Casablanca*. But many of its immortal lines, such as 'Play it, Sam', 'We'll always have Paris' and 'Round up the usual suspects', were Burnett's.

From the Villa Santo-Sospir, the coastal path turns north along the western Cap. The change of scenery and terrain is dramatic, with the new backdrop the wooded slopes of Mont Boron topped by its fortress, and the foreground the stunning Bay of Villefranche, with its opulent yachts and a natural harbour deep enough to welcome the *QE2* or the aircraft carriers of the US Sixth Fleet.

The literary circuit of the Cap Ferrat ends at the ancient harbour of Villefranche-sur-Mer, where many writers have berthed in the past. But it would be a pity to miss some of the cultural highlights along the way.

The turn-of-the-century Ephrussi Palace, for example, built by the daughter of multi-millionaire banker Baron de Rothschild, is the jewel of the Cap. It stands astride the narrowest part of the Cap, and the impression of being on the bridge of a ship is so strong that the Baroness named it the Île de France and dressed her 34 gardeners in sailor suits.

Pont-Saint-Jean, where the path turns left towards Villefranche, was the home of painter Graham Sutherland. On his first visit to the Mediterranean in the spring of 1947, he had lunch with Maugham and it was suggested that he paint Maugham's portrait. Sutherland had never painted a portrait before, but Maugham was delighted with the result. Sutherland must also have been pleased, because it led to many important commissions, including Lord Beaverbrook and Winston Churchill, a portrait that his wife hated so much that she destroyed it, despite the fact that it belonged to the government.

The opulent Villa Nellcôte in the avenue Louise Bordès has its own private harbour and its cosseted lawns stretch down almost to the water's edge. Here, in the 1970s, the Rolling Stones lived and recorded *Exile on Main Street* in their specially built recording studio: it was an exile whose main purpose was escape the maw of the Inland Revenue.

It is appropriate that the Stones should have come to Villefranche to avoid paying taxes, because that is how the town was born. In 1245, in order to populate the bay of Villefranche and provide a defence against invasion, Charles II of Anjou made a number of tax concessions to persuade people to come and live there – Villefranche means, literally, free town. To make them feel secure, he built a fortress – the Citadel – that dominates the town and was virtually impregnable from the sea. (It was, however, easily overpowered from the land, and, since no one had any reason to bombard it, has survived intact.)

Villefranche is so typical a Provençal port that it looks like a film set – and often is. The Riviera setting for the Disney theme park to be built in China will be a reconstruction of the port of Villefranche – made in California. The town's history is recorded as far back as 130 BC, but goes back further. Here Charles V stayed in the six-teenth century; a young Rimsky-Korsakov landed as a sailor in the Russian navy in 1864; George Bernard Shaw stopped off on a Medi-terranean cruise in 1896; Ernest Hemingway disembarked from the Swedish liner *Gripsholm* in 1934 on his return from the trip to Africa that inspired *The Green Hills of Africa* and *The Short Happy Life of Francis Macomber*; and the Irish navy corvette *Mocha* waited to take the bones of W.B. Yeats back home to Sligo.

On the waterline at the apex of the bay, the Hôtel Welcome has prime position, facing the harbour and with the old town at its back. ('We don't need to advertise,' said its present director, Monsieur Galbois. 'We're on every picture postcard of the town.') In 1947 Graham Sutherland paid for five weeks' bed and breakfast with a painting which still hangs in the hotel.

Jean Cocteau, who from 1924 onwards lived for much of the decade on the second floor overlooking the port, was dean of the Welcome 'school' of writers. It was, he said, not an hotel, but *'un autel* [an altar], a source of myth and inspiration for writers of every kind and every language'. 'Villefranche,' he said, 'is a theatre at which I watch as if in a box at the opera.' He wrote *Orphéus*, *Opéra* and *La Lettre à Maritain* there; with Stravinski, who lived on nearby Mont Boron, he completed his ballet *Oedipus Rex*; and he enter-tained Diaghilev in the Mère Germaine restaurant, a few doors away. On his balcony, he wrote his poem 'L'Hôtel', the first line of which is:

La chambre avec balcon s'envolait sur la mer
(The balconied room flew over the sea).

In Cocteau's time there, Villefranche was a base for the American and Russian navies, and the quiet Hôtel Welcome changed its character when the fleet was in. 'It's a funny place,' he wrote to a friend, 'I live in a brothel for American sailors. On the first floor of my hotel–brothel, the sailors dance and fight day and night. You hear nothing but loud jazz, each machine playing a different tune.'

At other times the Welcome was his muse. His dedication is still there: 'To my dear Hotel Welcome, where I have spent the best years of my life.'

Evelyn Waugh, author of *Brideshead Revisited* and *Officers and Gentlemen*, was a regular guest. He came to the Welcome with his older brother Alec in 1930, when Alec was the better-known writer. On this visit, the brothers dined with Maugham at the Villa Mauresque, an event of which Evelyn wrote later, 'he [Maugham] asked what someone was like and I said "a pansy with a stammer." All the Picassos on the walls blanched.'

As Alec was about to leave for the United States, it was a farewell trip, and they parted facing each other on Villefranche's Hornby-toy train station, Alec on the south side, heading for Paris, and Evelyn opposite, bound for an assignation in Monaco – he never said with whom.

The next year Evelyn was back at the Hôtel Welcome. He wrote from there in the summer of 1931, as if attending some scribes' convention: 'the district is full of chums, [Cyril] Connolly, Aldous H[uxley], Eddie S[ackville]-West ... – too literary by half'.

In 1989, a bust of Cocteau was placed on the quayside opposite the hotel. The words on the plinth read, 'When I see Villefranche, I see my youth again. Pray Heaven it may never change.'

His prayer has been answered only in part: Le Bar des Marins, Cocteau's favourite drinking place, is now one of a seemingly endless line of seafood restaurants; the US Sixth Fleet, on a whim of General de Gaulle, has been banished to Italy; cats bask on the sea wall where the *filles de joie* used to wait; and the classy villas of Villefranche now house stars of rock, cycling and football such as Tina Turner, Lance Armstrong and Arsène Wenger.

But some things have not changed: the Hôtel Welcome – now a model of respectability – still welcomes itinerant writers. The sight of the magnificent bay as one rounds the Cap de Nice is still breathtaking. And Villefranche, thankfully bypassed by the coastal highway, is a picturesque backwater again – except when the cruise liners call.

And penurious writers lucky enough to find a poky pension in the old town will be rewarded, in the words of Cocteau, with 'a veritable Lourdes – a fount of fables and inventions'.

CHAPTER SEVEN

... juts boldly out to sea as if on the look-out for prey.

(J.R. Green)

Monaco: City of Millionaires

It is easy to tell when you have entered Monaco. The signage is discreet, but suddenly the buildings are five times taller (Anthony Burgess called it a mini-Manhattan), the streets are cleaner, the policemen wear white hats and gloves – and there are more of them.

The borders themselves are hard to define. Even the natives get confused: the Monte Carlo Country Club – home of the Monte Carlo Tennis Open – and the Monte Carlo Beach Club, are in France. But they are in the Monaco telephone book.

The nomenclature can be confusing, too. The name 'Monaco' is used generically for the whole Principality, the three square miles – often compared in size with London's Hyde Park – that are bounded by the Mediterranean to the south and by France on the landward side. It is also used geographically to define Monaco *ville*, the old town that sits on a sheer-sided table of rock at the western end of the Principality, on which stand also the cathedral and the pastel-pink palace.

The high ground to the east of the state, surrounding the Casino and the neighbouring Hôtel de Paris, is known as Monte Carlo. There is also a portion of land to the west of the rock called Font-vielle, home of the football stadium, the new yachting port and some fairly monstrous apartment blocks.

The history of Monaco is encapsulated in the tall bronze statue that stands outside the royal palace, of a Franciscan monk wearing, not sandals, as would be the habit, but shoes and with a sword poking incongruously from beneath his cloak. The plinth is captioned: 'Francesco Grimaldi, 1297'.

He was known as *le Malice* – the Crafty One – and was the founder of the little state, and of the Grimaldi dynasty that still rules it. In 1297, when it was part of the Genoese empire, he turned up at the castle gates with a monk's habit thrown casually over his soldier's garb, asking for shelter. Once inside, he drew his sword, slew all about him and opened the gates for his colleagues.

The Monagesques are especially proud of this initiative, and their coat of arms still bears the picture of two Franciscan monks – wearing shoes and brandishing swords.

Since 1297 the Principality has retained its independence by more peaceful means. Today only the police are armed, and there is no petty crime – even if there is no shortage of the serious kind. On the books awaiting trial is the case of a unit trust manager who has allegedly absconded with a $130 million fund. A nurse convicted of causing the accidental death of his fabulously wealthy patient by setting his apartment on fire escaped from prison by climbing down a rope made from rubbish bags and checked into an hotel in Nice. He then phoned a friend in Monaco to ask for money. The French police were there within minutes.

The economic turning points for the modern state were the granting of the gambling franchise in 1863 and the arrival of the railway in October 1868. Suddenly, instead of a dangerous ride along unparapetted mountain roads, or a hazardous boat trip, Nice was 15 comfortable minutes away. (Today it is only six minutes by helicopter.)

The owner of France's biggest daily newspaper, *Le Figaro*, was given a villa and some land options, and soon glowing articles started to appear calling Monaco *le paradis sur terre* – heaven on earth. It became necessary to find a name for the burgeoning paradise on the hill, and the then Prince, Charles III, chose Monte Carlo – Mount Charles.

Like many of today's corporations, the franchise holders of the Casino chose a name which hid the real nature of its business, calling itself euphemistically La Société des Bains de Mer (SBM) – the Sea Bathing Company. It owns the Casino and most of the leading hotels, including the Hôtel de Paris.

Gaming profits soared and hotels, apartments and villas erupted, as the cream of Russian and British society – the affluent of the day – flocked to Monaco. The cost of the accommodation – the result of a shortage of land and a surfeit of buyers – ensured exclusivity. A year after the trains arrived, the Prince found he could afford to abolish direct taxation.

Even the 90-year-old Lord Brougham was wheeled from his beloved Cannes to Monaco, to be impressed by its literary abundance: 'In one week,' he said, 'I have been able to talk of books with authors in the public eye, pay compliments to the queens of salons and theatres, talk politics with statesmen and art with renowned artists.'

Monaco's earliest recorded writer-tourist was Casanova, who was there in 1763 as a guest of the then Prince. Casanova's report of his visit is not noted for its philosophical depth. He records that he was having a boring conversation with the Princess when a laughing chambermaid entered, pursued urgently by the Prince – whom she managed easily to outdistance.

Two years later, James Boswell, the Scottish writer who was later to be the biographer of Dr Johnson, climbed – or rather was carried in a sedan chair – up the steep hill to the palace of Monaco. He was just 25 and returning from his Grand Tour of Europe:

> The French have a garrison there, as it is of consequence for them to take care of the frontiers of Italy. The commandant, to whom I was carried, gave me permission to walk about freely. The court of the palace pleased me. The outside of this building is not good ... The present Prince of Monaco [presumably the one seen in Casanova's fleeting encounter two years earlier] lives almost always at Paris, so that the palace looks desolate, like the house of a Scots laird who lives in England.

Guy de Maupassant, in his *Sur l'Eau*, a record of his voyages along the coast in the 1880s, described the status of the Prince:

> Hail to this great pacific monarch, who without fear of invasion or revolution, reigns peacefully over his happy little flock of subjects, in the midst of court ceremonies which preserve intact the traditions of the four reverences, the twenty-six handkissings, and all the forms used once upon a time around the Great Rulers.

He also mused on the relationship between the Principality's two main institutions, the royal palace and the Casino, facing each other across the harbour:

Opposite to the palace, rises the rival establishment, the Roulette. There is, however, no hatred, no hostility between them; for the one supports the other, which in turn protects the first. Admirable example! Unique instance of two neighbouring and powerful families living in peace in one tiny state: an example well calculated to efface the remembrance of the Capulets and the Montagues. Here, the house of the sovereign; there, the house of play; the old and the new society fraternizing to the sound of gold.

The saloons of the Casino are as readily opened to strangers, as those of the Prince are difficult of access.

Between the Castle and the Casino is La Condamine, a flat stretch of promenade facing the harbour – one of the few straight sections of the Monaco Formula One Grand Prix course. Edith Wharton's description of the area in her *The House of Mirth* was written in 1905, but it is just as valid today:

Their destination was one of the little restaurants overhanging the boulevard which dips steeply down from Monte Carlo to the low intermediate quarter along the quay. From the window in which they presently found themselves installed, they overlooked the intense blue curve of·the harbour, set between·the verdure of twin promontories: to the right, the cliff of Monaco, topped by the mediæval silhouette of its church and castle, to the left the terraces and pinnacles of the gambling-house. Between the two, the waters of the bay were furrowed by a light coming and going of pleasure-craft, through which, just at the culminating moment of luncheon, the majestic advance of a great steam-yacht drew the company's attention from the peas.

And in 1882, Karl Marx wrote to his daughter:

Nature here is splendid, further improved by art – I mean the magical gardens on barren rocks that slope from steep heights all the way down to the blue sea, like the hanging terraces of Babylonian gardens. But the economic basis of Monaco-Gerolstein [*The Duchess of Gerolstein* was an Offenbach operetta about a musical-comedy republic] is the gambling Casino; if it should close up tomorrow, Monaco-Gerolstein would go into the grave – all of it! I do not like to visit the gambling hall.

But Marx had come for relief from his catarrh – 'this accursed English disease' – and was more preoccupied with his health: his stay in Monaco was marred by a medley of respiratory and liver ailments. Another chronic complaint was the cost of doctors and their various treatments:

> I do not expect to leave this robber's nest before early June. Whether or not to remain longer, Dr. Kunemann is to decide. The sensitivity of persons suffering respiratory diseases (that is, those liable to relapses) is heightened in a normally favourable climate. For example, who in the North would dream of immediately getting pleurisy, bronchitis, etc., at an unexpected draft?

But Baroness Orczy, the Hungarian aristocrat who wrote over 20 novels during her 30 years in Monaco, went there in 1915 *because of* its climate:

> We had tested the amenities of that delightful place and found them very much to our taste. The climate, for one thing, was a great attraction, perhaps the greatest, for my husband had in recent years developed a very delicate throat and English winters and English springs were 'playing old Harry' with that throat. So climate was the first attraction, and inclination a good second.

And Lady Margaret Brewster had written almost a hundred years earlier:

> The great dryness and exciting qualities of the climate, however, make it a most suitable one for those who require stimulating after severe illnesses, or who are suffering from chronic complaints; and many kinds of bronchial affections are cured here. It is not good for sufferers from nervous irritability, or congestive headaches, or consumptive complaints.

Indigenous Monagesque artists are rare: like more than 90 per cent of its residents, they are imported. Writers do come here, but they seldom stay: it is too expensive. The cost of land means that single villas are almost non-existent and that apartments cost two or three times what they would cost over the border in France. Only very successful immigrant writers can afford to live in Monaco, and then only when their excess housing costs are offset by tax savings.

One such tax migrant was the novelist John Anthony Burgess Wilson (he chose his two middle names as his pen name). He was born of poor Irish immigrants in Manchester. As university lecturer, novelist, scenarist, musician and composer, he travelled extensively after the Second World War, and in 1968 moved from England to Malta as a tax exile: 'you cannot live without cheating the state', he told an interviewer.

Anthony Burgess's best-known novel was *A Clockwork Orange*, but it was not until the book was filmed by Stanley Kubrick in 1971 that his works came to the notice of a wider audience. They have included an eclectic range of novels, screenplays, essays, critical works and two autobiographies, *Little Wilson and Big God* and *You've Had Your Time*. He was also a well-known musician, and is the only writer in this book who has had full-length symphonies performed internationally.

Burgess soon realized that there was no amount of tax savings that would justify having to live in Malta, but his aversion to paying taxes drove him on, and he tried the USA, France and Italy before finally settling in Monaco in 1975. He left Italy following a threat to kidnap his son. He lived in La Condamine, on the fourth floor of 44 rue Grimaldi, a modern apartment block with a busy street on one side and a railway on the other.

While in Monaco, he published a number of novels and essays, including *Abba Abba* and *Ernest Hemingway and His World*. He died there in 1994.

The destination of most visitors to Monaco – and its nearest approach to an architectural gem – is the Casino. Its pseudo-baroque exterior is a Paris Opera in miniature, which is not surprising, since it was built by the same architect: Charles Garnier. Its promise of easy money has been the theme of many novels and stories.

But many more writers came to gamble than to write.

Anton Tchekhov was a compulsive gambler. During his stays in Nice at the turn of the century, he wrote to his brother Ivan, 'If I had money to spare I would spend the whole year gambling.' He had a love–hate relationship with the wheel: he liked to win but had an aversion to easy money. 'The roulette wheel puts me in mind of a sumptuous water closet,' he said, 'there's something about it that offends propriety and vulgarises nature.'

By the winter of 1897–98, Tchekhov had decided that gambling was an expensive distraction from work. It was also, in his tubercular condition, exhausting. But then his friend Potapenko came to stay at the Pension Russe. Potapenko was immediately addicted, and so confident of having worked out a winning system that he bought his own roulette wheel to test it. At the end of his visit, Tchekhov had to pay Potapenko's train fare back to Moscow.

Rational, deductive Arnold Bennett, who always knew how many words he had written that day, month and year, was someone one would never have expected to succumb, but he fell victim while working in Menton in collaboration with Eden Phillpotts. 'All the time I thought of gaming, gaming,' he said. 'The idea of gambling quite absorbed my thoughts; obsessed me.'

He did not get rich, but one of his characters, Henry Knight in *A Great Man*, breaks the bank. Bennett himself, after a more modest win of 45 francs, said, 'The art of literature seemed a very little thing.'

A fellow writer who lived in nearby Roquebrune, Alice Williamson, who in 1921, with her husband Charles, co-wrote *Berry Goes to Monte Carlo*, the story of a hard-up English aristocrat who makes his living running a guest house there, assured Bennett that it was possible to make a living at the tables. She believed that systems that enabled clients to win modestly were even encouraged by the Casino management as good public relations, provided they did not get too rich. Fortunately Bennett decided that writing offered better odds, and went back to Menton and Phillpotts.

Dorothy Parker, who wrote for a lifetime but is best remembered for a nine-word poem:

Men seldom make passes
At girls who wear glasses

visited the Casino while staying with the Murphys on Cap d'Antibes in 1926. The 'dress police' at the door refused her admission because she wasn't wearing stockings. 'So,' she said, 'I went and found my stockings, then came back and lost my shirt.'

Two years later, in 1928, Harpo Marx, like Parker, fell foul of the dress code. The comic actor and writer was turned away for not wearing a tie. 'Fortunately,' he wrote, 'I was wearing black socks':

I went outside into the shadows, I took off my socks, tied one of them into a bow beneath my shirt collar, stuffed the other one in a shoe, stuck my shoes inside my belt, and went back to the entrance. This time he smiled and said, 'Forgive the inconvenience, monsieur, but you know – the regulations. Please go in. Your friends will be expecting you.

He won a lot of money wearing his makeshift tie, but the next night he did not do well, and asked for directions to the cliff from which one is supposed to jump. Apparently there had been a real suicide the day before, and the image-sensitive Casino refunded his losses and sent him away.

The dress code is slightly less strict today, and one can enter the outer, less formal casino tie-less, but jackets are still desirable – and shorts are a guarantee of a swift exit.

The other Marx was scornful of gambling systems. On his visit in 1882, Karl Marx wrote:

> In reality, the great majority of gamblers, male and female, believe in the science of this pure game of hazard; gentlemen and ladies sit in front of this Café de Paris or on benches in the wonderful garden which belongs to the Casino, hold little tablets (printed) in their hands, head bent, scratching and calculating, or one explains importantly to the other 'which system' he prefers, whether one is to play in 'series', etc., etc. One has the impression of seeing inmates of a lunatic asylum.

He was even less impressed with the roulette tourists themselves:

> the *table d'hôte* [inclusive deal] comrades of the Hôtel de Russie, are much more interested in what happens in the *salles de jeu* [gambling rooms] of the Casino (*tables de roulette et de trente-et-quarante* [roulette and other gaming tables]). I am particularly amused by a son of Great Britain, thoroughly morose, sullen, demented, *and why?* Because he lost a certain amount of gold pieces.

Strangely, the aristocratic Baroness Orczy found herself in agreement with the proletarian Marx:

> To me there is no romance in the casino or even in the adventures, so often ending in tragedy, of its *habitués*; somehow this throwing money about (it was gold when first we visited Monte Carlo) on the chance of a diminutive ball tumbling into one tiny groove rather than into another, always seemed to me rather sordid and certainly futile.

Whether in Monte Carlo, Cannes or Le Touquet, P.G. Wodehouse was a regular contributor to Casino profits, but, true to the compulsive gambler's code, he never admitted to a losing stint. It was his friend, crime writer E. Phillips Oppenheim, who described his unorthodox techniques at roulette. One consisted of 'backing in *mille* notes a special combination of his own of red or black associated with the columns'. Another was 'of covering the board so that only five numbers remained on which he had not staked. I imagine that one or other of those five numbers turned up a little too often, for it is a system that he afterwards abandoned.'

Oppenheim himself spent many years on the Riviera between the wars, and used it as a setting for many of his 150 crime and spy novels. He refused a place on the last coal ships to leave before the German occupation in 1940 because he thought the journey would be dangerous, and it took him another year to get back to England. He was a regular visitor to Monte Carlo, either by car from his homes in Cagnes-sur-Mer or Roquefort-les-Pins, about 30 miles west of Monaco, or on his yacht *Echo*. Every summer, he spent a month at the de luxe Hôtel de Paris.

'Oppy', as his friends called him, inherited the family leather business from his father but, preferring to be a writer, sold the company and became independently wealthy. He was a keen golfer, and his first villa on the Riviera was on the 18th hole of the Cagnes-sur-Mer golf course.

Oppenheim, in his autobiography *The Pool of Memory*, claimed to have lived modestly – to have been 'on the Riviera but not of it ... I lived in a simple villa.' But the book features more titled gentry than *Burke's Peerage*, and contains passages like, 'My most pleasant memories of her [Suzanne Lenglen, French tennis champion] were of the days when she swam from the beach out to my small yacht, which I kept there for many summers, for cocktails and gossip.' He also had homes in the Channel Islands and England.

Many Casino customers were fictional: Edith Wharton's heroine in *The House of Mirth*, the ill-fated social climber Lily Bart, gets out of her depth with her wealthy fellow passengers:

> Lily was tempted, after luncheon, to adjourn in the wake of her
> companions to the hectic atmosphere of the Casino. She did not

mean to play; her diminished pocket-money offered small scope for the adventure; but it amused her to sit on a divan, under the doubtful protection of the Duchess's back, while the latter hung above her stakes at a neighbouring table.

The rooms were packed with the gazing throng which, in the afternoon hours, trickles heavily between the tables, like the Sunday crowd in a lion-house. In the stagnant flow of the mass, identities were hardly distinguishable; but Lily presently saw Mrs. Bry cleaving her determined way through the doors, and, in the broad wake she left, the light figure of Mrs. Fisher bobbing after her like a row-boat at the stern of a tug. Mrs. Bry pressed on, evidently animated by the resolve to reach a certain point in the rooms; but Mrs. Fisher, as she passed Lily, broke from her towing-line, and let herself float to the girl's side.

Another fictional gambler was Bertram, the hero in Graham Greene's *Loser Takes All*, also set in Monaco. Unusually for Greene, it has no criminal activity; its crime is a moral one – greed. *Loser Takes All* is an allegorical tale about a middle-aged accountant who takes his bride to Monaco on their honeymoon as guests of his wealthy boss. When the employer fails to show up, Bertram uses his numeric skills to work out a gambling system to pay his hotel bills while waiting for the boss to arrive – and wins five million francs. But it only makes him hungry for more.

When Bertram starts to imitate his autocratic boss, the bride, Cary, decides she doesn't like him any more and goes off with a young, romantic pauper. When the boss arrives, he advises Bertram how to win back his bride: give the money to the pauper, and the bride will respect him again. The plan works and the loser, Bertram, takes all.

The irony is that Greene wrote the character of Bertram's patriarchal boss as a tribute to the film producer Sir Alexander Korda, whom he greatly admired and who in fact played a similar role of *eminence grise* in Greene's own life. Not only had Korda hired Greene as a scenarist for *Fallen Idol* and *The Third Man*, but he also introduced him to the Côte d'Azur, taking him to the Cannes Film Festival on his yacht in 1952.

Korda also sailed with Greene to the yachting resort of Antibes. And in 1965, when the Inland Revenue suggested to Greene that he should leave the country, he went directly to Antibes and bought an apartment – 'off the train' – overlooking the yacht harbour. Was Greene still being influenced by Korda, nine years after his death?

Colette lived in the Palais Royale in Paris but visited the Principality as a tourist until her 80th year and was a friend of Prince Rainier. Having first stayed there in 1908 as a nearly nude dancer, her visits to the Hôtel de Paris in the early 1950s were as France's most successful woman novelist. It was long after her St-Tropez frolics: deaf and arthritic, she was in a wheel chair, having come south in the hope of some relief from the Paris winter.

By then her novel *Gigi* was being adapted for Broadway and the producers were having difficulty in casting the title role. As Colette was being wheeled through the hotel, she noticed a young actress in the process of shooting a film there. 'There,' she said, 'is our Gigi.'

The show was a Broadway triumph, and Audrey Hepburn never forgot her debt to Colette. But in 1958, when the film version won a record nine Oscars, the role of Gigi was played by a French actress, Lesley Caron.

Cocteau came to see Colette on her last visit to the Hôtel de Paris, but he was no stranger to the hotel: he had met Coco Chanel there in the 1920s, had worked there with Orson Welles and was introduced to opium there in 1924 as solace after the death of his friend Radiguet and remained a lifelong user.

In 1955, two Kellys attended the Cannes Film Festival – dancer Gene and actress Grace. Grace Kelly's studio arranged a number of photo calls to promote the film *Country Girl*, in which she starred with Bing Crosby.

One was a visit to Picasso at his workshop in Vallouris, but he failed to show up, so they photographed her in the Matisse Chapel in Vence, kneeling at the feet of St Dominique.

Her meeting the following day was with Prince Rainier III of Monaco. Less than a year later, in April 1956, she became Her Serene Highness Princess Grace of Monaco when they were married in Monaco Cathedral. Cocteau and the English-born Canadian poet who lived in Monaco, Robert W. Service, wrote poems to celebrate the wedding. Thrifty Somerset Maugham wore a morning suit made for him in 1906 – at 82 he saw no point in investing in another. The birth of Prince Albert in March 1958 ensured the preservation of the ruling dynasty.

Princess Grace was killed in a car accident in Cap d'Ail, just outside Monaco, in 1982, and was buried in the cathedral in which she had been married 26 years earlier.

The last book she read was Anthony Burgess's novel *Earthly Powers*, published in 1980, a fictional autobiography of an ageing homosexual. After Princess Grace's death, Burgess suggested that the Prince set up a library to house the many hundreds of books and manuscripts on all aspects of Irish life that the Princess – who like Burgess was of Irish descent – had collected in her lifetime. When the Princess Grace Irish Library opened in Monaco in November 1984, the music for the event was provided by Anthony Burgess.

Despite its glamorous image, Monaco has evoked strong feelings among writers, often not untinged with envy. Burgess once said 'Monaco suggests an immorality to the puritanical north that is not there ... The wealth and sheer success of Rainier's realm gets under the skin of some people.'

Katherine Mansfield called it 'real Hell, the cleanest, most polished place I've ever seen ... a continual procession of whores, pimps, governesses in thread gloves ... old hags, ancient men, stiff and greyish, panting as they climb, rich fat capitalists'.

To Karl Marx it was a 'den of genteel idlers or adventurers'.

American Paul Theroux, who writes of the world as seen through train windows, called the Monagesques 'anal-retentive tax exiles', which is rather perceptive considering that he only stopped there for lunch and never spoke to anyone.

The British columnist A.A. Gill called it 'Europe's bloated, pendulous haemorrhoid. Only the very, very rich could invent a slum this corpulently arid.'

And American journalist Mary Blume called it 'a place for people who have retired from the world in the sense that they have taken from it what they wished'.

During the occupation of the Riviera by Italian and German troops in the Second World War, the English writer Richard Le Gallienne and his wife, prevented from returning to their home in Menton after a trip to England, had to see out the war in Monaco. Unable to earn a living, and having refused to help the German and Italian authorities, who tried to enlist him to write and broadcast propaganda, they barely survived the war, Le Gallienne at one time collapsing in the street for lack of food.

Meanwhile his house in Menton was occupied by German troops. When he heard that his 'tenants' were planning to send his lifetime collection of books back to Germany as war trophies, he appealed to a German officer in Monaco, who allowed him to go back to Menton to collect them.

Baroness Orczy saw two world wars in Monaco. She had lived in England from the age of 15 until she first went to Monaco in 1915 at the age of 50.

It seems appropriate that she wrote her most famous work, *The Scarlet Pimpernel*, a story of the rescue of innocent victims from the reign of terror of a totalitarian regime, when, like the rest of the Côte d'Azur, Monaco was occupied by Axis armies. A flotilla of German navy ships took shelter in the harbour, making the Principality a legitimate target for the RAF and the submarines of the Royal Navy.

In the last paragraphs of her autobiography, *Links in the Chain of Life*, written in 1945, the Baroness recalls her villa being bombed twice during the liberation of France in 1944. ('The damage in the garden was devastating.')

Perhaps it showed the esteem in which her title was held when, the morning after the second raid, her doorbell rang. The commanding German officer had come to ask whether 'the Baroness had not been too frightened by the bombardment, and was well'.

The Baroness has described the subsequent changes in the Monaco landscape as 'heartbreaking', the new buildings being:

just immense blocks of stone with row upon row of small windows and mean-looking front doors, Germanic in character and wholly void of artistic features.

The place might have been made so beautiful; Nature had done her best for old Monaco, had expended her priceless treasures of beautiful colour, of mountains bathed in mists of rose and purple and delicate grey, of blue sea and sky and the varied greens of olive and palm, of orange and lemon with their shiny metallic leaves, of tall cypresses and distant horizons of silvery moonlight and the glint of sunshine through the trees, of fiery sunsets and of pearly dawns.

*

A number of other writers have made short stays in Monaco over the years. Vita Sackville-West stayed with Lady Sackville during the winter of 1910-11 at the Château Malet on the outskirts of the Principality. Her six months there were 'a perfection of happiness' for Vita. She returned with her lover Violet Trefusis in the winter of 1919, starting at the Hôtel Bristol; but they lost so much money that Vita had to pawn her jewels to pay their bill and they moved to the less expensive Hôtel Windsor.

Virginia Woolf and her biographer husband Leonard made a cursory visit when returning from an Italian holiday in 1933:

> A bright blue and white day: carved parapets gleaming; little em-bayed town on the sea. I saw domes & pillars & told L. this was the Casino; so we went in, & had to produce passports, & sign a paper, & give up hat & umbrella, & then paid nothing but went into a florid but dingy hall, set with seven or eight tables, something like great billiard tables, at which sat a dingy sweaty rather sordid crew, with their faces all set & expressionless watching the gold bars sweeping this way & that in the middle. They had something pecu-liar. One couldn't place them. Some were dingy old governesses in spectacles, others professors with beards; there was one flashy adven-turess; but most were small business men – only rather, not very vicious. It was a blazing hot Sunday morning about 12, & this, we thought is the way our culture spends its holidays. Vicious, dull, & outside lurid. So on.

Hans Christian Andersen visited the 'rocky little kingdom of Mon-aco, lying in the sunshine like a toy', in the spring of 1862; during the late 1950s, Marcel Pagnol lived at No. 2 boulevard d'Italie, at the eastern end of the basse Corniche; and the wife of the American writer Paul Gallico, author of *The Snow Goose* and *The Poseidon Adventure*, was lady-in-waiting to Princess Grace.

It is a measure of the Principality's capacity for change that, with the spread of gambling casinos in France, the UK and the USA, it has set out to develop other industries in order to make its economy less dependent on gaming. Between 1887 and 1962, the contribution of gambling to the state budget fell from 95 per cent to less than 5 per cent. Its big money earners now are tourism and financial services.

Today, the over-full Monte has no room for growth inland, and not much sky left: expansion can take place in only one of two directions: downwards – the railway station has just been moved underground to free up some ground space – and seawards. The state has reclaimed 75 acres from the sea, increasing its land surface by 20 per cent. Now, a ruined gambler leaping from the terrace of the Casino would simply land on the roof of another hotel.

The ivory stone for Monaco's Romanesque cathedral was mined in La Turbie, the ancient hilltop village that looks down on the Principality from the Grande Corniche, 1,500 feet above.

This is the ancient Roman Turbia, the point of entry into Gaul of the Emperor Augustus, in whose honour a huge monument was erected there in 7 BC. It was originally 165 feet tall and was topped by a statue of Augustus. Its plinth bore the names of all the 44 tribes subdued in the conquest.

After the fall of Rome, the monument, known as the Trophée des Alpes, or the Tower of Augustus, fell into disrepair for a couple of thousand years. When Smollett came by in 1764, it had 'the appearance of a ruinous watch-tower, with Gothic battlements; and as such stands undistinguished by those who travel by sea'. Francophile Tennyson, whose preferences were for the south-west corner of France, wrote of the 'Roman strength Turbia showed, in ruin by the mountain road'.

The ruin also distressed a wealthy American, Edward Tuck, who agreed to finance its restoration. Rebuilt using 3,000 of the stones from the original monument, plus the same local white stone that was used for the cathedral, the tastefully restored monument now shines like a beacon above the little town.

La Turbie is mentioned by one of the earliest of the area's immigrant writers. Dante, the Florentine author of The Divine Comedy, passed through early in the fourteenth century on his way into exile in Provence, and was daunted – as today's drivers are – by the vertiginous road down to the coast. His remarks are engraved in stone in the rue Comte de Cessole, which leads up to the monument:

Meanwhile, we'd reached the mountain's foot – and dead
Upright it rose, a cliff so steep and sheer
'Twould make the nimblest legs seem dull as lead.

The craggiest way, the most remote and drear
Between Turbia and Lerici, you'd call,
Compared with that, a broad and easy stair.

(*Inferno*, Canto III)

The street that runs parallel with the rue Comte de Cessole is called the rue Edward Tuck.

A young writer-to-be passed through in 1309: the five-year-old son of a Florentine lawyer, Petracco. Like Dante, the family had been exiled from their native city for having supported the Ghibellines in their losing war against the Guelphs. The boy was to become the poet, traveller and scholar Petrarch, whose unconsummated love for Laura, a married woman he met when he was 23, inspired his most famous works: the *Canzoniere* love poems.

On the opposite, northern side of La Turbie, where a more gentle incline slopes down towards Nice, there is a chapel and shrine dedicated to the Madonna of Laghet.

The hero of Marcel Proust's *Remembrance of Things Past*, Charles Swann, having fallen in love with the Niçoise courtesan Odette, asks her to pledge her fidelity. Even when she gives him the answers he wants, he is sceptical, until he gets the idea to ask if she would be prepared to swear to it on her medal of the Notre Dame de Laghet, because, says the narrator, 'Swann knew that she would never perjure herself on that medal.'

The shrine of the Madonna of Laghet has been a place of pilgrimage for centuries, and welcomes more supplicants than any other sanctum in Provence – except, of course, for the pilgrims who frequent the green baize shrines of the Casino, 1,500 feet below.

CHAPTER EIGHT

*I call to mind Mentone, the warmest and
healthiest of these winter residences.*

(Guy de Maupassant)

Menton: Sanatorium City

Menton is the most Italianate of French towns. Its eastern suburbs abut the Italian border, and its Italian name, Mentone, is heard almost as frequently as the French one, especially at weekends, when trippers from Milan and Turin crowd its beaches and cafés. And if, architecturally, it has not escaped the concrete contamination, it has managed to keep it in harmony with the predominant mix of Romanesque and French *Belle Époque*.

Almost every Riviera town claims that theirs has the best climate, but the Mentonnais present evidence. They argue that, because the Maritime Alps are closest to the sea at this point on the coast, their town is best shielded from northern and western winds.

Certainly, the sub-tropical fauna here are more luxuriant. The citrus crop – so abundant that they can afford to use 200 tons of oranges, lemons and grapefruit to decorate the floats during Mardi Gras week – comes into fruit earlier and stays longer; and the olive trees think they are still Italian, and grow upwards, unlike their gnarled and twisted cousins farther west.

The heart of the town is Old Menton, where narrow streets steep enough to deter mountain goats lead up to cobbled squares and ancient churches. Adjoining this quarter are the more gentle hills of the suburb of Garavan, with its elegant villas. Here, in the early 1920s, Katherine Mansfield, the New Zealand novelist and short-story writer, lived in the Villa Isola Bella, and the Spanish novelist, Vicente Blasco-Ibáñez, author of *The Four Horsemen of the Apocalypse*, made his home in the Villa Fontana Rosa for most of the decade.

But writers discovered Menton long before that. In the early 1300s, the Italian poet Dante travelled extensively in the region after being exiled from Florence. He recorded his journeys in a number of epic poems, most notably *The Divine Comedy*, completed in 1321.

Menton owes much of its late nineteenth-century prosperity to the misplaced faith of northern European doctors in the curative powers of its climate. In those pre-antibiotic times, British and Russian doctors who should have been sending their tubercular patients to Blackpool or the Black Sea shipped them off to Menton, convinced that all that they needed was a spot of sunshine.

A paper in the medical journal *The Lancet* on 7 July 1860, by Dr James Henry Bennet, an English doctor living in Menton, claimed that its climate was warmer, not only than Nice, but than 'any part of the northern or central parts of Italy', and ideal for anyone with respiratory disorders.

The bacilli certainly flourished. After the coming of the railway in 1868, pulmonary migrants were packed into its steamy carriages to be carried southwards in their coughing hundreds. Menton became a middle-class Switzerland – what Guy de Maupassant called 'the hospital of society and the flowery cemetery of aristocratic Europe'.

The ornate necropolises of Menton were among the most scenic in the world, competing for the corpses of the bronchial Britons and Russians who spluttered their last here. Their tombstones attest to the brevity of their lives. As de Maupassant put it:

Just as in warlike cities, the fortresses can be seen standing out on the surrounding heights, so in this region of moribunds, the cemetery is visible on the summit of a hill.

What a spot it would be for the living, that garden where the dead lie asleep!

... All those who lie there, were but sixteen, eighteen, or twenty years of age. One wanders from tomb to tomb, reading the names of those youthful victims, killed by the implacable disease. 'Tis a children's cemetery ... where no married couples are admitted.

The cultural windfall from this myth was immense. Sculptors and musicians came: Bac, Paganini and Rubinstein, painters such as Aubrey Beardsley and Matisse, and, above all, writers, of every nationality and genre: France's de Maupassant and Guyau, Russia's Tchekhov, Germany's Nietzsche, England's Sillitoe and Swinburne, Scotland's Thomas Carlyle and Robert Louis Stevenson, Ireland's Laurence Sterne and W.B. Yeats, and New Zealand's Katherine Mansfield – all trekked to Menton in the hope of a miracle. Carlyle called the town 'Britain's main overseas sanatorium', and Stevenson's first published work was a study in hypochondria called *Ordered South*.

But although Menton – and indeed the whole of the Riviera – profited from the widely held belief in its remedial powers, many doctors today believe that to winter in the south was of dubious benefit to consumptives, especially in view of the lower standards of hygiene of the time. Mansfield, Stevenson and many others were not diagnosed as tubercular until *after* they reached the Mediterranean.

A few months after *The Lancet* article appeared, the English essayist and travel writer Augustus Hare decided to take Bennet's advice and came to Menton for the winter. His book, *A Winter in Mentone*, published in 1862, was dedicated to, 'My fellow sojourners in beautiful Mentone ... in grateful remembrance of the many happy hours passed in their society'. Hare wrote that twice daily, at dawn and dusk, 'a lovely fairy vision salutes us: Corsica reveals itself across the sapphire water, appearing so distinctly that you can count every ravine and indentation of its jagged mountains'. He was luckier than the present residents: today, thanks either to Mediterranean mist or urban smog, or sometimes both, sightings of 100-miles-away Corsica are much less frequent. The last was 18 years ago.

Robert Louis Stevenson had first visited the Côte d'Azur in 1863 as a boy of 12, when he stayed with his family in Nice at the beginning of a European tour, and later that year visited his mother, who by this time had moved to Menton on medical advice and was staying at the Hôtel Russe.

When he returned to Menton ten years later, it was for his own health. His doctor, Sir Andrew Clark, with some collusion, one suspects, from Stevenson himself, prescribed in writing not only that he should move to the south of France, but that his mother should not accompany him. Stevenson was euphoric: 'Clark is a trump. He said I must go abroad and that I was better alone – "Mothers", he said, "just put fancies into people's heads, and make them fancy themselves worse than they are". My mother (with some justice) denied this soft impeachment.'

He stayed at the Hôtel Mirabeau on Menton's eastern bay, two miles from the Italian border, where he finished *Ordered South*, and sought relief from his symptoms in the town's opium den – a treatment of which his mother would surely not have approved.

On 30 March 1874, the eve of his departure, he wrote, 'My last night in Mentone. I cannot tell you how strange and sad I feel', and later:

> Mentone is one of the most beautiful places in the world and has always had a warm corner in my heart, since I knew it eleven years ago.

Stevenson's next visit to the Riviera was a further ten years on. He had made his arduous trip by immigrant ship and train across America in pursuit of his beloved Fanny, and married her as soon as she was divorced in 1880. He had brought her and her son Lloyd back to England in 1884 and settled in Bournemouth.

He was now a famous author, but a sick one, and although he spent the next two winters in Davos, Switzerland, he found that the improvement in his health there was only temporary, and decided to try the Riviera again.

As we have seen in Chapter 1, that blissful and productive stay in Hyères was to be his last visit to France. After his death in Samoa in 1894, he was buried at the summit of Mount Vaea. The epitaph on his simple tomb is from his own poem, *Requiem*, the last lines of which are:

> Here he lies where he longed to be;
> Home is the sailor, home from the sea,
> And the hunter home from the hill.

While in Menton, Stevenson had been treated by the same Dr Bennet whose article in *The Lancet* had encouraged Augustus Hare to come. By this time, Bennet, a tuberculosis sufferer himself, had written *Winter and Spring on the Shores of the Mediterranean*, a tubercular tour of the Riviera which concluded that, for the well-off consumptive, a winter in the South of France would be, if not curative, therapeutic. Coming just after the extension of the railway to Monaco, the publication of Bennet's book was a major boost to sano-tourism for the whole of the Côte d'Azur. Menton awarded him its highest accolade: the rue Henry Bennet. It was said that local medics could tell, from the ethnic mix of their patients, into which languages the book had most recently been translated.

*

Another early recruit was the Irish writer Laurence Sterne, author of *Tristram Shandy*. Sterne suffered his first lung haemorrhage while a student at Cambridge. The great-grandson of an archbishop of York, he followed family tradition and became Anglican vicar of Shillington, and later Coxwold, in Yorkshire.

He became a novelist by default. A book he produced in support of a Church friend was deemed so politically incorrect that it was ordered to be destroyed, but in writing it he found his true metier, and in 1759, at the age of 46, he finished the first part of *The Life and Opinions of Tristram Shandy, Gentleman*. When a London publisher rejected the manuscript, he decided to publish it himself, and, finding he had spare copies, sent some to the same publisher, who sold them and ordered more, and the book was an immediate success.

Tristram Shandy is a satirical novel purporting to be an autobiography. Its major theme is the tragedy of the breakdown of communication between intimates.

The narrator tells his life story from the moment of his own conception. His father, 'the most regular of men in every thing he did', was in the habit of carrying out certain 'family concernments' – among them sex and winding the clocks – on the first Sunday of each month, 'to get them all out of the way at one time'. At the precise moment of impregnation, Shandy's mother reminds his father that he has not wound the clocks – a distraction that results in the hero's foetus being impaired, leaving him ill equipped, both physically and mentally, for life.

While the novel does not pretend to be a true autobiography, the parallels with Sterne's own life are unmistakable. He was a life-long invalid, his relationships with women were disastrous, and his writing suggests a depressive and paranoid state of mind.

In 1762, Sterne's worsening condition had caused his doctors to recommend that he move to France for his health, where he completed the last volume of *Tristram Shandy* and started *A Sentimental Journey through France and Italy by Mr Yorick*.

In it, Sterne attacks Tobias Smollett's *Travels through France and Italy* of 1766, comparing it unfavourably with his own work, and calling Smollett 'the learned Smelfungus' for his complaints about the locals:

> The learned SMELFUNGUS travelled from Boulogne to Paris –
> from Paris to Rome – and so on – but he set out with the spleen and
> jaundice, and every object he passed by was discoloured or distorted.
> He wrote an account of them, but 'twas nothing but the account of
> his miserable feelings.

If published today, *A Sentimental Journey through France and Italy* would probably infringe the Trade Descriptions Act: starting in Calais, it tells of the Reverend gentleman's amorous exploits, but gets no further south than Lyons. He presumably intended to write more, but he finally succumbed to tuberculosis in London on 18 March 1768, aged 53, and *Sentimental Journey* was published after his death.

Even then he did not rest in peace. After his funeral in London, his body was removed by body snatchers and sold. Fortunately it was sent to Cambridge for research, where it was recognized, returned, and eventually buried in the churchyard of his old parish in Coxwold.

On a leafy hillside in the eastern suburb of Garavan, in the Villa Isola Bella (beautiful island) within coughing distance of the Italian border, lived another consumptive author, the New Zealand short-story writer, Katherine Mansfield. She was born in the capital city, Wellington, on 14 October 1888, and at the age of 19 left its 'singular charm and barrenness' for London, never to return.

In pre-war London, Mansfield and her husband John Middleton Murry had been close friends of D.H. Lawrence, and were witnesses at his marriage to Frieda in 1914. Frieda gave Mansfield the wedding ring from her previous marriage, which, despite subsequent disputes – such as her calling Frieda 'a great fat sod' – Mansfield wore until she died. (The rift was mutual: while she was at Isola Bella, an embittered Lawrence wrote to her from Capri, 'I loathe you. You revolt me stewing in your consumption.')

Mansfield had first come to the south of France in 1915, grieving the death of her brother on the Western Front. Her tuberculosis was first diagnosed in 1917, and she reached Menton in January 1920, having spent the last years of the war in a number of coastal towns in the Toulon area – in particular Bandol – then in the Italian Riviera towns of San Remo and Ospidaletti. Soon after moving into Isola Bella, Mansfield wrote that, when she died, 'You will find ISOLA BELLA in poker work on my heart.'

Despite her illness, her stay there was highly productive, resulting in a succession of short stories (including *Bliss and Other Stories*), book reviews, articles and a translation from Tchekhov. She had also found contentment ('this little place is and always will be for me – the only place'), some relief from her symptoms and, judging by the frequency of Murry's visits, a rekindling of her fragile marriage. During his visits she would invent elaborate reasons to send her maid out of the house: 'What is one to do? The house is so small.'

Late in 1922, Mansfield decided to attend a course at the pretentiously titled Institute for the Harmonious Development of the Mind, in an old monastery near Fontainebleau, 40 miles south of Paris. Unfortunately, the course – or the northern winter – did not harmonize with her body, and she died there of tuberculosis on 9 January 1923, at the age of 34. A few days earlier she had written, 'I simply pine for the S. of France.'

She was buried in a nearby village, and her gravestone bears the words that she had chosen as an epigraph for one of the works she completed in Menton, *Bliss and Other Stories*. It was a quotation from Shakespeare's *Henry IV*: 'out of this nettle, danger, we pluck this flower, safety'. The name of the village, appropriately, is Avon.

Today's Menton is still, as Mansfield observed: 'a lovely little town, small and unreal ... The colour and movement everywhere make you continually happy.' The colour and movement are still there: oranges and lemons flourish unpicked and shrub-like geraniums cascade from sunny balconies, while the bustle of the town centre contrasts with the lonely shuffle of pensioners, walking their dogs along the elegant promenade.

The street where she lived – the avenue Katherine Mansfield – is now dotted with luxury apartment blocks. The faded plaque to her memory is barely readable, but the *isola*, despite its crumbling stuccoed walls and overgrown garden, is still, in its dishevelled way, *bella*.

The avenue Katherine Mansfield adjoins the rue Webb Ellis – juxtaposing New Zealand's most famous cultural export with its most cherished import. (William Webb Ellis was the boy at Rugby School who, in 1823, according to school legend, picked up and ran with the ball, thereby 'inventing' the game of rugby. After a career as vicar of St Clement Dane's Church in London's Strand, he became the Anglican vicar of Menton and his grave, in the little cemetery of the Vieux Château that overlooks the town, has become a place of pilgrimage to lovers of the sport.)

A short climb from the Vieux Château, yet another cemetery, the Trabuquet, looks down on the Byzantine dome of the Church of St Michel and the narrow streets around it. The Trabuquet is the resting place of two English writers who were at one time literary collaborators.

Aubrey Beardsley was one of what de Maupassant called the 'youthful victims'. His grave perches on the edge of a ravine overlooking the port, the Mediterranean and, on exceptionally clear – but increasingly rare – days, the distant island of Corsica. He was born in Brighton in 1872 and was consumptive from the age of seven. He published some poetry and one novel, Under the Hill, in 1896.

He had the precocity and work rate of those who do not expect a long life. Although a novelist and poet, he achieved his fame as an illustrator. He won his first major commission, to illustrate Flaubert's Madame Bovary, at the age of 15.

With the exception of some evening classes at the Westminster School of Art, he was largely self-taught. At 20 he produced 500 ink drawings for Sir Thomas Malory's Morte d'Arthur, and, a year later, provided the illustrations for Oscar Wilde's Salomé.

At 22 he was art director of The Yellow Book, a prestigious literary review whose contributors included Arnold Bennett and Henry James. After Oscar Wilde's arrest in 1895, the offices of The Yellow Book were attacked – despite the fact that he never wrote for it – the mob having made the same association that John Betjeman was to make half a century later. Beardsley was one of a number of its staff and contributors who left the country.

Beardsley's artistic style was, for its time, revolutionary and iconoclastic. Strongly influenced by the sensuality and frankness of Japanese woodcuts, he was a key figure in the art nouveau movement – what the French call art nouille (noodle art). His prose was as provocative as his art, and although *Under the Hill* was published clandestinely in 1896, the unexpurgated version, renamed *The Story of Venus and Tannhäuser*, did not appear until nine years after his death.

His last two years were spent in Menton, where, after being baptized into the Roman Catholic faith, he died of tuberculosis on 16 March 1898, at the age of 25.

Another expatriate writer, Richard Le Gallienne, is buried nearby. He and Beardsley have other things in common than sepulchral proximity: Le Gallienne was a contributor to *The Yellow Book*, both were friends of Wilde, and although Le Gallienne survived Beardsley by half a century, both were medical migrants to Menton.

Le Gallienne was born Richard Gallienne in Liverpool on 20 January 1866, his Gallic-sounding surname deriving from a mariner grandfather who was born in Guernsey. Too poor to send their son to university, the Galliennes articled him to a Liverpool firm of accountants at the age of 15. He stayed with the firm for eight years, but he was more interested in book collecting than bookkeeping and spent most of his time and money in local bookshops.

Le Gallienne began to write for publication after being inspired by a lecture given by Oscar Wilde in Birkenhead in 1883, and on failing his accountancy finals, he left the family home to make a career as a writer in London. He became a member of the Rhymers' Club, a group of poets, including the likes of Wilde and W.B. Yeats, who met in the Cheshire Cheese in Fleet Street to critique each other's work, and was a regular contributor to the club's anthologies. Swinburne called him 'Shelley with a chin'.

After publishing several volumes of poetry and some inauspicious attempts to succeed as a playwright, he went to the USA in 1895. The stigma of Wilde's disgrace contaminated his associates, whatever their sexual orientation, and many years later, in *The Romantic '90s*, Le Gallienne summed up the hypocrisy of the Wilde era:

> In him the period might see its own face in a glass. And it is because it did see its own face in him that it first admired, then grew afraid, then destroyed him.

On his return from the USA, he married a woman he had known in Liverpool with whom he had a daughter, and in 1900 went to Hyères to both ease his asthma and write a book. Neither objective was achieved, and soon afterwards he left his wife and emigrated permanently to the United States.

Unfortunately, Le Gallienne's style did not keep pace with the changing fashions of the new century. In the USA he made a precarious living as part-time actor and lecturer, and published critical reviews, travel and biographical works, and a novel, *The Quest of the Golden Girl*.

He returned to Europe in 1929, and at first lived in Paris with his third wife, Irma. He had already discovered the Côte d'Azur, having also stayed in Cagnes-sur-Mer and Nice on earlier visits, and decided to try Menton, 'where', he told his father, 'it will be sunny and clear, and where I shall have the sea, which always agrees with me'. After spending four winters in Menton, he moved there permanently in 1935. He bought the Castel Fleuri on the quai Laurenti in the Garavan quarter, where he published a number of books, including *From a Paris Garret* and *From a Paris Scrapbook*, which won a French government award for the best foreign publication about France.

The couple's stay in Menton was interrupted by the Nazi occupation in the Second World War and they took refuge in Monaco, where, as we saw in Chapter 7, although poor and often hungry, he turned down lucrative German offers to broadcast pro-Axis propaganda.

On their return to Menton after its liberation, they learned that the town planned to tear down the 200-year-old Castel Fleuri to make room for a sports stadium, and they were given the nearby Villa Béatrice, in the rue Albert Premier, in its place.

It was there that the former accountant from Liverpool, who in his long life had known generations of fellow writers, from Ibsen, Stevenson and Wilde to Joyce, Hemingway and Pound, died in penury and obscurity on 15 September 1947, aged 81. His artistic life had been as long and relatively anonymous as Beardsley's had been brief and meteoric: one wonders which life he would have chosen. His grave is not as scenically located as his former colleague's – but then he died 50 years later.

A table in the lounge of the Villa Béatrice provided an unlikely link with Oscar Wilde: Le Gallienne bought it in Paris at an auction on the closure of the Hôtel Alsace (the hotel in which Wilde died in 1900). It was the table at which Wilde wrote his very last words.

In the year in which Le Gallienne - and H.G. Wells - were born, 1866, the Scottish historian Thomas Carlyle arrived in Menton at the age of 71. His most significant works were his *History of the French Revolution* and the marathon *Life of Frederick the Great*. His only copy of *History of the French Revolution* was accidentally used to light the fire while on loan to a colleague, and he had to write it all again.

Yeats called him 'the chief inspirer of educated men', and his contemporary, George Eliot, said:

> there has hardly been a superior or active mind of this generation that has not been modified by Carlyle's writings; there has hardly been an English book written for the past ten or twelve years that would not have been different if Carlyle had not lived.

In Menton he stayed at the villa of the second Lady Ashburton, recovering from the 13-year slog of completing *Frederick the Great*, and coming to terms with the death, eight months earlier, of his long-suffering wife Jane, whose death, he said, 'shattered my whole existence into immeasurable ruin'.

At first his writing, in the pleasant surroundings and relative calm of Menton, went well. He was working on his *Reminiscences*, and was able to write, in January 1867: 'things continue all well, and as it were at their best for me'.

But he caught a cold in February, and soon his morale was at its more customary depressive level, so that, by March, on finishing a memoir on Wordsworth, he noted: 'Won't begin another ... it is wearisome and naught even to myself ... ETERNITY cannot be far off.'

In fact, it was 14 years off. Although not tubercular, Carlyle, a serial hypochondriac, was prone to most other ailments known to science, and by the end of the month he was back in his house in Cheyne Row, Chelsea.

There was a strange sequel to his spell in Menton. His friend and fellow writer John Ruskin published an article saying that Carlyle had told him that he could not walk in London without being abused by the 'common people' because he was well dressed, whereas the peasant class in the South of France treated him with great courtesy. When Carlyle wrote denying having said any such thing, the paranoid Ruskin, ever ready to take offence at real or imagined slights, demanded a retraction. The trifling argument raged for some weeks before Carlyle finally issued a statement.

It was not exactly the one that Ruskin wanted. It began: 'I never told you, nor could tell or have told any mortal, that "Mr Carlyle" was liable to be insulted on the streets of London.' But apparently it was the statement, not its content, that was important. Pride was satisfied, the 'common people' of London were exonerated and the friendship resumed.

Carlyle remained in Chelsea, continuing to write, to acknowledge the deaths of friends – including that of his friend of 30 years, Charles Dickens – that are concomitant with longevity, to receive honours – including a doctorate from Harvard University – and to sit for portraits. Despite his earlier visions of eternity, he remained in relatively good health until his peaceful death while sleeping, at the age of 85.

Although Carlyle's work has inspired a heterogeneous range of readers – his *French Revolution* was Dickens's inspiration for *A Tale of Two Cities*, and Hitler had Goebbels read *Frederick the Great* to him in his Berlin bunker as the Russians closed in – it has taken some time for his contribution to literature to be widely acknowledged. In his lifetime, he refused a knighthood on the grounds that it was 'out of keeping with the tenour of my own poor existence hitherto', and, on his behalf, his niece refused a tomb in Westminster Abbey. But the Dean of the Abbey, in his obituary sermon, quoted Matthew viii:24. 'The seed that fell onto good soil ... yields a hundredfold.'

The rue William Webb Ellis, at the other end from its junction with the avenue Katherine Mansfield, runs into another road commemorating an internationally known writer: the avenue Blasco-Ibáñez.

Vicente Blasco-Ibáñez, best known as the author of *The Four Horsemen of the Apocalypse*, was born in Valencia, Spain, in 1867, while Thomas Carlyle was in Menton writing his *Reminiscences*.

He ran away to Madrid at the age of 15, but returned to Valencia to finish his studies and qualified as a lawyer at 19. He turned first to political writing and, in the great tradition of Spanish literature, was soon deported for anti-royalist incitement. He spent much of his long life either in prison – he was jailed 33 times in all – or in exile, mostly in Paris, where he wrote a history of the Spanish revolution, or Argentina, where he founded two vast agricultural communities to provide work for the poor of Buenos Aires. He called them Nueva Valencia and Colonia Cervantes.

Much of his early fame was won abroad. He returned during the amnesty of 1891 to found *El Pueblo*, Spain's first socialist newspaper, and represented Valencia in parliament, all the time maintaining his prolific output. Many of his works became films, among the most famous being *Blood and Sand* and *The Four Horsemen of the Apocalypse* (written in 1916 in support of the Allied cause), which originally starred Rudolph Valentino – but spawned many imitations.

Eventually, his opposition to the military dictatorship led him to choose voluntary exile, believing, like his friend and mentor Émile Zola, that he could better serve his people as a writer than as a political prisoner. He spent most of the First World War in the neutral state of Monaco, later moving to the boulevard Carnot in Nice, where the evening walk-about on the promenade inspired his story *The Old People of the Promenade des Anglais*.

But despite his success, one dream remained unfulfilled: he was looking for the ideal spot to build a mansion to house his vast art collection and libraries, and where he would establish a writers' colony, where novelists of different nationalities could meet in an atmosphere of mutual understanding and inspiration. He found it in Menton, on the wooded slopes of Garavan, and dedicated the rest of his life to the project.

It was to become a corner of Spain on the Côte d'Azur. He called the house Fontana Rosa (Pink Fountain) and for its gardens he imported Spanish flowers, shrubs and citrus trees – and Spanish gardeners to plant and tend them.

Above its wrought-iron entrance gates, the name of the garden, El Jardin de los Novelistas, appears in brightly coloured tiles, flanked by its name in English (The Garden of the Novelists) and French (Le Jardin des Romanciers). Above the signs, in blue tiles, are large portraits of three novelists: Dickens, Balzac and Cervantes, whose picture is the largest of the three.

The Garden of the Novelists was a writers' retreat, laid out in the style of the gardens of Moorish Spain, with fountains and frescoes. Scattered around beneath tall shady trees were informal sitting areas, tiled – for coolness – with colourful ceramics made in Valencia to Blasco-Ibáñez's own designs.

Writers of any genre were free to use the gardens as a reading-room, and to take books from his library of over 50,000 books. For added inspiration, there were busts of the three novelists portrayed at the entrance, plus those of Dostoievski and Flaubert.

He hired a leading French sculptor, Ferdinand Bac, to design a floral terrace, the purpose of which was to conceal the Cadillac that he had ordered from New York, which was parked discreetly beneath the terrace because he deemed it out of keeping with the monastic tone of the gardens.

Blasco-Ibáñez was awarded the French Legion of Honour in 1906, and when he died in 1928, he bequeathed to the city of Menton his beloved Fontana Rosa and the gardens in which he wrote:

> Eleven o'clock in the evening. The autumn is a second spring on the Côte d'Azur. It is November, yet I stroll in my garden, breathing the fresh evening air heavy with the fragrance of flowers and fruit. All that is missing are the blue flashes of the glow-worms, weaving their nocturnal dance in the springtime darkness.

Amazingly, the local authorities closed the gates and left it to decay for the next 60 years. The first items to go were the moveable ones: the art galleries and the library were pillaged, and the busts of the authors were removed. (Those of the Spanish writers have been replaced, but the plinths of those of Dickens and Dostoievski still stand headless.)

Ibáñez's palatial residence has had to be pulled down as a danger to public safety. The Doric columns that once lined floral groves lie in crumbled heaps, and the frescoes look like badly distempered walls. The site was finally designated a national monument, but not until 1990 – too late to prevent the construction of the two apartment blocks that overshadow it.

The authorities have renovated the amphitheatre dedicated to Cervantes, with its cartoon-strip presentation of *Don Quixote* in ceramic tiles, and are in the process of restoring the rest of the property, including the library and Ibáñez's private cinema, but at the present rate of progress one wonders whether the remaining structures will have fallen down completely before the reconstruction is half finished.

Blasco-Ibáñez was buried an exile in the same hilltop Trabuquet cemetery in which Aubrey Beardsley had been buried 25 years earlier, but in 1933, five years after his death, his body was disinterred and, as if in a gesture of contrition by the city, laid in state in Menton's town hall. It was then transferred to a cruiser of the Spanish Navy and taken to its final resting place – his natal town of Valencia.

At the northern end the avenue Blasco-Ibáñez meets the boulevard de Garavan at an historic junction. Here in the pink Chalet des Rosiers, overlooking the bay of Garavan, Queen Victoria spent the winter of 1882. This most Victorian of French cities put on a *fête de nuit* for her enjoyment – a Venetian carnival in which more than 100 illuminated boats bobbed across the bay below like a fiery serpent.

A few years later, the Chalet des Rosiers became part of the Clos Roman Gris, the five-acre residence of the First Marquis of Milford Haven (father of Lord Mountbatten of Burma), where, early in the twentieth century, the gatekeeper's lodge was lent to a young writer who dreamed of becoming a successful crime novelist.

The writer's name was Agatha Christie.

Vladimir Nabokov was another pulmonary pilgrim. Although he had been a regular visitor to the Côte d'Azur since he was four, his first recorded visit to Menton was in his 38th year.

Still a relatively unknown writer, he had spent the summer of 1937 in Cannes with his wife Vera and son Dmitri, and in October moved to the Pension Hespérides in Menton, where he completed his novel *The Gift* and a number of smaller works, including *Lik*, a short story set on the coast, and *Visit to the Museum*, inspired, not surprisingly, by a trip to the Menton Museum.

Apart from its more obvious charms, an undoubted attraction of Menton for Nabokov was the variety of its butterflies. Like his Mentonnais contemporary Richard Le Gallienne, he was a passionate lepidopterist – he taught entomology at Harvard's Museum of Comparative Zoology and published many papers on the subject. (The names of Lolita's classmates are all classifications of insect.) During his time in the area, he added considerably to his collection.

From Menton the Nabokovs moved to Moulinet, a remote mountain village some 15 miles inland.

Nabokov may not have made much use of the Riviera as a setting (except that one of Humbert's dalliances with Lolita takes them to Antibes), but the Côte d'Azur survives in Nabokov's writing. His sensitivity to its plants and perfumes, his descriptions of coastal scenery, twilit skies and the effects of light on limpid seas, are unmistakable and permanent souvenirs of his Mediterranean sojourns. In *Ada or Ardor*, one of his last books, the hero Van describes a sunset:

> as if the artist had wished to include a very special example of light, the dazzling wake of the westering sun pulsated through a lakeside lombardy poplar that seemed both liquefied and on fire.

On 19 December 1916, a frozen body was pulled from the Neva River in St Petersburg with five bullet holes in it. It was the body of Grigory Efimovich Rasputin.

In his book *Lost Splendour*, Prince Félix Yusupov, who, like Nabokov, was born in St Petersburg, tells how he killed Rasputin, the Siberian peasant who rose to wield extraordinary influence over the Tsarina Alexandra through his ability to alleviate the symptoms of her haemophiliac son, the Tsarevich Alexei.

According to Yusupov, he and a small group of aristocrats, fearing Rasputin's increasing power while Tsar Nicholas II was away commanding the Russian army, hatched a plot to assassinate him.

To call it a 'plot' is to flatter it. Prince Félix was to invite Rasputin to his house and offer him a poisoned glass of Madeira wine and some cakes sprinkled with potassium cyanide.

Surprisingly, Rasputin accepted. He even asked for a second glass of the wine and ate two cyanide cakes. But he just kept on talking – and was still talking when Yusupov's co-conspirators, including his cousin Dmitri, arrived to help dispose of the body. After frenzied discussion, it was decided that Yusupov would have to shoot him. 'I slowly raised the revolver,' wrote Yusupov. 'I aimed at his heart and pulled the trigger. Rasputin gave a wild scream and crumpled up on the bearskin.'

But Rasputin was still not dead, and with 'the green eyes of a viper – staring at me with an expression of diabolical hatred' he leapt to his feet, and, mouth foaming, lunged at Yusupov's throat. Yusupov pushed him away and shot him four more times.

Again Rasputin got up. He staggered outside and fell on the pavement, where another conspirator shot him again. They wrapped the body in heavy linen and dropped it through a hole in the ice covering the River Neva.

When the frozen body was taken from the water, it was clear from the position of the hands that Rasputin, still alive, had struggled to free himself while in the water.

Yusupov's story sounds barely credible, yet much of it is supported by external testimony – from police reports of hearing the shots to the photographs of the body. Although the assassins were exiled, the Tsar, fearful of political unrest, had the charges dropped.

Later Felix collected a couple of Rembrandts, hid the family jewellery in a secret place, and caught the train to Paris. In Paris he and his wife Irina set up a successful fashion business, selling haute couture and perfumes under the label Irfe (the first two letters of their names). Dmitri went to Florida and became a champagne salesman.

Yusupov later sued MGM for what he claimed was the defamation of his wife's character, in suggesting, in their film *Rasputin and the Empress*, that he had used the promise of Irina's favours to lure Rasputin to his palace. So confident was he of winning the case that, while waiting for the result of the trial, he and his family came to the Côte d'Azur on vacation and crossed to the island of Corsica, which they liked so much that they bought not one, but two properties in the Calvi area. He won a handsome settlement from MGM, and, with the proceeds of the sale of the jewellery, was able to live in reasonable comfort for the rest of his life. (Recently discovered correspondence shows that he and Irina had indeed agreed that she should be the 'lure' to attract Rasputin.)

Yusupov and his wife and daughter travelled extensively in Europe and the USA, and were regular visitors to Biarritz and the Riviera. The title of his book, *Lost Splendour*, seems to show more concern for his family's loss of status than any remorse for the murder of Rasputin.

Rasputin's curse – that, should he be murdered, the assassin would die soon afterwards – was not fulfilled. Fifty years later, just before he died, Prince Félix said in an article in *The Guardian* that he would do it again. He died a great-grandfather at 80 and is buried alongside Irina in the Russian cemetery in Ste Geneviève-les-Bois, near Paris. The Rembrandts are in the National Gallery in Washington DC.

Sandwiched between Monaco and Menton is the commune of Roquebrune-Cap-Martin. It is so close to Menton that you have to be alert to notice when you have passed from one to the other, and the *Centre Ville* signs can easily direct you to the centre of the wrong town.

Roquebrune is part modern seaside resort and part medieval village. The village hangs above the town, clinging to the brown rocks that give it its name, and boasts one of the oldest castles in France. Built in the tenth century, it stands 1,000 feet above the town, its narrow streets offering sudden glimpses of sea or cape.

The Cap Martin itself has been a favourite resort of royalty, Empress Eugénie, wife of Napoleon III, England's King Edward VII, and Emperor Franz-Josef of Austria, to name a few; of politicians from Lloyd George to Winston Churchill (who was made a Citizen of Honour and is commemorated with a statue and a scenic boulevard); and, of course, of writers.

On a two-storey yellow-and-white building overlooking the sea near the peak of the Cap, in a quiet street named after a pioneer French yachstwoman, Virginie Hériot, a plaque, placed there by the Princess Grace Irish Library of Monaco, reads:

> William Butler Yeats
> Nobel Prize Winner
> Lived and died here
> 1938–1939

The Irish poet and playwright spent the last flagging months of his life there, in a first-floor room overlooking the sea. He had won the Nobel Prize for Literature in 1923, and, on being informed of the honour, famously said, 'How much is it worth?'

Yeats knew the Riviera well, and had been a regular *hivernant* there since the mid-1920s – after he had first begun to cough blood. Whether or not he was tubercular no one knows, for, like Lawrence a decade earlier, he had never had an X-ray, and the dreaded word was never uttered in his presence.

Again like Lawrence before him, Yeats had already haemorrhaged his way along the Mediterranean coast. He had tried Barcelona, where a young protégée who had followed him there to read her poetry to him thought he was insufficiently impressed with either her or her work, and jumped out of a first-floor window. Another year he tried Cannes, then spent two winters in Rapallo on the Italian Riviera as a guest of the American poet Ezra Pound.

On this last visit, Yeats and his wife Georgie reached the coast late in 1938. Their initial destination was Monaco, but a severe attack of food poisoning there left him wary of his hotel's cuisine, and Georgie found a more suitable retreat in nearby Roquebrune, at what was then the Hôtel Idéal-Séjour.

His *séjour* was far from *idéal*. There was nothing wrong with the hotel, but Yeats's condition worsened, and, although he continued to work until within hours of his death, writing On the Boiler and his last work, The Black Tower, he lived for only another ten weeks.

A master of PR before the term was invented, Yeats choreo-graphed his death as meticulously as he had stage-managed his life. He had planned that, on 27 January, his currently favoured lover, Edith Heald, should replace Georgie as his nurse and guardian. Hearing that he was fading, Edith arrived early, and wife and mistress watched over him as he died, a scene that he had also programmed in his poem, The Only Jealousy of Emer:

> Of all the people in the world we two
> And we alone, may watch together here
> Because we loved him best.

The precise location and orientation of his Irish grave had also been specified in his literary epitaph, the poem 'Under Ben Bulben' (a mountain in his adopted home county, Sligo). The famous cryptic epitaph:

> Cast a cold eye
> On life, on death
> Horseman, pass by

even the type of stone – 'limestone quarried near the spot' – had already been decreed, as had the timing. The re-interment was to take place one year after his death – after the initial wave of global grief had died down.

That was where his plans started to go wrong. In his illness, he appears not to have noticed that Europe was on the brink of war at the time. Seven months later, Hitler invaded Poland, and by June of the following year France had surrendered. By the scheduled exhumation date, the export of corpses – not an easy matter even in peacetime, as Frieda Lawrence had found ten years earlier – was out of the question until after the war.

But French burials are seldom eternal. The headstone may say *Rest in Peace*, but if grave rentals are unpaid, the incumbent bodies are removed, their skulls detached and the bones sent to a communal ossuary, to make room for paying tenants. This was the fate of those of Yeats, despite the fact that the grave had been paid for *en perpétuité*. By the end of the war, almost a decade after the original burial, it would have been impossible, in those pre-DNA times, to say which remains were those of Yeats.

But after some political pressure, despite delays and confusion, the appropriate number of body parts were collected, the playwright was re-assembled and the montage certified by local *fonctionnaires* as authentic if not complete.

On 6 September 1948, after military ceremonies in Roquebrune and Nice, what the local *Nice-Matin* diplomatically called the 'ashes' of W.B. Yeats were taken on board the Irish Navy's corvette *Macha* in the port of Nice, and the putative remains of one of Ireland's greatest poets began their belated journey to their final resting place, under Ben Bulben.

Had Yeats foreseen even this fiasco 20 years earlier? In his 1919 play, *Dreaming of the Bones*, he had written:

> Have not old writers said

That dizzy dreams can spring
From the dry bones of the dead?

Not surprisingly, Menton's climate and location have attracted a number of itinerant writers.

The English poet, biographer and historian Algernon Swinburne was an important influence in the work of many twentieth-century writers, including Nabokov. Swinburne came to Menton in an attempt to recover from the excessive use of alcohol and masochistic abuse of his body. His verse may have been melodious and his changes of pace and rhythm dazzling, but the problem was its content. Its lasciviousness and atheism offended the refined taste of the literary establishment – *Punch* called him 'Mr. Swineborn'.

In spite of these eccentricities – or perhaps because of them – many younger writers saw him as a mentor. F. Scott Fitzgerald, when drunk, would recite him at the top of his voice. (Menton is unique in the complete absence of American writers – which makes the bust of Henry Wadsworth Longfellow that glowers across the rue de la République at the town hall all the more mysterious.)

Swinburne stayed at the Villa Laurenti in 1861, but was less than impressed with Menton, and what he called its 'scorched', 'leprous' countryside, peopled with 'hunch-backed women with necks twisted from carrying heavy loads', and he hurried on to his beloved Italy, where he travelled extensively. Three years later, he passed through Menton again – this time leaving no trace.

In February 1914, A.A. Milne, creator of Winnie the Pooh, and his wife Daphne stayed in the home of Anne Williamson on Cap Martin. The loan came 'complete with staff, food, the cellar and even the cigars, together with letters of introduction to everybody and the company of that delightfully wheezy bull-dog, Tiberius'. The Williamsons were American, 'to whom', wrote Milne, 'such gestures are natural'.

It was Milne who once suffered a scathing review from Dorothy Parker, who, as critic for *The New Yorker* under the pen name Constant Reader, ended her article, 'Tonstant Weader fwowed up'. Milne did not respond at the time, but saved his response until his autobiography, written ten years later: 'The books were written for children ... no writer of children's books says gaily to his publisher, "Don't bother about the children, Mrs. Parker will love it".'

Kenneth Clark, author and television presenter of *Civilization*, was a regular visitor to Menton, staying first at the Hôtel des Anglais, and later as a guest of Graham Sutherland at his Maison Blanche in the hills outside the town. Sutherland's vast tapestry for Coventry Cathedral – made up of 39-foot-long strips – was assembled in a disused department store in the town.

In January 1952, in the avenue Cernuschi, a few steps from where Sutherland built his Maison Blanche, lived the novelist and short-story writer Alan Sillitoe, who came to the Riviera, as had his fellow Nottingham consumptive, D.H. Lawrence 24 years earlier, in the hope of relief from tuberculosis. But in style, Sillitoe's house was a long way from the custom-designed Maison Blanche. It was a stone cottage called Le Nid, but it was a nest whose water came from a pump in an olive grove 200 yards away, and whose plumbing, like its staircase, was outside.

The 23-year-old Sillitoe, epitomizing the struggling writer, would walk the 14 kilometres to Ventimiglia in Italy to buy food more cheaply, and 'stood in line for stale bread at the baker's, on days when it was sold at half price'. He spent just over a year in Le Nid, during which he wrote a number of short stories – one of them called *Saturday Night*, about a drunken night out – and poems, but his health, like that of Lawrence before him, got worse, and for that reason – and also because he was told it was cheaper – he decided to move to Majorca.

There he met the English poet Robert Graves, who told him he should write about what he knew, so he merged some of the 'Nottingham' stories that he had written in Menton into a novel. He called it *Saturday Night and Sunday Morning*.

The Villa Le Souco, home of Simon and Dorothy (sister of Lytton Strachey) Bussy in Roquebrune, welcomed artists and writers for more than half a century from 1904 onwards, including Matisse, Paul Valéry, Virginia Woolf, and no less than four Nobel Laureates: Gide (1947), Martin du Gard (1937), Yeats (1923) and Rudyard Kipling (1907). Kipling, who visited in 1933, was warning that the Germans were already preparing for war, and that Monaco was their listening post. He was at least half right.

And in June 1947, the Irish novelist and playwright Samuel Beckett, author of *Waiting for Godot*, was in Menton with his wife Suzanne, where they rented the Villa des Cuses in the avenue Aristide Briand. Beckett had lived in France since before the Second World War and had been awarded the Croix de Guerre for his work in the Resistance, but he did not become famous until he turned to plays: 'to relieve myself of the awful depression prose led me into. I thought theatre would be a diversion'. He was not to win the Nobel Prize until 1969, which Suzanne described as 'a disaster' for the reclusive Beckett. He did not attend the presentation ceremony, and his publisher accepted the award from the king on his behalf.

At the Villa des Cuses, conditions were less than luxurious: the furniture was rickety and sparse, and for presumably financial reasons, there was no power supply, so they cooked all their meals outdoors on a charcoal brazier. But the weather was fine, Beckett was able to work and they spent six happy and productive weeks there.

The villa is still there, overlooking the Mediterranean within yards of the Italian border. It seems somehow ironic that its Swedish owner should have been unaware that the winner of one of his countryman Alfred Nobel's prizes had barbecued on his terrace.

The avenue Aristide Briand is the last street of the Côte d'Azur, and Samuel Beckett is its last author. Well, he did write *Endgame*.

Epilogue

Two hundred yards east of Beckett's villa the journey ends: it is the Italian frontier.

Today it is more a border than a frontier, marked only by a huddle of deserted buildings, already with an air of dereliction. A faded sign still says *Carabinieri*, but there is no barber's-pole barrier to raise, no smartly uniformed policeman asks for your passport. All those *Bureaux de Change* have gone: a single shed can easily cope with the trickle of travellers wanting to exchange pounds or dollars. We are in Euroland.

Does this mean that the Riviera has become just another corner of a vast homogenized continent? Will there be no tingle of excitement at that first sight of the Mediterranean? No *dépaysement* – the agreeable sensation of finding oneself in a strange country?

It has become fashionable to claim so. In 1978, Lawrence Durrell wrote to Henry Miller, 'But of course Provence has now been discovered as a subsidised tourist playground.' Ten years ago, Dirk Bogarde complained, 'Alas the area of France about which I write [Grasse] has now been drastically altered, almost beyond recognition.' But then people have been forecasting the demise of the Côte d'Azur for as long as it has existed. In 1887, the very year in which Liégeard gave it its name, de Maupassant wrote, 'I love it ... because the Parisian, the Englishman, the American, the man of fashion, and the adventurer have not yet poisoned it.'

Everyone regrets changes to a cherished place. But do we have a right to ask that it remain quaint for our occasional enjoyment? Did Dirk Bogarde, like Stevenson, travel with a donkey to his home in the hills, or did he drive along the autoroute?

There have certainly been changes. Sandwiched between sea and mountains, the Riviera's population density is four times the national average. Two hundred and fifty years ago, Smollett reported that the population of Nice was 12,000. Today it is almost half a million.

Tourism has followed the same pattern. Antibiotics may have staunched the flow of the tuberculosis trippers, but package deals and no-frills airlines have more than made up the difference. In 1957, 800,000 tourists arrived in Nice. In the year 2002, more than nine million visitors arrived in Nice by air alone.

But, despite its summer influx and creeping urbanization, the Côte d'Azur will always have its rocky coasts, its empty islands and its mountains. For every tripper-jammed St-Paul-de-Vence, there are many hundreds of perched villages as yet undiscovered. The green spaces between the towns may be getting smaller, but the cultural amenities of the towns themselves – art galleries, theatres and libraries – are expanding.

The Côte d'Azur will last because it is not so much a place as an environment. It inspires writers just as its light galvanized its migrant painters – so much so that many were unable to channel its intensity until after they had left. As Colette said, 'One does not write a love story when one is making love.'

And the writers of the Côte d'Azur, just as they survived the book-burners, will outlive demographic change, falling frontiers and the bulldozers.

Author Profiles

Louisa May Alcott (1832–88)
American author known for her children's books, but whose early works were adult novels written to support her improvident parents and siblings. Her stories appeared in *The Atlantic Monthly*, and, because of pressing family needs, she wrote the semi-autobiographical *Little Women* in 1868, which was an immediate success. She visited Nice in the winter of 1865–66.

Richard Aldington (1892–1962)
English poet, novelist, critic and biographer. His best-known works include the novels *Death of a Hero* and its sequel *All Men Are Enemies*, his book of poems *A Dream in the Luxembourg* and biographies of Voltaire, both D.H. and T.E. Lawrence, and Wellington. He stayed at Port Cros in the Îles d'Or in the winter of 1928–29 before moving to La Rochelle.

Hans Christian Andersen (1805–75)
Danish writer. He was the son of a cobbler who trained as an actor, but achieved international recognition as a master of the fairy tale. He also wrote plays, novels, poems, travel books and autobiographies. His fairy tales, such as *The Little Mermaid* and *The Emperor's New Clothes*, are among the most frequently translated works in literary history. He visited Monaco in 1862, and Toulon and Nice in 1869–70.

Jacques Audiberti (1899–1965)
French poet, novelist and playwright. A native Antibois, he was a clerk for the local justice of the peace, and began his writing career with the collections of verse *Race des hommes* (*The Race of Men*) and *Des Tonnes de semence* (*Tons of Seed*). He wrote more than 20 plays,

and the novels *Abraxas, Carnage* and *Monorail.* He is commemorated in his home town by an annual literary award.

James Baldwin (1924–87)

American essayist, novelist and playwright. The eldest of nine children, he grew up in poverty in New York's Harlem. As a teenager, he followed his father as a preacher, at the same time writing his autobiographical first and finest novel, *Go Tell It on the Mountain.* His later works, such as *Giovanni's Room,* deal with issues of homosexuality and racism. He lived in Paris and St-Paul-de-Vence, where he died in 1987.

J.G. Ballard (1930–)

English novelist and short-story writer born in Shanghai, who began his career writing science fiction. As a boy he spent four years in a Japanese prison camp near Shanghai during the Second World War, a story told in his novel *Empire of the Sun.* His later novels, such as *Crash* and *Cocaine Nights,* deal with the psychological problems associated with disasters and closed communities. He based his novel *Super-Cannes* on the Riviera science park, Sophia-Antipolis.

Marie Bashkirtseff (1860–84)

A Russian émigrée who was the daughter of Russian nobility, and spent her childhood in Germany, on the Riviera and in Paris. Although initially a singer, she studied painting in Paris, but is best known for her autobiography *Journal de Marie Bashkirtseff.* From 1872 she lived on the Promenade des Anglais in Nice, where she died of tuberculosis just before her 24th birthday.

Aubrey Beardsley (1872–98)

A leading English illustrator of the 1890s who won early acclaim with his illustrations for Flaubert's *Madame Bovary* at the age of 15, and his revolutionary art nouveau illustrations for Oscar Wilde's play *Salomé.* He also published some poetry and one novel, *Under the Hill.* A lifelong consumptive, he moved to Menton in 1896, where he died in 1898.

Simone de Beauvoir (1908–86)

French novelist and essayist, most often associated with French feminism, who, with her lifelong partner, Jean-Paul Sartre, whom she met at the Sorbonne, helped to establish the Existentialist movement. Her most influential work was *Le Deuxième Sexe* (*The Second Sex*), which challenged the cult of 'femininity'. She frequented many parts of the Côte d'Azur, mostly Antibes, for decades from the 1930s onwards.

Samuel Beckett (1906–89)

Irish author and playwright. From 1932 onwards he worked mostly in France and Italy, and after his first two novels *Murphy* (1938) and *What* (1953) wrote almost exclusively in French. His reputation as a playwright was established with *En attendant Godot* (1953), performed in 1956 as *Waiting for Godot*, and he was awarded the Nobel Prize for Literature in 1969. He stayed in Menton in 1947.

Robert Benchley (1889–1945)

American critic, actor and humorist. Although best known for film acting, his essays and film scripts were his finest achievement. During the 1920s he was a member of the Round Table, the urbane and witty literary group who lunched in the Algonquin Hotel in New York, and whose participants included his friend Dorothy Parker and Harpo Marx. Occasional guest at the Villa America on the Cap d'Antibes in the 1920s.

Arnold Bennett (1867–1931)

English novelist, playwright, critic and essayist. In 1889 he went to London where he worked as a solicitor's clerk, but soon gained a footing writing popular fiction and editing a women's magazine. After his first novel *A Man from the North*, he became a professional writer and is best known for his novels of the 'Five Towns' (the Potteries) in his native Staffordshire. He visited Cannes and other coastal towns from 1912 onwards.

James Gordon Bennett (1841–1918)

Newspaper magnate who took over the management of the *New York Herald* from his father in 1867, and funded newsworthy events, including Stanley's search for Dr David Livingstone, a failed exploration of the North Pole and trophies for international yachting and road races. He moved to Paris in 1877 and established the international edition of the *Herald*, now the *International Herald Tribune*. He established a reputation for extravagant behaviour and ran the newspaper from his yacht and villa in Beaulieu.

Vicente Blasco-Ibáñez (1867–1928)
Spanish novelist and politician. His best-known work was his novel *The Four Horsemen of the Apocalypse*. Other novels include *The Cabin*, *The Fruit of the Vine* and *Woman Triumphant*. He served several terms of imprisonment for his Republican beliefs and later represented Valencia in parliament, but went into voluntary exile in France, where he received the French Legion of Honour in 1906. He settled in Menton, and on his death, left his home to the town.

Dirk Bogarde (1921–99)
British film actor originally best known for his role in the film *Doctor in the House* and its sequels, but who later excelled in darker, more complex roles, such as the blackmailed homosexual lawyer in *Victim*, the sinister manservant in *The Servant* and the doomed von Aschenbach in *Death in Venice*. His 11 books included autobiographies and novels. He also wrote essays and book reviews. He was knighted in 1992 and from 1968 he lived in St-Sulpice, near Grasse, for 20 years.

James Boswell (1740–95)
Scottish writer famous for his biography of Samuel Johnson. The publication of his journals also proved him to be a great diarist. He met Johnson in 1763 and, despite the 30-year age gap, began a great friendship. He visited Corsica in 1765 to meet Pasquale Paoli, its new president, and returned via Monaco and Nice.

Paul Bourget (1852–1935)
French novelist and critic. He studied medicine and philosophy before becoming an author, and began his writing career as a poet: several of his poems were set to music by Claude Debussy. His best-known work was the novel *Le Disciple*. He lived and worked in

Hyères, where he established a reputation for supporting Catholicism and other conservative causes.

William Boyd (1952–)

English novelist and film and television scenarist, born in Accra, Ghana, and educated at the universities of Nice, Glasgow and Oxford. He lived in Nice while attending its university. His early works – *A Good Man in Africa* and *An Ice Cream War* – were set in Africa, the latter winning the Rhys Memorial Prize for young writers. His later work has included collections of short stories, film and television scripts, simulated biographies and novels on a wide range of subjects, including violence in Africa (*Brazzaville Beach*) and a diary of amorous adventures in *Armadillo*.

Bertolt Brecht (1898–1956)

German poet and playwright who worked to establish a theatre for leftist causes. After losing his German citizenship in 1933 for his Stalinist sympathies, he moved to Scandinavia and then the USA, returning in 1949. His most famous work was *The Threepenny Opera*, first staged in 1928, an adaptation of John Gay's *The Beggar's Opera*. In 1949 he returned to Berlin to stage *Mother Courage*. He visited Le Lavandou in 1928 and Sanary-sur-Mer in 1937.

Rupert Brooke (1887–1915)

English poet. His early poems included 'The Old Vicarage, Grantchester' which celebrated his love of the countryside. He became a national hero with his war poems which appealed to the early wartime idealism. He joined the Royal Navy but died of septicaemia in Greece. He is best remembered for 'The Soldier' ('If I should die, think only this of me'). He visited Cannes in 1912.

Ivan Bunin (1870–1953)

Russian poet and novelist. In 1903 he was awarded the Pushkin Prize for his translation of Longfellow's *Hiawatha* and in 1933 he was the first Russian to receive the Nobel Prize for Literature. He made his name as a short-story writer with such works as *Gospodin iz San-Frantsisko* (*The Gentleman from San Francisco*). After the Revolution in 1918 he travelled extensively and lived in Grasse from 1923 to 1945.

Anthony Burgess (1917–93)
English novelist, critic, composer and man of letters. Born in Manchester of Irish parents, he wrote three novels with a Malayan setting while working in Malaya and Borneo. He wrote more than 50 books, but is best remembered for A Clockwork Orange, filmed in 1971. He also wrote literary criticism, television scripts, translations and biographies and produced dozens of musical compositions. He travelled extensively before settling in Monaco in 1975.

Murray Burnett (1911–97)
American writer who began his career as a teacher, but who is known primarily for plays. He co-wrote (with Joan Alison) Everybody Comes to Rick's, an unproduced play that was bought by Warner Brothers for the unprecedented sum of $20,000 and became the basis for the 1942 film Casablanca. The play was finally brought to the stage in 1991. He stayed at the Grand Hôtel du Cap on Cap Ferrat in the late 1930s.

Albert Camus (1913–60)
French novelist, essayist and playwright. His early years were lived in poverty in Algeria, but after university he wrote novels of which the best-known are L'Étranger (The Stranger), La Peste (The Plague) and La Chute (The Fall). He edited Combat, the journal of the French Resistance during the Second World War. In 1957 he received the Nobel Prize for Literature at the exceptionally young age of 44, but was killed in a car accident three years later. He spent some years on the Riviera, especially near Grasse, seeking relief from tuberculosis.

Thomas Carlyle (1795–1881)
Influential Scottish historian, biographer and essayist. His Calvinist father intended him to enter the ministry but he became a mathematics teacher. His major works include History of the French Revolution and the six-volume history Frederick the Great, which took him 13 years to complete. He worked in Menton in 1866–67.

Giacomo Casanova (1725–98)

Italian writer, ecclesiastic, soldier, spy and diplomatist, he is chiefly remembered for his sexual adventures. He was expelled from his seminary for scandalous conduct, escaped from a prison in Venice and travelled widely in Europe under the name of Chevalier de Seingalt. His best-remembered work was the journal of his adventures, first published as *Mémoires de J. Casanova de Seingalt*. He visited Monaco in 1763 as the guest of the Prince.

Bruce Chatwin (1940–89)

English novelist and travel writer, best known for his travel-based books. He gave up his career as art consultant at Sotheby's to study archaeology, and in 1976 began the journeys that resulted in his award-winning *In Patagonia*. Several of his books were filmed, including *On the Black Hill* and *The Viceroy of Ouidah*. He worked in Seillans during his last years and died from AIDS in Nice.

Dame Agatha Christie (1890–1976)

English detective novelist and playwright whose books have sold more than 100 million copies and have been translated into some 100 languages. Many have been adapted for film and television, including *Murder on the Orient Express* and *Death on the Nile*. She created the well-known detectives Hercule Poirot and Miss Marple. Her plays include *The Mousetrap*, which has run for a record 50 years. She was created a Dame of the British Empire in 1971. Early in the twentieth century she worked at the villa of the First Marquis of Milford Haven (father of Lord Mountbatten of Burma) in Menton.

Lord (Kenneth) Clark (1903–83)

English author and art historian whose first book *The Gothic Revival* ruffled feathers in traditional circles. His exposure to art as director of the National Gallery for 11 years from 1934 helped him to develop ideas for his various books on art and the television series *Civilization*, which he wrote and presented. He was a regular guest of Maugham and also stayed in Menton, where he visited the English artist Graham Sutherland.

Jean Cocteau (1889–1963)

French poet and artist. He established his reputation with the novel *Les Enfants terribles* (*The Incorrigible Children*) and sketches for Diaghilev's ballet company such as *Parade*. He wrote poetry, for example *L'Ange Heurtebise* (*The Angel Heurtebise*), and produced plays such as *Orphée* (*Orpheus*) and surrealist films such as *La Belle et la bête* (*Beauty and the Beast*). Living on Cap Ferrat from 1950 until his death, he painted frescoes in public buildings and villas throughout the south of France. He decorated the town halls of St-Jean-Cap-Ferrat and Menton, and chapels in Villefranche and Fréjus.

Colette (Sidonie-Gabrielle) (1873–1954)

French novelist. A former musical artist of the 1890s whose talent for writing was discovered and developed by her first husband, the writer and critic Henri Gauthier-Villars. She wrote reviews and short stories with a special sensitivity to the woman's viewpoint. She is best remembered for the *Claudine* novels (written under her husband's pen name of Willy) and the well-known novel *Gigi* which was adapted for both stage and screen. In the 1920s and 1930s she lived in St-Tropez with her third husband, writer Maurice Goudeket (imprisoned by the Gestapo in the Second World War), and in later life was a regular visitor to Monaco. Goudeket wrote his memoir of their life together, *Près de Colette* (*Close to Colette*). During her time in St-Tropez, she wrote *La Naissance du jour* (*Morning Glory*).

Cyril Connolly (1903–74)

English critic, novelist and founder and editor of *Horizon*, a magazine of contemporary literature in 1939. He began writing as a contributor to the *New Statesman* and broadsheet newspapers and became literary editor of the *Observer* in 1942, later producing collections of essays, which included *Enemies of Promise*, *The Condemned Playground* and *The Evening Colonnade*. He lived in Sanary-sur-Mer in 1930 and 1931 and stayed in Antibes in 1938, setting his only novel, *The Rock Pool*, in Antibes and Cagnes-sur-Mer.

Joseph Conrad (1857–1924)

Polish novelist and short-story writer. He was introduced to English at an early age by his father, who translated Shakespeare into Russian. He obtained his master's licence in the British merchant navy and wrote *Almayer's Folly* in 1889 while waiting for a command; he went on to write the novels *Lord Jim*, *Nostromo* and *The Secret Agent*. His best-known work, *Heart of Darkness*, has been filmed in a number of versions. He visited Hyères as a youth and continued to visit the Riviera for the next 50 years.

Noël Coward (1899–1973)

English playwright, actor and composer, known for highly polished comedies of manners. His successes include *Private Lives*, *Cavalcade*, *Present Laughter* and *Blithe Spirit*. He rewrote his *Still Life* as the film *Brief Encounter*. He was knighted in 1970 and spent his last years chiefly in the Caribbean. He visited his friend Maugham on Cap Ferrat.

Dante Alighieri (1265–1321)

Italian poet. He is best known for his epic poem *The Divine Comedy*, which he wrote in Italian rather than in Latin to encourage the use of Italian as a literary language. He was exiled from Florence because of the political struggles of the time and travelled extensively in Provence.

Alphonse Daudet (1840–97)

French short-story writer and novelist. He is best remembered for his tales of provincial life in southern France, particularly *Lettres de mon moulin* (*Letters from My Mill*). He lived in western Provence and spent his honeymoon in Cassis in 1867.

Charles Dickens (1812–70)

Probably the most famous English novelist of the Victorian era who began his career contributing to popular magazines. His prodigious output included *The Pickwick Papers*, *Oliver Twist*, *A Tale of Two Cities*, *Great Expectations* and *Nicholas Nickleby*. In July 1844 he travelled with his family by steamer along the coast from Marseilles to Genoa, but was prevented by bad weather from entering Nice harbour. He remained in Italy until June 1845, visiting Pisa, Rome, Leghorn, Florence and Naples, and making brief visits into and through the

Riviera. Towards the end of his life he made many tours in Britain and abroad, giving readings from his works.

John Dos Passos (1896-1970)
American novelist of Portuguese descent. He travelled extensively in Spain, Mexico and the Near East as a journalist. His major work was the trilogy *U.S.A.* comprising *The 42nd Parallel*, *1919* and *The Big Money*. He visited Cap d'Antibes in the 1920s.

Alexandre Dumas-père (1802-70)
French author best remembered for his historical novels *Le Comte de Monte Cristo* (*The Count of Monte Cristo*), *Les Trois Mousquetaires* (*The Three Musketeers*) and *La Tulipe noire* (*The Black Tulip*). He worked in the household of the future King Louis-Philippe, but took up writing and wrote successful plays such as *Napoléon Bonaparte* and *Antony*. He was in Nice in 1835 visiting his friend Alphonse Karr.

Lawrence Durrell (1912-90)
English novelist, poet and travel writer who spent most of his life outside England, moving in 1935 to Corfu. He is best known for his tetralogy *The Alexandria Quartet*. His other major work, the *Avignon Quintet*, a series of five novels set in Provence, won him awards in France. His last book, *Caesar's Vast Ghost: Aspects of Provence*, was published in 1990. He carried on a 45-year-long correspondence with American writer Henry Miller. He visited Nice, Antibes and Cannes but settled near Nîmes in south-west France.

T.S. Eliot (1888-1965)
American-English poet and playwright. His major works include *The Waste Land*, *The Four Quartets* and plays like *Murder in the Cathedral* and *The Cocktail Party*. He became a British citizen in 1927, and was awarded the Order of Merit and the Nobel Prize for Literature in 1948. He made occasional visits to Somerset Maugham on Cap Ferrat.

John Evelyn (1620-1706)
English author of books on fine arts, forestry and religious topics. His diary is an important source of information on the social, cul-

tural, religious and political life of seventeenth-century England. He visited Fréjus and Cannes in 1644.

Lion Feuchtwanger (1884–1958)
German novelist and playwright, best known for his historical romances. After Hitler came to power he moved to France, where he was interned by the Vichy government, spent some months in a concentration camp but escaped to the United States in 1940. After leaving Germany in 1933, he settled in Sanary-sur-Mer until his internment.

F. Scott Fitzgerald (1896–1940)
American short-story writer and novelist famous for his depictions of the 1920s Jazz Age and his lavish lifestyle with his wife, Zelda. He first went to the Riviera in 1924 prior to the publication of his best-known novel *The Great Gatsby*. There he joined the group of American expatriates hosted by Gerald and Sara Murphy, whom he used in his last completed novel, *Tender Is the Night*. During this period, despite his struggle with alcoholism, he wrote stories, scripts and part of a novel, *The Last Tycoon*, before his death from a heart attack. He visited the Antibes area from 1924 to 1929.

Gustave Flaubert (1821–80)
French novelist best known for his controversial novel *Madame Bovary*, about the adulterous wife of a country doctor. His major works include *Salammbô*, *L'Éducation sentimentale* and *La Tentation de Saint Antoine*. He adopted Guy de Maupassant as his pupil and assisted him in his career. The poet Louise Colet became his mistress, but they parted in 1855. In 1845 he visited Antibes with his sister, who later moved there.

Ian Fleming (1908–64)
British author famous for his creation of the secret service agent 007, James Bond. He had a varied career, working as a banker, stockbroker, naval intelligence officer and journalist. His James Bond novels have been translated into many languages and filmed, as was his children's book, *Chitty Chitty Bang Bang*. He occasionally visited Somerset Maugham on Cap Ferrat.

Paul Gallico (1897–1976)

American author who, as a sports writer, sparred with and was knocked out by the world heavyweight boxing champion Jack Dempsey. After writing *Farewell to Sport*, he went to Europe where he wrote his best-known work *The Snow Goose*. He lived in Monaco and in Antibes where he died just before his 79th birthday.

Max Gallo (1932–)

French journalist, historian and socialist politician, he began his literary career with biographies of Mussolini, Napoleon and De Gaulle, followed by historical novels and novels on topical themes, in particular *Le Cortège des vainqueurs* and his trilogy set in Nice, *La Baie des Anges*. He was born in Nice, which he represented as a Deputy and later MEP.

André Gide (1869–1951)

French novelist and critic. Much of his work reflects his conflict with conventional and religious morality. His novels include *Les Caves du Vatican* (*The Vatican Cellars*, earlier *The Vatican Swindle*) and *Les Faux-monnayeurs* (*The Counterfeiters*). His *Journal*, which he kept from 1885 until his death, is a major work of literary autobiography. A former Stalinist, he was disillusioned by a visit to Russia in 1936 and wrote *Retouches à mon retour* (*Afterthoughts*). He won the Nobel Prize in 1947. He was a regular visitor to the Côte d'Azur, especially Grasse and Cabris, for the last 30 years of his life.

Graham Greene (1904–91)

English novelist, short-story writer and playwright. He began his career in journalism and worked for *The Times* from 1926 to 1930. He converted to Roman Catholicism in 1926 to marry his first wife, and Catholicism is a theme in many of his books, including *The Power and the Glory*, *Brighton Rock*, *The Heart of the Matter*, *Monsignor Quixote* and *The Human Factor*. His extensive travels took him to seedy and remote locations, and he wrote thrillers and screenplays like *The Third Man* and *Our Man in Havana*. He lived in Antibes from 1966 until his death and wrote his last seven novels there.

Jean-Marie Guyau (1854–88)

French philosopher, author and translator. Precocious and multi-talented, he published his first philosophical work *La Morale d'Épicure* in 1878, and although he wrote prolifically on this subject throughout his short life, his published works also included poetry, music and books on art, religion and education. A lifelong sufferer from tuberculosis and asthma, he moved to Nice, where he was a contemporary of Nietzsche, and later Menton, where he died in 1888 aged 33.

Frank Harris (1856–1931)

Irish-born American journalist and biographer who emigrated to the United States at the age of 14. On his return he edited newspapers and magazines and wrote his four-volume autobiography, *My Life and Loves*, which was banned by censors in the USA and Britain because of its sexual frankness. As editor of the *Saturday Review* he was an early publisher of George Bernard Shaw and Oscar Wilde and wrote biographies of both. He moved to Nice in 1922 and died there nine years later.

Ernest Hemingway (1899–1961)

American novelist and short-story writer, awarded the Nobel Prize for Literature in 1954. He worked as a journalist in Paris, associating with a number of contemporary American writers. In 1926 he published his first successful novel, *The Sun Also Rises*. He supported the Republican cause during the Spanish Civil War, and wrote about it in *For Whom the Bell Tolls*. His other works include *A Farewell to Arms*, *The Old Man and the Sea* (for which he received the Pulitzer Prize), *To Have and Have Not* and *Islands in the Stream*. After he left Cuba in 1960 he settled in Idaho, where after severe bouts of illness and depression, he shot himself. He was a visitor to the Murphys, a wealthy Boston couple who lived on the Cap d'Antibes during the 1920s and who liked to entertain writers and artists. He also toured the region in 1954.

Victor Hugo (1802–85)

French poet, dramatist and novelist, considered the most important of the French Romantic writers. He is best known abroad for such novels as *Notre-Dame de Paris* (*The Hunchback of Notre-Dame*) and *Les Misérables*. During the 1840s he became involved in republican politics and went into exile after the *coup d'état* by Napoleon III in 1851. He returned from Guernsey in 1870 and became a senator. He visited Antibes and the Arrières-Pays both before and after his exile.

Aldous Huxley (1894–1963)

English novelist and critic. He developed keratitis at Eton and became partially blind. His first two published novels, *Crome Yellow*, which caricatured the country house lifestyle, and *Antic Hay*, established him as a major author, and were followed by *Those Barren Leaves* and *Point Counter Point*. His best-known work, *Brave New World*, portrayed a prophetic and concerned vision of the future. After spending much of the 1930s in France and Italy, he moved to the USA in 1937. Between 1930 and 1937 he lived in Sanary-sur-Mer, near Toulon.

Henry James (1843–1916)

American novelist, short-story writer and critic. After education in London, Paris and Geneva, he studied law at Harvard and moved to Europe in 1875, becoming a British citizen in 1915. He received the Order of Merit in 1916. The central theme of many of his novels is of Americans confronting European culture, and his major works include *Daisy Miller*, *Portrait of a Lady*, *Washington Square*, *The Bostonians* and *The Ambassadors*. He visited the Riviera throughout his adult life, especially the home in Hyères of his friend Edith Wharton.

James Joyce (1882–1941)

Irish novelist, best known for his collection of stories, *The Dubliners*, and his novels *Ulysses* and *Finnegans Wake*, which helped to establish the 'stream of consciousness' technique. He achieved early notice with an essay, *The Day of the Rabblement*, attacking the Irish Literary Theatre (later the Abbey Theatre) for populism. He went to Paris in 1902 and afterwards lived in Trieste, Zurich and Paris. His novel *Ulysses* was written and published in Paris because it was deemed obscene in Britain. He visited Nice in 1922.

Alphonse Karr (1808–1890)

French journalist, poet, novelist and essayist of Bavarian descent. He made his journalistic reputation in Paris as editor of the *Figaro* daily newspaper, and started his own monthly magazine, *Les Guêpes* (*The Wasps*). His most successful novel was *Sous les Tilleuls* (*Under the Linden Trees*). Because of his opposition to Louis-Napoleon after the latter's accession to the throne as Napoleon III in 1852, he left Paris in voluntary exile as a protest and moved to Nice, where he became a strong advocate of life on the Riviera, moving to St-Raphaël.

Nikos Kazantzakis (1885–1957)

Greek writer whose best-known work is his novel *Zorba the Greek*. He also wrote essays and travel books, and translated Dante's *Divine Comedy* and Goethe's *Faust* into modern Greek. He travelled widely in Spain, England, Russia, Egypt, Palestine and Japan, served as a Greek government minister and worked for UNESCO in Paris until 1948, when he moved to Antibes.

Rudyard Kipling (1865–1936)

English short-story writer, poet and novelist, born in India and brought up by a foster mother in England. He is best known for his stories and poems of military life in India, where he published *Departmental Ditties* and *Plain Tales from the Hills*. He received the Nobel Prize for Literature in 1907, the first English writer to do so. He married in 1892 and moved to Vermont, returning to England in 1896. His novel *Kim* became a classic, as did his children's books, particularly *The Jungle Books*. He wintered regularly in Cannes and Hyères after the First World War.

Ring Lardner (1885–1933)

American short-story writer and humorist. He was educated in Chicago and trained as an engineer before switching to sports writing. He later moved into short stories and humorous essays, musical comedy and an autobiography. He was hailed by the New York *Daily News* as 'America's foremost humorist of the 1920s' and lauded by Hemingway, Virginia Woolf and Scott Fitzgerald. A close friend and neighbour of the Fitzgeralds, he stayed with them in Antibes in 1924.

D.H. Lawrence (1885–1930)

English novelist, poet and short-story writer, best known for his controversial novel *Lady Chatterley's Lover*. He began his career teaching, but his talent was recognized by the *English Review* and led to the publication of his first novel, *The White Peacock*, in 1911. His other novels include *Sons and Lovers*, *The Rainbow* and *Women in Love*. In 1914 he married Frieda Weekley and they travelled extensively during the 1920s, settling for a time in New Mexico. After a year in Bandol, in 1930 he moved to Vence, where he died a few weeks later.

Richard Le Gallienne (1866–1947)

English poet and man of letters. He had his first poems, *My Ladies Sonnets and other Poems*, printed privately, and worked with Aubrey Beardsley on *The Yellow Book*. He wrote verse and literary criticism, and a novel, *The Quest of the Golden Girl*. After a stay in Hyères in 1900, he settled in the USA in 1901 but returned in 1929 to live in Paris and later Menton and Monaco. He is buried in Menton.

Edward Lear (1812–88)

English landscape painter, best known for his four books of nonsense verse for children, first produced for the Earl of Derby's grandchildren. A compulsive traveller, he published three volumes of bird and animal drawings and seven illustrated travel books. He spent the winter of 1864–65 in Nice and the next two winters in Cannes.

Jean Lorrain (1856–1906)

Pen name of Paul Duval, French poet, dramatist and novelist whose sadistic and erotic style – supposedly ether-induced – found favour with turn-of-the-century Parisian society. His poetic works included *Le Sang des dieux* (*The Blood of the Gods*) and his best-known novel was *Monsieur de Phocas*. He lived in Nice at the beginning of the twentieth century.

Katherine Mansfield (1888–1923)

New Zealand short-story writer who greatly influenced the short-story format. She left New Zealand for good at the age of 19 to establish a

musical career in England, but switched to writing. Her first collection of stories, the result of a stay in Bavaria, was *In a German
Pension*. Her first stories were published in *Rhythm*, edited by John
Middleton Murry, whom she later married, and the two formed a
close association with D.H. Lawrence and his wife. She had a close
relationship with Virginia Woolf, whose Hogarth Press published
Prelude. Other collections included *Bliss*, *The Garden Party* and *Daughters of the Late Colonel*. From 1915 onwards, she travelled the Riviera
coasts of France and Italy trying to alleviate her consumption, finally
settling in Menton.

Roger Martin du Gard (1881–1958)

French author and winner of the 1937 Nobel Prize for Literature.
He is best known for his eight-part novel *Les Thibault*, chronicling
the social and moral issues of the French bourgeoisie. His other
works include a study of the author André Gide and a drama about
repressed homosexuality. He spent time in Grasse and the Îles d'Or,
off Hyères.

Harpo (Arthur) Marx (1888–1964)

American comic actor and script-writer. He was the mute harpist in
the famous Marx Brothers act, appearing in vaudeville, plays and
films, such as *A Day at the Races*, *A Night at the Opera* and *A Night in
Casablanca*. He wrote an autobiography, *Harpo Speaks*. He stayed on
the Cap d'Antibes in 1928 where he met Maugham, Shaw and
Wells.

Karl Marx (1818–83)

German philosopher and revolutionary. After the suppression of the
radical paper which he edited in Germany, he spent the rest of his
life in exile in Paris, Brussels and London. He published much of his
work in collaboration with Friedrich Engels, who also provided
financial support. In 1849 he moved to London where he spent the
rest of his life. His most famous work was *Das Kapital*, published
between 1867 and 1894. He travelled around the Mediterranean in
1882, spending a month in Monaco.

W. Somerset Maugham (1874–1965)

English novelist, playwright, and short-story writer. He qualified as a doctor in 1897, but the success of his first novel *Liza of Lambeth* encouraged him to abandon medicine. His plays were outstandingly successful in Edwardian London, with, at one time, four plays running in the West End at once. He is best known for his novels *Of Human Bondage*, *The Moon and Sixpence*, *Cakes and Ale* and *The Razor's Edge*. In 1926, after extensive travel, he settled in Cap Ferrat on the French Riviera, where, with the exception of the war years spent in the USA, he remained until his death 39 years later.

Guy de Maupassant (1850–93)

French short-story writer and novelist. He served in the army during the Franco-Prussian War which provided him with the material for some of his best stories. He was introduced into literary circles by Flaubert and, following the success of *Boule de suif* (*Ball of Tallow*) in 1880, he wrote about 300 short stories and six novels, including *Une Vie* (*A Woman's Life*) and his well-known *Bel-Ami*. He suffered from syphilis and died in an asylum at the age of 42. He spent considerable time sailing the northern Mediterranean in the 1880s in his yacht *Bel-Ami*, and lived in Antibes and Cannes.

Prosper Mérimée (1803–70)

French dramatist, historian, archaeologist and short-story writer. Interested in the Greek, Spanish, English and Russian languages and their literatures, he was an early interpreter of Russian literature into French. He began writing plays at 19, then his famous novellas: *Colomba*, which dramatized the vendetta culture of Corsica, and *Carmen*, which inspired Bizet's opera. He came to the Côte d'Azur in 1834 as Inspector of Historic Monuments, and settled in Cannes in 1861, where he spent every winter for the rest of his life.

Henry Miller (1891–1980)

American novelist and essayist. Born in Brooklyn, he went to France in 1930 where his best-known books *Tropic of Cancer* and *Tropic of Capricorn* were published. His major works were banned in Britain and the USA because of their sexual frankness, and his *The Air Conditioned Nightmare*, based on a tour of the USA, was considered unpatriotic, but after his return to the USA in 1942 he was acclaimed by the beat generation. He travelled regularly in Provence, especially Cannes, where he was a juror at the film festival in 1960.

A.A. Milne (1882-1956)

English novelist and dramatist best known for his books *Winnie-the-Pooh* and *The House at Pooh Corner*, written for and about his son Christopher Robin. He worked on *Punch* magazine and wrote a number of plays, including *Mr Pim Passes By*; he also adapted Grahame's *The Wind in the Willows* for the stage as *Toad of Toad Hall*. He stayed on Cap St Martin with his wife Daphne in 1914.

John Milton (1608-74)

English poet who supported the Puritan revolution and wrote defending civil liberties. After the Restoration he became blind but wrote his best-known works, including his master work *Paradise Lost*, its sequel *Paradise Regained* and *Samson Agonistes*. He travelled to Italy in 1638-39, meeting Galileo in Florence, and called into Nice.

John Middleton Murry (1889-1957)

English journalist and critic. He edited a number of literary magazines and wrote at least 40 books, including studies of Keats and Blake and an autobiography, *Between Two Worlds*. He was married to Katherine Mansfield until her death in 1923 and published her letters. He made many visits to the Riviera while Mansfield was living in Bandol and Menton.

Vladimir Nabokov (1899-1977)

Russian-born American novelist, poet and critic. After leaving Russia he studied at Trinity College Cambridge and travelled in Europe. A keen butterfly collector, he was also a professor of entomology. His fame came with the publication of *Lolita*, after he had worked in American universities for 15 years. Thereafter his earlier works were reappraised. His visits to the Riviera covered over 50 years from 1904 to the winter of 1960-61 when he wrote *Pale Fire* in Nice.

Friedrich Nietzsche (1844–1900)

German philosopher who influenced generations of intellectuals. He studied Schopenhauer in Leipzig, where he met Wagner. His *The Birth of Tragedy* argues that Wagnerian opera was the successor to Greek drama. His best-known work, *Thus Spake Zarathustra*, much of which was written in Nice, advances one of his most widely accepted philosophies, the concept of *Übermensch*. Zarathustra rejected absolute moral values, in particular what he called the 'slave morality' of Christianity. His 'Super man' would impose his totalitarian will upon the weak. Although he was against nationalism and anti-Semitism his name was invoked by the Nazis in support of Aryanism. He spent a number of winters in Nice in the late nineteenth century.

Anaïs Nin (1903–77)

French-born author of novels and short stories who won recognition with the publication of her personal diaries in New York. This provoked interest in her other works, including the five-volume *Cities of the Interior*. She visited a number of Riviera towns, particularly St-Tropez.

David Niven (1909–83)

British actor who made his reputation in Hollywood in the 1930s. In a film career covering over 40 years, he is best known for his films *Around the World in 80 Days*, *The Moon is Blue*, *The Guns of Navarone*, *The Pink Panther* and *Death on the Nile*. He also won an Academy Award for his dramatic role in *Separate Tables* in 1958. He settled in St-Jean-Cap-Ferrat, where he wrote two popular autobiographies, *The Moon's a Balloon* and *Bring on the Empty Horses*, and remained there until his death.

E. Phillips Oppenheim (1866–1946)

English novelist and short-story writer. He inherited his father's leather business, but was bought out by a wealthy New York businessman who made him a director so that he could concentrate on writing. Between 1887 and 1946 he wrote more than 150 books, many set on the Riviera, featuring gentlemen thieves and glamorous spies. Among his best-known works are *The Moving Finger* and *The Great Impersonation*. He decided to make his home on the Riviera in

1926 and remained until after the German occupation in 1941, living in Cagnes-sur-Mer and Roquefort-les-Pins.

Baroness Orczy (1865–1947)

Hungarian-born British novelist. She came to England at the age of 15 with no English, and at first studied art and exhibited at the Royal Academy. She became famous in 1905 with her swashbuckling adventure story *The Scarlet Pimpernel*, set in the time of the French Revolution. Her sequels were less successful, but she wrote 20 novels in all, including several detective stories. She first came to Monaco in 1915, and remained for more than 30 years.

John Osborne (1929–94)

English playwright and scenarist whose play *Look Back in Anger* gave rise to the phrase 'Angry Young Men'. He continued to criticize contemporary Britain in plays like *The Entertainer*, *A Patriot for Me* and *West of Suez*, and won an Academy Award for his screenplay of *Tom Jones*. He wrote two volumes of autobiography: *A Better Class of Person* and *Almost a Gentleman*. He stayed in Valbonne, where he wrote most of the prose collection *Damn You, England* and attended the Cannes Film Festival in June 1959.

Marcel Pagnol (1895–1974)

French poet, novelist, playwright and producer-director who became the first film-maker to be elected to the French Academy in 1946. He began his film career in 1931 and set many of his films in Provence, including *Lettres de mon moulin* (*Letters from My Windmill*), an adaptation of Alphonse Daudet's novel, and *Manon des Sources*, which he wrote and directed. He wrote extensively about Provence, lived in Grasse and Monaco, and was the president of the jury at the Cannes Film Festival in 1955.

Dorothy Parker (1893–1967)

American short-story writer, poet and critic, famous for her acerbic wit and satirical verse. Her first book *Enough Rope* was a bestseller in 1926, and in 1929 she won the O. Henry Award for the best short story of the year with 'Big Blonde'. She was the only regular woman member of the famous Algonquin Hotel's Round Table. In the

1920s she was a regular visitor to the Villa America on the Cap d'Antibes, the home of wealthy Bostonians Gerald and Sara Murphy, with whom she travelled to Switzerland to take care of their invalid son Patrick.

Petrarch, Francesco Petrarca (1304–74)
Italian poet and humanist, considered the greatest scholar of his time. His best-known surviving poems are about the death of his mother and his *Canzoniere*, proclaiming his chaste love for 'Laura', whose identity he never revealed. He fled with his parents from political conflict in Florence and settled in Avignon until 1353.

Sylvia Plath (1932–63)
American poet and novelist. While at Smith College, Massachusetts, she underwent periods of psychiatric hospitalization. In 1956 she married the English poet Ted Hughes, later Poet Laureate, and lectured at Smith for two years before returning to England in 1959 where her first collection of poems, *The Colossus*, was published. She became something of a cult figure with her best-known collection *Ariel*. Her only novel, *The Bell Jar*, was published in 1963. A month later she committed suicide in London. She spent time in Nice in 1956 while a Fulbright scholar in Cambridge.

Ezra Pound (1885–1972)
American poet and critic who moved to Paris in 1920 and four years later to Italy, settling in Rapallo, where he was host to Yeats, Aldington and other writers, and made occasional visits to St-Raphaël. He published his first book of poems, *A Lume Spento*, at his own expense. His pro-Fascist and anti-Semitic broadcasts from Rome during the Second World War led to his arrest in 1945 by American troops and his confinement for 12 years in a Washington DC asylum for the criminally insane. On his release, he returned to Italy, where he lived in Venice for the rest of his life. In addition to his influence on the work of his contemporaries, most notably his critical role in the construction of T.S. Eliot's *The Waste Land*, his own later works, in particular *Cantos* and *Hugh Selwyn Mauberley*, were widely acclaimed.

Jacques Prévert (1900–77)

French poet, script-writer and ballad composer. Some of his best-known works include his collection of poems *Paroles* (*Words*), *Histoires* (*Stories*) and *Charmes de Londres* (*Charms of London*). Among the best of his many film scripts are *Drôle de drame* (*Odd Drama*) and *Les Enfants du paradis* (*The Children of Paradise*). He lived in the old town of Antibes during the Second World War.

Marcel Proust (1871–1922)

French novelist, famous for his masterpiece *À la Recherche du temps perdu* (*Remembrance of Things Past*). In 1912 he published the first volume, *Swann's Way*, at his own expense and won the Prix Goncourt for the second volume, *Within a Budding Grove*. Graham Greene called him 'the greatest novelist of the twentieth century'. Severely asthmatic, and a closet homosexual, with a charismatic yet reclusive personality, he was an obsessively perfectionist writer. His chauffeur and close friend Agostino (Alfred) Agostinelli was killed in an aeroplane crash in Antibes in 1914.

Jean-François Regnard (1655–1709)

French comic playwright who wrote for both the Comédie-Italienne and the Comédie-Francaise. Along with *Le Joueur* (*The Gambler*) and *Les Folies amoureuses*, his best-known play is *Le Légataire universel* (*The Sole Heir*). He was widely travelled, and his early experiences included ten months in slavery after being captured by pirates off the Corsican coast.

Vita Sackville-West (1892–1962)

English novelist and poet, daughter of the 3rd Baron Sackville and married to the diplomat and author Harold Nicolson. Her best-known works include the novels *The Edwardians* and *All Passion Spent*, and her poem about the English countryside, *The Land*, although she gained her reputation in part through her friendship with Virginia Woolf, who based her character Orlando on Vita. She stayed in Sanary-sur-Mer and spent the winter of 1918–19 and 1919–20 with Violet Trefusis in Monaco.

Françoise Sagan (1935–)

French novelist and dramatist who took her name from the Princess of Sagan in Proust's *Remembrance of Things Past*. She has written many novels including *Un Certain Sourire* (*A Certain Smile*), *Les Merveilleux Nuages* (*Wonderful Clouds*) and *Un Profile perdu* (*Lost Profile*) but is best known for her first novel *Bonjour Tristesse*, which she wrote in four weeks at the age of 18. It became a bestseller and a film. Since her first visits in the early 1950s, she has been a regular visitor to St-Tropez and to the Cannes Film Festival, of which she was jury president in 1979.

Antoine de Saint-Exupéry (1900–44)

French aviator and writer, best known as the author of the popular French children's book *Le Petit Prince* (*The Little Prince*). He obtained his pilot's licence in 1922 and became a military reconnaissance pilot. His love of adventure and flying are reflected in his novels *Courrier-Sud* (*Southern Mail*) and *Vol de nuit* (*Night Flight*). He also wrote two autobiographical works, *Terre des Hommes* (*Wind, Sand and Stars*) and *Pilote de guerre* (*Flight to Arras*). While in America he wrote *Lettre à un otage* (*Letter to a Hostage*), a call to unity among Frenchmen. He worked in Cabris in 1939 and went missing while flying over the Mediterranean in 1944.

George Sand (1804–76)

French Romantic writer, noted both for her so-called rustic novels such as *La Mare au diable* (*The Haunted Marsh*) and *François le Champi* (*François the Waif*) and numerous love affairs with, among others, Prosper Mérimée, Musset and Chopin. She spent the spring of 1861 at Tamaris, near Toulon.

Jean-Paul Sartre (1905–80)

French novelist, playwright and critic, best remembered for his lifelong association with Simone de Beauvoir, whom he met at the Sorbonne, in establishing the Existentialist movement, and his general intellectual leadership after the Second World War. His many philosophical works include *L'Être et le néant* (*Being and Nothingness*) and novels such as *Les Chemins de la liberté* (*The Roads to Freedom*), *La Nausée* (*Nausea*) and *L'Imagination* (*Imagination: A Psycho-*

logical Critique). He was a prisoner of war in 1939–40. He visited the Riviera over most of his life, particularly Grasse.

Robert W. Service (1874–1958)
English-born poet who emigrated to Canada in 1894 and became popular with his ballads describing life in the frozen north, particularly 'The Shooting of Dan McGrew', and *Ballads of a Cheechako*. From 1912 he lived in Europe, mainly in Monaco.

George Bernard Shaw (1856–1950)
Irish dramatist and critic. He made his mark in London when Frank Harris recruited him to the *Saturday Review* as theatre critic. He was an executive of the Fabian Society from 1885 to 1911. He wrote more than 50 plays, some of the best-known works being *Pygmalion* and *St Joan*. He won the Nobel Prize for Literature in 1925 and visited the Cap d'Antibes in 1928.

Simone Signoret (1921–85)
French actress and writer, mostly famous for her films *Casque d'or* (*Golden Helmet*) and *Room at the Top* (for which she won Best Actress Award from both the British and American film academies.) She wrote a bestselling autobiography, *Nostalgia Isn't What It Used To Be*, and a novel, *Adieu Volodia*. She and her second husband Yves Montand were wartime communists and campaigned against the wars in Vietnam and Algeria. They met and married in St-Paul-de-Vence and were regular visitors to the village.

Alan Sillitoe (1928–)
English novelist, short-story writer and poet. Brought up in Nottingham, he left school at 14 and worked in a cycle factory before doing National Service with the RAF in Malaya. On demobilization he was found to have tuberculosis and spent 18 months in hospital. On release from the RAF, he travelled in France, Spain and Italy and in 1959 married the American poet Ruth Fainlight. His first novel *Saturday Night and Sunday Morning* was an immediate success, as was the film starring Albert Finney. He has followed it with a collection of short stories, *The Loneliness of the Long Distance Runner* (1959), the title story of which was also filmed, a large number of collections of

stories and articles and an autobiography, A Life without Armour, in 1995. He lived in Menton from January 1952 to March 1953.

Georges Simenon (1903–89)

Belgian-French novelist. A prolific writer who wrote more than 200 books of fiction under 16 pseudonyms. He introduced his best-known character Inspector Jules Maigret in Pietr-le-Letton (The Strange Case of Peter the Lett) in 1930 and wrote 83 more detective novels featuring Maigret, as well as 136 psychological novels. He was a frequent visitor to the Riviera and set many books there, staying on the Îles d'Or, at Cannes and on Cap d'Antibes.

Tobias Smollett (1721–71)

Scottish novelist, best known for his novels The Adventures of Roderick Random, The Adventures of Peregrine Pickle and The Expedition of Humphry Clinker, whose writing influenced Charles Dickens. His works include translations of Voltaire and of Don Quixote and, in 1757–58, his successful Complete History of England. While editor of the Critical Review, he libelled Admiral Sir Charles Knowles and was sentenced to three months' imprisonment. In 1763, following the death of his 15-year-old daughter, he went to Nice in the hope of alleviating his respiratory problems and stayed for two years. In 1766 he published his still-read book Travels through France and Italy.

Gertrude Stein (1874–1946)

The eccentric American writer who became a legend in Paris, throwing open her home to the leading artists and writers of the period. Her literary and artistic judgements were revered and her portrait was painted by Picasso. Her works include Three Lives, The Making of Americans and her widely read The Autobiography of Alice B. Toklas (her lifelong companion). She befriended Hemingway and Fitzgerald and joined them as guests of Gerald and Sara Murphy, an American couple who kept 'open house' to writers at their home on the Cap d'Antibes.

Stendhal (1783–1842)

Pen name of Henri Marie Beyle, French novelist and critic, whose major works were the novels Le Rouge et le noir (The Red and the Black) and *La Chartreuse de Parme* (*The Charterhouse of Parma*). He also wrote books on travel, music and painting. After the fall of the French First Empire in 1814 he settled in Italy, during which time he toured the Riviera, staying in Cannes and Grasse.

Laurence Sterne (1713–68)

Irish-born English novelist and humorist. He began his career in the Church, becoming canon of York Minster, but in 1759, in supporting his dean in a Church squabble, he wrote *The History of a Good Warm Watch-Coat*, which was so barbed that it ended his ecclesiastical mission. He became famous with his novel *Tristram Shandy*, and later with his Rabelaisian travelogue, *A Sentimental Journey through France and Italy, by Mr. Yorick*, which was published, unfinished, after his death. In 1765, on the recommendation of his doctors, he travelled to Menton as part of his 'sentimental journey', which took him as far south as Naples.

Robert Louis Stevenson (1850–94)

Scottish novelist, essayist and travel writer, best remembered for his novels *Treasure Island*, *Kidnapped* and *The Strange Case of Dr Jekyll and Mr. Hyde*. To please his father he studied law, but although called to the bar, he never practised. His frequent journeys abroad, in search of climates beneficial to his tuberculosis, were the source of his travel books *An Inland Voyage* and *Travels with a Donkey in the Cévennes*. He married Fanny Osbourne in California in 1880 and lived in Hyères and Menton before moving to Samoa, where he died.

Algernon Swinburne (1837–1909)

English poet and critic. He left Oxford without a degree, but was able, with an allowance from his father, to follow a literary career. His successful works include the verse drama *Atalanta in Calydon* and *Poems and Ballads*, but many readers were troubled by their anarchistic content, and his penchant for excessive drinking and self-abuse seriously damaged his health. He came to Menton in 1861 and 1864 in the hope of recovery, but it was not until he came under the charge of his friend Watts Dunton in 1866 that his health was restored.

Anton Tchekhov (1860–1904)

Russian dramatist and short-story writer. He wrote hundreds of stories while studying medicine at the university of Moscow, but is best remembered for his plays, which he wrote after he developed tuberculosis. His most famous works include *Uncle Vanya*, *The Three Sisters* and *The Cherry Orchard*, which he wrote for the Moscow Art Theatre, where he met and married the actress Olga Knipper. He stayed in Nice on a number of occasions, beginning in 1891, when he wrote *The Three Sisters*.

Alfred, Lord Tennyson (1809–92)

English poet who was one of 12 children, brought up in a Lincolnshire rectory. At Trinity College Cambridge he began a lifelong friendship with Arthur Hallam and in 1830 they went to Spain to help in the unsuccessful revolution against Ferdinand VII. He became Poet Laureate in 1850 and published *In Memoriam*, mourning the death of Hallam. His best-known work was *Idylls of the King*. A favourite of Queen Victoria, he received a peerage in 1884. A regular visitor to the eastern Pyrenees, he passed through La Turbie.

James Thurber (1894–1961)

American writer and cartoonist. He worked for *The New Yorker* in both capacities and remained a leading contributor even after he left in 1933. He was eventually forced to give up drawing because of his blindness. His most famous work was *The Secret Life of Walter Mitty*, which was made into a successful film starring Danny Kaye. He worked as a journalist for the *Chicago Tribune* in Nice in the 1920s and later stayed on the Cap d'Antibes.

Count Leo Tolstoi (1828–1910)

Russian writer and novelist, famous for his epic novels *War and Peace* and *Anna Karenina*, although he also wrote shorter works such as *The Death of Ivan Ilyich*. Around 1879, he underwent a spiritual crisis and became a vegetarian and pacifist, working and dressing as a peasant. He visited Beaulieu and Hyères in 1840 with his brother Nicolas, who died in Hyères.

Ivan Turgenev (1818–83)

Russian novelist. He was an admirer of Western society and wrote critically of the Russian social system in *Sportsman's Sketches*. He also composed verse in the style of the poet Lord Byron as well as plays and the novel *Fathers and Sons*. He made a brief but unsuccessful visit to Hyères for his health in 1848.

Mark Twain (1835–1910)

Pen name of Samuel Langhorne Clemens, American humorist, writer and lecturer, best known for his stories *The Adventures of Tom Sawyer* and *The Adventures of Huckleberry Finn*. He lived close to the Mississippi river and worked as a steamboat pilot. After a petition by British writers, including Greene and Maugham, a commemorative stone was placed in Westminster Abbey. He visited the Château d'If near Marseilles and sailed along the coast to Genoa in 1867.

Paul Valéry (1871–1945)

French poet, essayist and critic. Although he wrote a great many essays and papers on literary topics, his best work is considered to be the poem *La Jeune Parque* (*The Young Fate*). He switched to essays in the 1920s but is best remembered for his 29 volumes of metaphysical speculations in his *Cahiers* (*Notebooks*) and was a much-sought-after society figure for his dazzling conversational gifts. He was born in Sète on the Mediterranean coast and was a frequent visitor to Grasse, Nice and Vence.

Jules Verne (1828–1905)

French novelist and scenarist. He achieved worldwide popularity with fantasy books which foresaw the submarine, the Aqua-Lung, television and space travel. His novels, many of which became stage and film productions, included *Voyage au centre de la terre* (*A Journey to the Centre of the Earth*), *De la Terre à la lune* (*From the Earth to the Moon*), *Vingt mille lieues sous les mers* (*Twenty Thousand Leagues under the Sea*) and his most popular, *Le Tour du monde en quatre-vingt jours* (*Around the World in Eighty Days*). For several winters in the 1870s he worked in the Villa Les Chênes Vertes on the Cap d'Antibes.

Sir Hugh Walpole (1884–1941)

British novelist, critic and dramatist. Born in New Zealand, he taught at an English prep school before becoming a writer, an environment he used as background for *Mr Perrin and Mr Traill*. His major works were *The Dark Forest* and a family saga, *The Herries Chronicle*. He also wrote critical works on Trollope, Scott and Conrad. He was knighted in 1937. He was an old friend of Maugham, whom he followed as pupil at King's School Canterbury, but the friendship suffered a setback when he was caricatured in Maugham's first Riviera-written novel, *Cakes and Ale*.

Evelyn Waugh (1903–66)

English novelist who served in the army in the Second World War. His best-known works include the satirical novels *Decline and Fall*, *Vile Bodies* and *The Loved One*. His conversion to Catholicism in 1930 gave rise to novels with religious themes such as *Brideshead Revisited*. Later novels include his war trilogy *Men at Arms*, *Officers and Gentlemen* and *Unconditional Surrender*. With his brother Alec, he dined with Maugham at the Villa Mauresque in June 1930 and stayed in nearby Villefranche.

H.G. Wells (1866–1946)

English novelist and journalist. Although he left school at 14 with very little education, he won a scholarship at 18 to the Royal College of Science. He is best known for his science fiction novels *The Time Machine* and *The War of the Worlds* and his many comic social novels, including *Kipps* and *The History of Mr Polly*. Although married to Catherine Robbins, he set up home with Odette Keun in a villa near Grasse in the 1920s and 1930s.

Rebecca West (1892–1983)

British journalist, novelist and critic who began her career with a critical biography of Henry James in 1916. Among her novels are *The Judge*, *The Thinking Reed*, *The Return of the Soldier* and *The Fountain Overflows*. In 1946 she reported for the *New Yorker* magazine on the treason trial of William Joyce (Lord Haw-Haw), but she is best known for her reports on the Nuremberg trials, collected as *A Train of Powder.* She made many visits to the Riviera, especially Cannes, often with her son by H.G. Wells, Anthony West.

Edith Wharton (1862–1937)

American author best known for her stories and novels about the upper-class society into which she was born. Her major literary model was Henry James and she acknowledged her debt to him in her manual, *The Writing of Fiction.* She published more than 50 books, including fiction, short stories and travel and historical works. Her best-known work was *Ethan Frome* but others include *The House of Mirth, The Reef, The Custom of the Country, Summer,* and *The Age of Innocence,* which won a Pulitzer Prize. She lived her last 30 years in Paris and Hyères.

Oscar Wilde (1854–1900)

Irish poet, wit and dramatist. He was born in Dublin, but became a leading society figure in London. He became as famous for the trial arising from his homosexual relationship with Lord Alfred Douglas and subsequent two-year prison sentence, as for his works, which include his social comedies such as *Lady Windermere's Fan, An Ideal Husband* and *The Importance of Being Earnest,* a novel, *The Picture of Dorian Gray,* and *Poems.* While in exile in Paris he produced his best-known poem, *The Ballad of Reading Gaol.* In 1898, with the patronage of his friend Frank Harris, he lived in La Napoule and Nice, but returned that same year to Paris, where he died two years later.

Tennessee Williams (1911–83)

American novelist and dramatist. He is best remembered for his works depicting southern family life with recurrent themes of sex and violence, including *The Glass Menagerie, A Streetcar Named Desire* (for which he won a Pulitzer Prize) and *Cat on a Hot Tin Roof.* He was an occasional visitor to the Riviera and was president of the Cannes Film Festival in 1976.

Godfrey Winn (1908–71)

British actor, novelist and journalist, best remembered for his tabloid columns and whimsical articles in women's magazines. In 1928 he stayed with Maugham on Cap Ferrat, where they became lovers; they remained friends until Maugham's death. Maugham's unflattering portrait of Winn in *Strictly Personal* was deleted in Britain for fear of a libel action.

P.G. Wodehouse (1881–1975)

English-born comic novelist, short-story writer and playwright, best known for his caricature of upper-class British society through the characters of the inept Bertie Wooster and his manipulative manservant Jeeves. After 1909 he lived and worked for long periods in the USA but was living in northern France when the Germans invaded in 1940. His radio broadcasts to the United States while a German prisoner caused great resentment in Britain. After the war he settled in the United States. He was knighted in 1975. He visited Cannes, Auribeau and Monaco between 1925 and the Second World War.

Virginia Woolf (1882–1941)

English novelist who was a central figure in the Bloomsbury group. Her best-known works include *Mrs Dalloway*, *To the Lighthouse* and her historical fantasy *Orlando*. With her husband Leonard Woolf she founded the Hogarth Press and published her own works. She also wrote biographies and criticism. She was frequently prey to depression and committed suicide by drowning. Together with Leonard she made a number of visits to her sister Vanessa Bell in Cassis, and passed through Nice on journeys to Italy.

W.B. Yeats (1865–1939)

Dublin-born poet, dramatist and prose writer. He received the Nobel Prize for Literature in 1923. He espoused the Irish nationalist cause, and his unrequited love for the Irish nationalist actress Maud Gonne influenced many of his works. Together with his friend Lady Gregory, he founded the Irish Literary Theatre (eventually the Abbey Theatre) whose first performance in 1899 was Yeats's play *The Countess Cathleen*. Many of his better-known works had the themes of the Easter Rising and the Irish Civil War. In later life he spent the winter months on the French or Italian Rivieras, and died in Roquebrune-Cap-Martin in January 1939.

Prince Félix Yusupov (1887–1967)

Best remembered as the Russian who arranged the murder in 1916 of Rasputin. Heir of the wealthiest family in Russia, he received the title of prince by virtue of his marriage to the tsar's niece, Irina Romanov. The murder helped precipitate the 1917 Revolution, after which most of the Romanovs were executed. Yusupov sought asylum in the USA and later Menton. He wrote his memoirs, *Lost Splendour*, in 1953.

Émile Zola (1840–1902)

French novelist. His major work was a 20-volume series entitled *Les Rougon-Macquart*, which includes *La Terre* (*Earth*), *Germinal* and *Nana*. He achieved notoriety when he intervened in 1898 in the Dreyfus Affair, publishing *J'Accuse*, an open letter to the president denouncing the rigged trial of a Jewish French army officer for treason. He was found guilty of libel and fled to England. He was an occasional visitor to Monaco.

Bibliography

Ackroyd, Peter, *Charles Dickens* (London: Minerva, 1990)

Alcott, Louisa M., *Little Women* (Oxford: OUP, 1998)

Amoretti, Louis N., *Partage de mémoire* (Menton: Société d'Art et d'Histoire du Mentonnais, 2001)

Bair, Deirdre, *Samuel Beckett: A Biography* (London: Jonathan Cape, 1978)

Baker, Carlos, *Ernest Hemingway* (London: Penguin, 1972)

Ballard, J.G., *Super-Cannes* (London: Flamingo, 2000)

Bedford, Sybille, *Aldous Huxley: A Biography*, Vol I (London: Chatto & Windus, 1973)

Benchley, Nathaniel, *Robert Benchley: A Biography* (London: Cassell, 1956)

Bernstein, Burton, *Thurber: A Biography* (London: Gollancz, 1975)

Berthoud, Roger, *Graham Sutherland: A Biography* (London: Faber & Faber, 1982)

Birkenhead, Lord, *Rudyard Kipling* (London: Weidenfeld & Nicolson, 1978)

Blume, Mary, *Côte d'Azur: Inventing the French Riviera* (London: Thames & Hudson, 1994)

Boddy, Gillian, *Katherine Mansfield, the Woman and the Writer* (Australia: Penguin, 1988)

Bogarde, Dirk, *A Short Walk from Harrod's* (London: Viking, 1993)

Brady, Frank and Pottle, Frederick (eds), *Boswell on the Grand Tour* (London: Heinemann, 1955)

Brewster, Margaret M., *Letters from Cannes and Nice* (Edinburgh: Thomas Constable, 1857)

Bruccoli, Matthew J. (ed), *Ever, Scott-Fitz* (London: The Woburn Press, 1973)

——, *Fitzgerald and Hemingway: A Dangerous Friendship* (London: André Deutsch, 1995)

Calder, Jennie, *Robert Louis Stevenson* (London: Hamish Hamilton, 1980)

Calder, Robert, *'Willie': The Life of W. Somerset Maugham* (London: Heinemann, 1989)

Cane, André, *Anglais et Russes à Villefranche* (Nice: self-published, 1988)

Carrington, Dorothy, *Granite Island* (London: Penguin, 1984)

Châteauneuf, Charles de, *Un Siècle à Menton* (Nice: Éditions du Dabris, 1998)

Christie, Agatha, *An Autobiography* (London: HarperCollins, 1993)

Coale, Samuel, *Anthony Burgess* (New York: Frederick Ungar, 1981)

Cocteau, Jean, *Past Tense, Diaries*, Vol I, translated by Richard Howard (London: Hamish Hamilton, 1983)

Colette, *La Naissance du jour* (*Morning Glory*) (London: Victor Gollancz, 1932)

Colvin, Sydney (ed), *The Letters of Robert Louis Stevenson*, Vol II (New York: Scribners, 1911)

Connolly, Cyril, *The Unquiet Grave* (London: Penguin, 1967)

——, *The Rock Pool* (Oxford: OUP, 1981)

Cooper, Artemis and Diana (eds), *Mr Wu and Mrs Stitch: The Letters of Evelyn Waugh and Diana Cooper* (London: Hodder & Stoughton, 1991)

Cronin, Anthony, *Samuel Beckett: The Last Modernist* (London: HarperCollins, 1996)

Crosland, Margaret, *Colette: The Difficulty of Loving* (London: Peter Owen, 1996)

Curtis, Anthony, *Somerset Maugham* (London: Weidenfeld & Nicolson, 1977)

Davenport, Hester, *Writers in Windsor* (Windsor: Cell Mead Press, 1995)

Decaux, Alain, *Les Heures Brillantes de la Côte d'Azur* (Paris: Perrin, 1964)

Donaldson, Frances (ed), *Yours, Plum: The Letters of P.G. Wodehouse* (London: Hutchinson, 1990)

Doyle, Charles, *Richard Aldington: A Biography* (London: Macmillan, 1989)

Drabble, Margaret, *Arnold Bennett: A Biography* (London: Weidenfeld & Nicolson, 1974)

Duran, Leopoldo, *Graham Greene, Friend and Brother* (London: HarperCollins, 1994)

Durrell, Lawrence, *Spirit of Place* (London: Faber & Faber, 1988)

Edel, Leon, *Henry James: A Life* (London: Collins, 1985)

Eglund, Steven, *Princess Grace* (London: Orbis, 1984)

Ellis, LeRoy, *Les Russes sur la Côte d'Azur* (Nice: Éditions Serre, 1988)

Ellman, Richard, *James Joyce* (Oxford: OUP, 1959)

——, *Oscar Wilde* (London: Hamish Hamilton, 1987)

Erlanger, Philippe, *Fascinant Monte Carlo* (Monaco: Bazzoli, 1983)

Faulk, Quentin, *Travels in Greeneland: The Cinema of Graham Greene* (London: Quartet, 1990)

Ferguson, Robert, *Henry Miller: A Life* (London: Hutchinson, 1991)

Field, Andrew, *VN: The Life and Art of Vladimir Nabokov* (London: Futura, 1988)

Fisher, Clive, *Noël Coward* (London: Weidenfeld & Nicolson, 1992)

——, *Cyril Connolly: A Nostalgic Life* (London: Macmillan, 1995)

Fitzgerald, F. Scott, *Tender is the Night* (New York: Simon & Schuster, 1995)

Franca, Michel, *Nice: La Baie des Requins* (Paris: Éditions AM, 1982)

Fuegi, John, *The Life and Lies of Bertolt Brecht* (London: HarperCollins, 1994)

Gallo, Max, *La Baie des Anges, Vol 3: La Promenade des Anglais* (Paris: Robert Laffont, 1976)

Gide, André, *Journal 1939–1942* (Paris: Gallimard, 1946)

Gillespie, M.A. (ed), *Nietzsche's New Seas* (Chicago: University of Chicago Press, 1991)

Girard, Xavier, *Les Années Fitzgerald: La Côte d'Azur 1920–1930* (Paris: Éditions Assouline, 2001)

Glendinning, Victoria, *Vita: The Life of Vita Sackville-West* (London: Weidenfeld & Nicolson, 1983)

Goudeket, Maurice, *Close to Colette*, translated by Enid McLeod (London: Secker & Warburg, 1957)

Graham, Sheila, *The Real Scott Fitzgerald* (New York: Grosset & Dunlop, 1976)

Greene, Graham, *Loser Takes All* (Harmondsworth: Penguin, 1971)

——, *J'Accuse: The Dark Side of Nice* (London: Bodley Head, 1982)

——, *May We Borrow Your Husband?* (London: Penguin, 1984)

Guinsberg, Sylvia, *Perched Villages of the Alpes Maritimes*, Vol 3 (Aix-en-Provence: Edisud, 1983)

Hare, Augustus J.C., *A Winter in Mentone* (London: Wertheim, Macintosh & Hunt, 1862)

Harris, Frank, *Oscar Wilde* (New York: Carrell & Graf, 1997)

Hassall, Christopher, *Rupert Brooke: A Biography* (London: Faber & Faber, 1964)

Hemingway, Ernest, *A Moveable Feast* (London: Reprint Society, 1964)

Holt, Tonie and Valmai, *My Boy Jack* (London: Leo Cooper, 1998)

Howarth, Patrick, *When the Riviera Was Ours* (London: Century, 1977)

Jones, Nigel, *Rupert Brooke: Life, Death & Myth* (London: Richard Cohen, 1999)

Karl, Frederick R., *Joseph Conrad: The Three Lives* (London: Faber & Faber, 1979)

Kelly, Lionel (ed), *Tobias Smollett: The Critical Heritage* (London: Routledge & Kegan Paul, 1987)

Kelly, Richard, *Graham Greene* (New York: Frederick Ungar, 1984)

Kipling, Rudyard, *Something of Myself* (Cambridge: CUP, 1990)

Knowlson, Hames, *Damned to Fame: The Life of Samuel Beckett* (London: Bloomsbury, 1997)

Koteliansky, S.S. (ed), *The Life and Letters of Anton Tchekhov* (London: Cassell, 1925)

Kukil, Karen V. (ed), *The Journals of Sylvia Plath, 1950–1962* (London: Faber & Faber, 2000)

Lafourcade, Georges, *Swinburne: A Literary Biography* (London: G. Bell, 1932)

Le Gallienne, Richard, *The Romantic '90s* (London: Robin Clark, 1993)

Lear, Edward, *The Nonsense Verse of Edward Lear* (London: Jonathan Cape, 1984)

Lee, Hermione, *Virginia Woolf* (London: Vintage, 1997)

Lewis, Jeremy, *Cyril Connolly: A Life* (London: Jonathan Cape, 1997)

Lindsay, Jack, *Charles Dickens: A Biographical and Critical Study* (London: Dakers, 1953)

Lottman, Herbert R., *Albert Camus* (London: Weidenfeld & Nicolson, 1979)

——, *Flaubert: A Biography* (London: Methuen, 1989)

Lycett, Andrew, *Rudyard Kipling* (London: Weidenfeld & Nicolson, 1999)

Lynn, Kenneth S., *Hemingway* (London: Simon & Schuster, 1987)

Lyon, Sylvia, *The Life and Times of Prosper Mérimée* (New York: The Dial Press, 1948)

Maddox, Brenda, *Nora: A Biography of Nora Joyce* (London: Hamilton, 1988)

——, *D.H. Lawrence: The Story of a Marriage* (New York: Simon & Schuster, 1994)

——, *George's Ghosts: A New Life of W.B. Yeats* (London: Picador, 1999)

Mansfield, Katherine, *Bliss and Other Stories* (London: Penguin, 1974)

Marx, Harpo, *Harpo Speaks* (London: Robson Books, 1976)

Maupassant, Guy de, *Afloat*, translated by Marlo Johnston (London: George Routledge & Sons, 1889)

——, *Sur l'Eau* (Paris: Pocket, 1999)

McLynn, Frank, *Robert Louis Stevenson* (London: Hutchinson, 1993)

Meade, Marion, *Dorothy Parker: What Fresh Hell is This?* (London: Heinemann, 1998)

Mehew, Ernest (ed), *Selected Letters of Robert Louis Stevenson* (New Haven: Yale University, 1997)

Mellow, J.R., *Charmed Circle: Gertrude Stein and Company* (London: Phaedon Press, 1974)

Mille, Raoul, *Ma Riviera* (Nice: Giletta, 2002)

Morgan, Janet, *Agatha Christie: A Biography* (London: Collins, 1984)

Morris, Jan, *Travels with Virginia Woolf* (London: The Hogarth Press, 1993)

Murry, J. Middleton (ed), *Journal of Katherine Mansfield 1914–1922* (London: Constable, 1936)

Nabokov, Vladimir, *Ada or Ardor* (London: Penguin, 2000)

Najder, Zdziskaw, *Joseph Conrad: A Chronicle* (London: Criterion, 1992)

Oppenheim, E. Phillips, *The Pool of Memory* (London: Hodder & Stoughton, 1941)

Orczy, Baroness, *Links in the Chain of Life* (London: Hutchinson, c.1945)

Ozick, Cynthia, *What Henry James Knew* (London: Vintage, 1994)

Padover, Saul K. (ed & trans) *The Letters of Karl Marx* (New Jersey: Prentice-Hall, 1979)

Paul, Eric and Arthaud, Christian, *La Côte d'Azur des Écrivains* (Aix-en-Provence: Edisud, 1999)

Pemble, John, *The Mediterranean Passion: Victorians and Edwardians in the South* (Oxford: Clarendon Press, 1987)

Plath, Aurelia, *Sylvia Plath: Letters Home 1950–1963* (New York: Harper & Row, 1975)

Pope-Hennessy, Dame Una Constance, *Charles Dickens 1812–1870* (London: Chatto & Windus, 1945)

Pound, Reginald, *Arnold Bennet: A Biography* (Bath: Cedric Chivers, 1971)

Radzinsky, Edvard, *Rasputin: The Last Word*, translated by Judson Rosengrant (London: Weidenfeld & Nicolson, 2000)

Rayfield, Donald, *Chekhov: A Life* (London: HarperCollins, 1998)

Robinson, Marc (ed), *Altogether Elsewhere: Writers in Exile* (London: Faber & Faber, 1994)

Romer, Jean-Claude, *Cannes Memories* (Paris: Media Business, 1997)

Safranski, Rüdigir, *Nietzsche: A Philosophical Biography*, translated by Shelley Frisch (New York: W.W. Norton, 2001)

Sagan, Françoise, *Réponses: The Autobiography of Françoise Sagan*, translated by D. Macey (Godalming: Black Sheep Books, 1979)

Secrest, Mary, *Kenneth Clark: A Biography* (London: Weidenfeld & Nicolson, 1984)

Service, Robert W., *Why Not Grow Young?* (London: Ernest Benn Ltd., 1928)

Shakespeare, Nicholas, *Bruce Chatwin* (London: Harvill Press, 1999)

Signoret, Simone, *Nostalgia Isn't What It Used to Be* (London: Penguin, 1978)

Sillitoe, Alan, *A Life without Armour* (London: HarperCollins, 1995)

Smith, David C., *H.G. Wells: Desperately Mortal* (New Haven: Yale, 1986)

Smollett, Tobias G., *Travels through France and Italy* (London: John Lehmann, 1949)

Soames, Mary (ed), *Speaking for Themselves: The Personal Letters of Winston and Clementine Churchill* (London: Doubleday, 1998)

Stannard, Martin, *Evelyn Waugh: The Early Years* (London: J.M. Dent & Sons, 1986)

Stendhal, *Voyages en France* (Paris: Gallimard, 1992)

Sterling, Monica, *The Wild Swan: H.C. Andersen* (London: Collins, 1965)

Sterne, Laurence, *A Sentimental Journey through France and Italy* (London: Penguin, 1967)

Stevenson, R.L., *Travels with a Donkey in the Cévennes* (London: Folio, 1967)

Stuhlmann, Gunther, *Henry Miller: Letters to Anaïs Nin* (London: Sheldon Press, 1965)

Sugden, John, *Niccolò Paganini* (London: Midas, 1980)

Theroux, Paul, *The Pillars of Hercules* (London: Hamish Hamilton, 1995)

Thwaite, Anne, *A.A. Milne: His Life* (London: Faber & Faber, 1990)

Tomkins, Calvin, *Living Well is the Best Revenge* (London: André Deutsch, 1972)

Touche, Hugues de la, *Sur les Pas de Jean Cocteau* (Nice: ROM Édition, 1998)

Troyat, Henri, *Maupassant* (Paris: Flammarion, 1889)

Vestri, René, *Ballades des trois corniches* (Nice: Éditions YPA, 1985)

Wells, Herbert G., *H.G. Wells in Love* (London: Faber & Faber, 1984)

West, Anthony, *H.G. Wells: Aspects of a Life* (London: Hutchinson, 1984)

Wharton, Edith, *The House of Mirth* (London: Everyman's Library, 1991)

Whittington-Egan, Richard and Smerdon, Geoffrey, *The Quest of the Golden Boy: The Life and Letters of Richard Le Gallienne* (London: Unicorn Press, 1960)

Wheen, Frances, *Karl Marx* (London: Fourth Estate, 1999)

White, Edmund, *Proust* (London: Weidenfeld & Nicolson, 1999)

Wickes, George (ed), *Henry Miller and James Lauchlin: Selected Letters* (London: Constable, 1996)

Williamson, Charles N. and Alice M., *Berry Goes to Monte Carlo* (London: Mills & Boon, 1921)

Wright, Sara B. (ed), *Edith Wharton Abroad* (London: Robert Hale, 1995)

Yardley, Jonathan, *A Biography of Ring Lardner* (New York: Random House, 1977)

Yusupov, Prince Félix, *Lost Splendour*, translated by Ann Green and Nicolas Katkoff (London: Jonathan Cape, 1953)

Index

Also available from Tauris Parke Paperbacks

Egypt's Belle Epoque
Cairo and the Age of the Hedonists
Trevor Mostyn

Egypt's belle époque was a period of incredible extravagance during which the Khedive Ismail's Cairo became the mirror image, both architecturally and socially, of decadent Paris. The glamour and hedonism of the era reached its peak during the magnificent celebrations for the opening of the Suez Canal in 1869. But the splendour was short-lived. Only a year after the Suez Canal opened, the Second Empire in France collapsed and the Khedive's excesses plunged Egypt into crippling debt. Ismail was eventually forced to abdicate, leaving Cairo to the British who occupied Egypt in all but name.

Paperback, 216pp
ISBN 978 1 84511 240 0

'*This is an enthralling account of a period in Egypt's history now too often forgotten. Trevor Mostyn brings to life a glittering near century which opened with the Suez Canal and launched Cairo as one of the world's great cities.*'
Lisa Appignanesi

'*Egypt's Belle Epoque has the immediacy of oral history. This narrative depicts with wit and elegance the grandeur and decadence of a not so distant past. Trevor Mostyn writes as if he was himself a witness to the extraordinary events.*'
Moris Farhi

www.taurisparkepaperbacks.com

Also available from Tauris Parke Paperbacks

Queen Victoria and the Discovery of the Riviera

Michael Nelson

Queen Victoria fell in love with the Riviera when she discovered it on her first visit to Menton in 1882 and her enchantment with this 'paradise of nature' endured for almost twenty years. Victoria's visits helped to transform the French Riviera by paving the way for other European royalty, the aristocracy and the very rich, who were to turn it into their pleasure garden. Michael Nelson paints a fascinating portrait of Victoria and her dealings with local people of all classes, statesmen and the constant stream of visiting crown heads. In the process we see an unexpected side to Victoria: not the imperious, petulant, mourning widow but rather an exuberant girlish old lady thrilled by her surroundings. *Queen Victoria and the Discovery of the Riviera* is an absorbing and revealing account that makes an important contribution to both our understanding of Victoria's character and personality and our view of the late Victorian period.

Paperback + 24 black and white plates
ISBN 978 1 84511 345 2

'Michael Nelson fully appreciates the subtle relationships between the private and the public, even in the life of imperial sovereigns, and his highly readable book will interest different kinds of readers. For me it is rich in texture as, I believe, it will be for them.'
Asa Briggs

'A distinctly original contribution to the studies of Queen Victoria. Those sections covering the extraordinary people the Queen met on the Riviera are most moving and human.'
Elizabeth Longford

www.taurisparkepaperbacks.com